Noemi!!!

Thank you so much for being a friend to me, for letting your truth radiate and for being a blessing to this Earth.

I wish you sweet success
I wish you spectacular health
I wish you divine spiritual growth
I wish you true happiness

I believe you really can have it <u>all</u>

SEX, DRUGS & JESUS

A MEMOIR OF SELF-DESTRUCTION & RESURRECTION

Cover design by CHRIS AND CON DESIGNS, Greece

Copyright © 2022 De'Vannon Hubert. All rights reserved.

ISBN 979-8-9858963-0-5 (eBook)
ISBN 979-8-9858963-1-2 (Paperback)
ISBN 979-8-9858963-2-9 (Hardcover)

No part of this publication may be reproduced, distributed, stored in a database or retrieval system, or transmitted in any form or by any means, including photocopying, recording, or other electronic or mechanical methods, without the prior written permission of the publisher, except in the case of brief quotation embodied in reviews and certain non-commercial uses permitted by copyright law.

DE'VANNON HUBERT

SEX, DRUGS & JESUS

A MEMOIR OF SELF-DESTRUCTION & RESURRECTION

I became a drag queen 13 years ago after a friend dared me to hop on stage and put on a show. I'm not one to back down from a challenge and so here we are. In a world where the 2SLGBTQIA+ Community is often overlooked, marginalized, and demonized, it is refreshing to find people like us included, in a loving way, within these pages. The love that I feel reverberating throughout this read is inclusive of many backgrounds and lifestyles. This memoir contains a lot of thrilling content, and I feel like it was fast paced as I read through so many intense experiences. I sincerely hope the truth contained within this memoir is shared across the world and reaches the most unreachable of us.

-Amanda Rose Andrews, Miss Apollo 2015

CONTENTS

Prologue: S.W.A.T.	I
Part I (1982-2000)	**1**
Dream	3
Chapter 1: Gemstones	4
Chapter 2: Changes	23
Part II (2000-2006)	**37**
Chapter 3: Basic Training	39
Chapter 4: Rank 'N' File	46
Chapter 5: Into the Aurora Sea	58
Chapter 6: Curiosity	78
Chapter 7: Money	91
Part III (2006-2012)	**103**
Dream	105
Chapter 8: Welcome to Houston	107
Chapter 9: Aspirations	117
Chapter 10: Debtors & Collectors	127
Chapter 11: Dehumanized	148
Part IV (2010-2012)	**159**
Chapter 12: A Fucking Wreck	161
Chapter 13: Tina	171
Chapter 14: The Crucible	182
Chapter 15: Let's Make A Deal	200
Chapter 16: Mortality	217
Part V (2012)	**237**
Chapter 17: Not Like The Pornos :(	239
Chapter 18: Where Do You Live?	249
Chapter 19: Stunt Queens	271
Chapter 20: Not Again	287
Epilogue: Bittersweet	311
Wisdom & Witchery	**331**
About the Author	341

For confidentiality, safety, and security, the names of most characters have been changed. Some events and locations have also been modified.

HONORS

My memoir is dedicated to God first and then to the three women who raised me and carried me throughout my life.

* * *

To my Mother. I am sorry I put you through so much. I cannot begin to comprehend what it is like for a mother to watch her youngest child flail and stumble in the terrible way that I did. It is a miracle you did not have to attend my funeral after all the foolish mistakes I made, but to God be the glory for his mighty hand and his outstretched arm. My enemies were not able to prevail over me and the Lord delivered me safely into your hands. Thank you for your sacrifices over the years and for always being in my corner no matter how wrong I was. I have never met a woman who took to motherhood quite as well as you. It seems like a kind of gift you have. Our bond is as though the umbilical was cut at my birth, but our connection was never severed. Thank you for reading all my teachers for filth who put their hands on me when I was in elementary school. Thank you for staying up late to finish my projects for me in high school even though you had to go to work the next morning. Thank you for doing the best you could with the hand that life dealt you. I am thankful for and look forward to the time we have left together in this life.

* * *

Evangelist Nelson, there is no one nor will there ever be anyone who is like you in all the Earth. You are literally impossible to replace, duplicate, mimic, or even come close to. Thank you so much for your tutelage, wisdom, and instruction throughout my life. I appreciate your patience with me as I was making countless bad decisions while being on and off drugs and in and out of jail. Your prayers and divine intervention saved my life. This second chance will not be wasted. It was my privilege to serve as your assistant and altar boy when I was a teenager. It was an absolute honor to be at your side at your death, even though I never thought that day would ever come. I wish you were still here.

* * *

Grandmother, I wish you were still here too, but I understand the need to rest after this life. I will never forget the summer we spent together just the two of us. I miss watching All My Children and The Young & The Restless with you. Thank you for teaching me about God, how to cook, how to read my bible, and all about how to pray. Thank you for not judging me for my sexuality and for being open-minded. When I was 4 years old, I would put on my Mother's heels and run around the little shack we called a home, and it was you who would be my lookout in case my parents returned. I miss your blue eyes and gray hair, but I know you will be there when I cross over.

A Special Thanks

Thank you, Theresa Hissong! It was at a gay bar in Memphis, Tennessee that you were first called "Mother Theresa" by some fabulous queens we had met, and the name could not be more fitting. Thank you for being my literary mother and friend by laying out the steps to make my memoir a reality. Thank you for sticking by my side and encouraging me throughout this whole process even though you were going through so much at the same time. Thank you for coaching me and cheering me on for the past few years until the deed was done and even unto this day. As I join the author ranks, I feel like it was you who birthed me into this moment, and I cannot wait to take some shots of tequila with you again in New Orleans!

PROLOGUE: S.W.A.T.

MAY 2012 - HOUSTON, TX

My white Mustang purred calmly under my seat as I stared across the street at Fancy's Bar in Montrose.

It was the first time in two weeks since I'd left my apartment in the Galleria Area. I could hear the music inside, and the urge to dance pushed its way to the forefront of my mind. I imagined skipping the line and walking in like I had so many times before, and the DJ throwing on my favorite song. Except when I heard Kylie Minogue's voice echo *"get outta my way"* in my head, the meaning sounded different. It was no longer my *Bitch, Move* anthem, but my medieval cry of *"Unclean! Unclean!"*

I felt disgusting; diseased. *Fucking HIV!*

I turned my gaze away from Fancy's, shifted my Mustang out of park, and drove.

Montrose at night was still as beautiful as I remembered it. The lights danced across my windshield. Fuck, I wanted to dance. But I couldn't think of anywhere to go. Every gay bar in Houston would know my face, and I couldn't be seen... not with the city's entire criminal underworld thinking I was a snitch.

I felt stuck. I needed to get high again. But I didn't want to go back to my apartment. Not yet. *Who can I trust?* I wondered. *Spaz? No. Suggs? No. Baker? Hell no. Thiago? Martino? Yes, but they'd be working right now. Ridley?*

Of course I could trust Ridley, my right hand man. I did a quick scan for any patrol cars as I waited under the glowing red of a stoplight before pulling out my phone and dialing.

"Token? Holy shit! What the fuck is up, man? Where the fuck have you been?"

"Oh, you know. Just sitting at home and getting fucked up."

"It's not like you to fall off the radar though."

"Oh, come on. It's not like you've been doing shit." I tried to shift the conversation. I didn't want to have to reveal my diagnosis.

"I'm always doing shit! You know me! Where are you now? What's going on?"

"I'm just driving around. Listen, I'm down to my last teener of Tina. You wanna split it before I stock up again?"

"Sure as shit, Token! You know where to find me."

* * *

I didn't recognize the two other tweakers in Ridley's apartment. Their eyes were glued to a porno on the TV, so I figured they weren't undercover cops, but I still wasn't sure if I could trust them. *What if they're snitches!* I trusted Ridley, but even he could be fooled. *No,* I told myself, *Ridley's one of the most careful guys I know. He wouldn't get caught out by two streetwalkers like these idiots.* Still, I uncomfortably avoided eye contact with them as I passed Ridley my pipe.

I struggled with the thought of telling Ridley about my HIV, but not with these strangers around. It had been almost five months since I found out I was infected but it still felt like only yesterday. Thankfully, Ridley didn't ask too many questions as he was also drawn to the porno. One meaty guy with an anchor tattoo on his neck thrusted furiously on top of a skinny guy's ass in the bed of a red pickup truck.

I tore my gaze away. I wanted to watch and enjoy the last of my meth, but the scene just reminded me of my disease. *My contamination.* I wanted to puke.

"Hey, Ridley, let's go back to my place."

"That's cool. Is it okay if Timmy and Z come with?"

I bit my lip, wishing he had not asked. I wanted to trust these guys, but I didn't trust them. I couldn't trust anyone I didn't know until this shit with the cops blew over. Still, I answered, "Sure. Why not." I loved enabling people to have a good time, and even though I hadn't seen anyone in a while, I had to uphold my reputation.

* * *

We drove temptingly past Fancy's Bar on the way back to my apartment. I gazed longingly at the lights through a crystal meth fog, my body craving the orgasm of the dance floor. I saw Ridley's sight was also fixed on the bar. I reminisced about a time when I wouldn't have hesitated to detour into the parking lot, skip the line with Ridley and our friends, and party the night away. My stomach tied up into a knot from the shame of driving away from Fancy's without even entertaining the thought with Ridley.

* * *

The man at the main entrance to my apartment complex didn't turn around when I pulled into the parking lot. His bald scalp glowed, even in the night, and he was dressed as if he was going to church. That was, except for the two black leather gloves on his hands which were working aggressively at the lock on the door. It was Little D.

I revved my Mustang's engine, and Little D turned. His two beady eyes burned with murderous intent at me through my windshield. I did not flinch. I knew he had come to kill me, but I didn't care. I was not afraid of my Tony Montana moment. But as I stared down the hitman, waiting for him to pull out a gun and shoot, his expression changed.

Little D's eyes widened in shock. The fear he so desired to instill in me before he took my life was absent, and that scared the hell out of him. Little D stepped away from the door to my apartment complex like a spider caught out when the lights switch on, suddenly eager to retreat to his carefully hidden web.

He could not scare me, and therefore he could not kill me. And so, he ran.

"Who the fuck was that?" Ridley asked when Little D was out of sight.

"Just an old, jealous church friend," I said.

"Oh. Are we going in?"

I still had the engine running. *What if Little D comes back? He could just be going to get backup.* Just moments ago I had been ready to die, but now that I had escaped I suddenly didn't want to die just yet.

"Yo, Token. Are we going in? What's up?"

"I'm horny as fuck, yo!" one of the tweakers in the back complained.

"Why don't I drop you guys off at Fancy's?" I offered. It was an excuse to get away from my apartment. I shifted into reverse and backed out of the parking spot.

"What do you mean, 'drop us off'?" Ridley butted in. "I thought we were hanging?"

"Nah," I said as casually as I could. "I'll drop you guys off. Then I'm gonna go cruising."

Ridley eased back into his seat. "Dirty motherfucker," he muttered whimsically. "A'ight. Works for me."

* * *

I loved cruising Montrose at night. My trans girls were all glammed up and the hottest trade boys in Houston were always out to play. But tonight my ass was not available. *Fucking HIV!*

I tried to just drive and not think about my infection. *In a few hours, Martino will get off work, and then I can crash the night at his place*, I figured. There was no way in hell I was going back to my apartment.

The buzz of my cell phone stole me mercifully from my thoughts.

"Do you know how many calls I've gotten in the past fifteen fucking minutes telling me your white fucking Mustang is cruising around all of fucking Montrose? What the fuck did I say about laying low?" Casey's domineering tone crackled violently through my phone.

"I don't give a fuck'!" I screamed back. "Also, I'm running dry. Can I come by for a pickup?"

"No! Listen, Token. I don't care if you've given up on life. Really, I don't. But I do care if one of my main business partners gets shot up in the middle of Houston! I'm having a hard enough time as it is keeping people on my books after your last run-in with the cops. So, do me a favor, will you? Lay fucking low! I'll arrange for a drop-off at your place tomorrow. Transfer payment in advance."

The connection dropped as Casey hung up. If his phone was on a wire,

I'm sure he would've slammed it. I sent the last of my money to Casey immediately, but he underestimated my apathy. If Casey wanted me to lay low, he could fucking put me down himself.

* * *

I intercepted Martino when he walked out of the back of F Bar, and he graciously let me crash at his place. I was his dealer, and he would do *anything* for a discount on my meth. But his curtains were shit, and as soon as the May sun was up, I was hissing like a cat.

"I'm sorry man," I told him, "but if you're not gonna get better blackout shades, then we gotta go back to my place. We are not spending the day in the fucking sun!"

"What do you mean *we*? If you don't wanna stay, then you can go."

"Fuck no, man! What if there's a hitman waiting back at my apartment?"

"Then I don't wanna fucking be there when he jumps you!"

"No, you're not thinking this through," I argued. "If there's two of us, he's more likely to think twice and bail."

"Token!" Martino complained. He didn't like disappointing me.

"Come on. Just walk in the door with me, and then when everything checks out you can leave. I'll even give you some free T for the road."

"Fuuuuck. Fine!"

I drove as fast as I could back to my apartment, eager to escape to the darkness of my blacked-out abode. But when we got back to my place, my front door wouldn't open.

"What the fuck?"

"What?" Martino asked.

"It's like it's been fucking deadbolted from the inside," I said. My key turned the latch, but the door wouldn't budge.

Martino whimpered. "This doesn't feel right. Token, I think we should go."

"Hell no. Don't worry, no one's gonna pull any stupid shit in the middle of the day."

"I feel like something bad is going to happen here."

"The worst thing that is going to happen," I explained, "is that *you* are going to have to go around back and climb into my apartment through the trash hatch."

"What the fuck?"

"It'll be fine!"

"Hell no!"

"I promise I will give you free T! Just do this for me!"

Martino fidgeted. He really didn't want to disappoint me, and he really wanted the drugs. "You better make this worth it," he said.

"I *promise*."

Around the backside of the apartment complex, I located my trash hatch and gave Martino a boost to get in. "It smells like shit!" he complained.

"Of course it smells like shit! It's fucking trash!"

"Fuck!"

With a loud CLUNK, Martino succeeded in getting in through the trash hatch. I hurried back around to the front door where Martino was waiting, scowling in the open doorway.

"Now was that so bad?"

"Give me my fucking dope so I can leave."

"Is the apartment clear?" I asked.

"How the fuck should I know?"

"Come on," I said and shoved Martino back into my apartment as I entered. He whimpered again as I checked the rooms and the corners. It took twenty seconds. I hadn't furnished the place beyond the absolute basics, and there was nowhere anyone could have realistically been hiding.

"Can I have my meth now, please?" Martino begged.

"Okay," I relented. "I suppose you've been a good friend. Thank you."

I opened my kitchen drawer where I kept my drugs to find that I only had half a gram of meth left, and that was it. That was the last of my drugs. *Fuck!* I didn't know when Casey's drop-off would arrive, and the thought of slowly sobering through the wait sounded like purgatory. Still, Martino had done everything I'd asked of him.

Accepting my momentary loss, I grabbed the small baggie and passed it to Martino. "Here, that's the last of everything I have." Martino looked disappointedly down at the bag, clearly expecting more, but he kept silent. "I'll get you another teener when I have more," I offered. Martino nodded.

"Okay, man," he said. "Thanks. Good luck not getting killed."

* * *

It was night again, and the drone of a distant helicopter seemed to make the time pass more slowly. Casey's drop-off was taking forever. With my nervous energy, I cleaned my bongs and pipes, and when they were all sparkling clean on my kitchen table the boredom made me want to scream. *I need a fucking Sprite.*

I started getting dressed. I was wearing just my underwear, and I'd managed to get on my jeans when there was finally a knock on my door. When I opened the door, Ridley walked in.

"Ridley?"

"Hey, Token! What's up? Cool if I hang for a bit?" Ridley threw his backpack on my couch and then instantly crashed next to it.

"Sure," I said. I had no objection to Ridley hanging out. I was just disappointed my meth hadn't arrived yet.

Ridley pulled a nine inch tall orange prescription bottle out of his backpack and put it on the table.

"What's that?" I asked. It was full of pills.

"Adderall," Ridley said. "It's like meth, but–"

"I know what fucking Adderall is."

"Right. Cool. Of course. Well, help yourself if you want. I'm gonna go grab some shit from Walmart. Want me to grab you anything?"

I want my fucking meth to arrive! "No, I'm good, Ridley. Thank you, though." I didn't feel like asking him for my Sprite.

"Okay." Suddenly, Ridley was up and back out the door. The sound of the helicopter droned loudly as the door swung open and then shut, leaving me alone again with an extra backpack and a bottle of Adderall.

That's weird. Ridley never goes anywhere without his shit... nobody ever goes fucking anywhere without their shit.

I tried to ignore the abnormality and go back to getting dressed, throwing on the nearest T-shirt I could find. I pulled one sock on and stopped. I heard the pitter patter of feet outside my door, like a family of mice running for cover. I walked to the door and looked through the peephole. What I saw made my heart jump.

A dozen men in black masks and bulletproof vests had lined up on either side of my door. Over their masks were face shields, and they all carried semi-automatic rifles. The one at the front suddenly raised his hands and gave the "1-2-3" signal.

I turned to run away from the door as fast as I could. I made it as far as my kitchen when I slipped on my one sock and face planted underneath the table.

BOOM!!!

My front door burst into the apartment, flying across my foyer. A shit ton of men swarmed in.

"Show yourself you dirty motherfucker!"

I curled up in a ball underneath my kitchen table, convinced that this would be my Tony Montana moment. *Any moment now… they're gonna start shooting any moment now.*

The lead man had his gun trained on me, and two others were coming alongside him and doing the same. But then he put a fist in the air, and the guns lowered. Behind the face shield, I could see his glaring eyes pinch in confusion, and then soften to pity. I was apparently not the ruthless, cutthroat drug dealer he seemed to be expecting. Instead, I was no more than a scared child in a near fetal position, missing a sock.

Another loud *BANG* reverberated from the back of my living room. Another dozen men swarmed into my apartment. By now I could read the "S.W.A.T." signage on the backs of these men's uniforms. The lead cop removed his face shield and mask to get a better look at me. "Fucking fairies. Get him on a fucking chair."

The other officers picked me up and sat me down forcibly on one of my kitchen chairs. Then they twisted my arms behind my back. I felt cold handcuffs clasp my wrists together. The lead cop took another chair and set it in front of me before straddling it and looking directly into my eyes, inches from my face.

"Now, listen to me, you scumfuck faggot," he said, baring his teeth as he spoke. His breath smelled like peppermint. "Where is the fucking dope?"

I stuttered and said nothing. For once, all the dope was gone. The cops would find nothing. And I didn't know what to tell them.

"WHERE ARE THE FUCKING DRUGS? ANSWER ME YOU ROTTEN FUCK!"

His hand flashed across my face. *SLAP!* The sting burned, but the handcuffs kept my hands from clasping my face. The cop grabbed my shoulder and pulled me upright again. He stared into my eyes.

"Where's he looking?" one of the other cops asked from another room. The cop in front of me didn't answer, but kept his gaze fixed on my eyes, watching closely. *He's trying to see if I look to where the drugs are!* I thought about the kitchen drawer right behind me that would normally be stashed with a glorious array of narcotics, but thanks to Martino that was now empty.

Finally, the lead cop got out of my face. "Bring in the other perp!"

I watched as two more cops dragged in Ridley and pushed him down on his knees. His hands were also handcuffed behind his back. He looked at me fearfully. *He's a snitch,* I suddenly realized.

Then the lead cop hoisted up his rifle and pointed it at Ridley's temple.

"Talk, faggot! Where is the fucking dope! Talk! Or I'll fuck your head up worse than your asshole's worse nightmare!"

I didn't buy the scene. *What the fuck kind of charade is this bullshit?*

Ridley stayed silent. He knew where I kept my drugs, but I could sense he had already told the cops where to look before he ever showed up. This was all a show to make him look like he wasn't an informant.

I looked to where his bottle of Adderall had been left on the kitchen table. It was gone. Likely picked up by one of the cops to be used as evidence against me later.

After a minute of cussing out Ridley, the lead cop lowered his weapon and told the others to take Ridley away. "Alright, tear this place apart! Find those fucking drugs!"

Cops started ripping up my couch and my mattress. Then I heard barking as two K-9 dogs were brought in on leashes. One immediately pounced on my pile of pipes and bongs, knocking one over and shattering it on the floor.

"See, that's what happens when you don't control your animal!" the lead cop said angrily. "Don't fuck up any more evidence!"

Then I heard another *CRASH!* I turned to see that a cop had smashed my mirror plaque that I'd received for being a Distinguished Graduate in the Air Force. "Hey!" I yelled.

"Shut the fuck up, bitch!" the cop snapped back. "Don't they teach you fags manners in Montrose?"

"Fuck you!"

"Don't worry, you'll have plenty of fuck-daddies in prison, bitch!"

What the fuck is wrong with these cops?

In the kitchen I heard more cops rummaging through all the drawers. I turned just in time to see a cop throw my military gold coin for Outstanding Volunteer Service into a black bag. "What's this, your tooth fairy money?" he teased. I opened my mouth to protest again, but one of the cops standing by me slapped me across the face first.

"Don't you fucking say another word, you piece of shit! Save that mouth of yours for the big dicks behind bars!"

In the kitchen, the cop continued to throw everything he found into the black bag. I watched as checks I hadn't cashed yet were taken along with my fake IDs. *What kind of robbery is this?*

"Look at this!" one cop yelled. "GODZILLAAAA! RAAAA!"

He stuffed my Godzilla doll into another black bag.

Finally, my tears emerged. The terror was too much.

"Aww, the fairy's sad!" one cop mocked.

"Awwwww," more cops jeered.

My shiny golden trophy for Academic Achievement that I earned in seventh grade was the next artifact to go into the black bag. After that I stopped watching. I stared at my feet and waited for the raid to be over.

After what seemed like hours, the lead cop came over to me and said, "Listen close, bitch. I'm gonna read you your fucking rights." He proceeded to read me my rights, and then motioned for the other cops to take me away.

"Can I put on another sock and shoes?" I asked.

"Fuck you!" one cop shouted. "I thought you liked being stripped down! I bet you like being tied up, too!"

As I was hauled out of my apartment, I saw several nosey-ass neighbors sticking their heads out of their doors, curious what all the commotion was about. When they saw me being arrested, they nodded their heads in agreement, like I was getting what I deserved.

Several white vans were parked outside. I looked up at the helicopter that had been droning overhead all night and saw that it was in fact a police chopper. *Who the fuck do they think I am? I'm not actually Tony fucking Montana. Fuck!*

A hand landed on top of my head and pushed me into the backseat of a cop car. Before the door slammed, the cop who had been escorting me said, "Hey. Your driver, Kenny, is a good man. Don't go letting your ass bleed all over his seat. You hear me, faggot?"

When the door clamped shut, the world became suddenly very quiet. The engine ignited to a quiet purr, and I was driven away. After a few minutes, the police officer driving me spoke up.

"Hey listen," he said. His voice was gravelly, but soft. "I've been on plenty of raids throughout my career, and I gotta say, you don't seem like the other kinds of drug dealers I'm used to seeing. You seem all right. Sensible. Maybe just caught up with the wrong crowd? I don't know. But listen, when all of this is over, give yourself a second chance, all right? Get out of this city and start over. Do that and you'll be alright. Okay?"

I just nodded along, listening to the gentle hum of the car's engine taking me away.

PART I
(1982-2000)

DREAM

"Tell me about your dreams, child," said Evangelist Nelson.

"I dreamed I was with my parents, and we were standing on the top of a super tall, slender mountain in the middle of the ocean," I said. "I stood in between my parents, and there wasn't much room to move. There was no way down that I could see. There was no sunshine. It was dark and foggy, like we were in a storm, but I could still see the ocean. The water was black, and the ocean was throwing a fit, but everything in the dream was completely quiet. We looked terrified."

Evangelist Nelson nodded. "Then what happened?" she asked.

I hesitated, but I could see in her eyes a promise to believe me, and so I continued. "A wave of black water, taller than the mountain, was headed for us, and we couldn't do anything about it. I just remember the look of horror on all our faces as we braced ourselves for it to hit. That's where the dream ended."

Afternoon sunlight blazed in through the open windows of Evangelist Nelson's kitchen, reflecting off the shiny black and white checkered tiles of the floor. I took a big gulp of her homemade lemonade, chilling in a glass sweating with condensation.

"You have challenging times ahead of you," she told me. "God has a calling for your life, and you will need all of your faith to make it through the difficult times ahead."

I nearly dropped the glass of lemonade. The thought terrified me more than the dream.

What did God want with me?

CHAPTER 1: GEMSTONES

1987 - BATON ROUGE, LA

I grew up in a neighborhood in Baton Rouge called Eden Park, and I learned at an early age: *little kids don't play in The Park.*

I was four years old, and my brother was teaching me how to pass a basketball in our front yard when a black car pulled up. I didn't think much of the polished hood and chrome grill of the vehicle, but even at the age of four I could tell the difference between a rich man's clothes and a poor man's clothes. The black boots that swung out of the passenger side door did not look cheap. The man who stood up was freakishly tall, and dressed all in black. I wondered where he got pants, a shirt, and a jacket cut to his gargantuan size. *And why does he only dress in black?* The only thing that wasn't black was his water bottle, which he dropped as he exited the vehicle. The bottle clanged to the ground and water gushed out.

Oh no, his water was spilling! I darted toward the man.

As I approached the front yard fence, my brother lunged for me. "DE'VANNON, STOP!"

I ran and skidded to a stop by the puddle of water, then I picked up the water bottle. *Victory!*

Before I could look up, the tall man's shadow moved. A large hand reached down, but not for the water bottle. Gravely fingers grasped beneath the collar of my shirt, and I felt the fabric tighten around my torso.

My brother *screamed*.

Something was very wrong. I panicked. I twisted my body to loosen the man's grip and flung his water bottle at him. I heard a heart wrenching *rip* as my shirt tore out of the man's grasp. I moved my feet to scamper away, but they slipped on the wet pavement. Now both the man and my brother were screaming.

I felt the man's gravely fingers start to wrap around my arm, and I swung and clawed at them with my free hand. Now I was screaming.

"What's going on out here?" cried the concerned voice of one of our neighbors.

The man's grip loosened from my arm, and I fell on my hands and knees. Tears flooded my vision and I curled up into a ball on the concrete. I heard the *roar* of an engine and the *screech* of tires burning rubber as the black car sped off down the street.

The next hand on my back was gentle. It was our neighbor. "Hey, sweetie, come on. Let's get you inside."

My brother and I were escorted back to our front door where my Mother was standing. My shirt was ripped up, and I tried to fix it in a hurry. Mother noticed right away.

"Some creepy-ass man just tried to nab your child," the neighbor told my Mother.

Dad appeared in the doorway out of nowhere. He scowled down at me and my brother. "Thank you, Jackie. Get inside, kids." We obeyed.

As soon as we were in the house the door slammed behind us.

"WHAT HAPPENED?" dad shouted.

Tears streamed down my face. Through shaky breaths I tried to explain as fast as I could. I tried to tell him that it wasn't my fault, because I knew what would happen if dad thought it was my fault.

"The man... dropped his water bottle... and... it was spilling out... all over his shoes... so I–"

"So you what?"

"Dad, I–"

My voice was cut off by the cold sound of leather flapping through belt loops.

I raised my hands just in time to stop the first blow from coming down on my face. My arm was still sore from where the man had grabbed me, and the sting of the belt whipping against bruised flesh erupted a new layer of pain. I screamed and cried but my dad didn't stop. Blows came down on my arms until I couldn't hold them up any longer. I curled into a ball on the floor and tried to protect my face with my knees.

Dad was panting. "Don't you ever play near the front yard fence again!"

* * *

"I had a strange dream, grandma," I said.

I loved spending time with grandma. Grandma was safe. She lived in the duplex adjacent to ours, and when my older siblings were in school I got to spend the days with her. Sometimes I even got to cuddle up next to her in bed while she read her Bible.

"What kind of a dream?" she asked. She stopped reading her Bible to look at me.

I looked into her eyes and could see there wasn't a hint of malice there. I felt safe. We were sitting in the living room, and autumn sunlight filtered through the heavy lace curtains, throwing diamond-shaped shadows across my grandmother's weathered face. She had the last visible traits of my family's Native American heritage. I hoped to learn more about our heritage from her one day. All I knew was that the Indigenous side of our family was on the receiving end of some unfair treatment but no details. Her most prominent traits were in her high cheekbones and dark blue eyes. I was captivated by her eyes. They weren't bright electric blue. They were deep blue, the color of the ocean at midnight under a full moon. I loved looking into those eyes.

"There's a cross," I told her, something I'd never told another human. "It's solid gold and speckled with jewels of all colors."

My grandmother nodded, urging me to continue.

"What else?" she asked. "Does anything else happen in the dream?"

"The cross was floating in the air vertically and spinning in circles," I said, "and it spun toward me until it was standing up right in front of me. I felt like it was pleading with me."

We sat in silence for a moment and then she explained the dream might be the voice of God speaking to me and it was my job to listen. I was blown away.

What did God want with me?

*   *   *

Any time spent with my dad was tense. One night dad decided to do a last minute run to the grocery story just before closing time. We were the last ones in the store which felt awkward in a sense. As we walked through the grocery store aisles I scanned the breakfast cereal shelves while he picked out the usual items: milk, coffee, cigarettes… I spotted the Fruity Pebbles, but my dad was moving on with the cart. I checked my pocket to see if I had enough allowance money to buy the Fruity Pebbles, but I only had a single dollar bill.

If I were with my Mother, I would have asked for the Fruity Pebbles and she would have gotten them for me. I always loved Fruity Pebbles. I was afraid to ask my dad, though, so I bit my tongue and hurried after him.

We remained silent all the way through the store, through checkout, and to the car. I waited patiently as dad loaded the groceries into the back of the truck. We got into the truck, closed the doors, and rolled the windows down for a breezy ride home. Before either of us knew anything there was a skinny white man who appeared to be homeless standing at my dad's window. His long, stringy hair was dirty and matted and so were his clothes. But his eyes shone a bright, electric blue that reminded me of lightning flashing in the middle of a thunderstorm. The color was both intense and intimidating. "You got a dollar?" he asked me. He spoke to me directly as though my dad wasn't even sitting there and as though he already knew exactly how much money I had.

I looked over at my little Velcro camouflage wallet sitting on the dashboard which had exactly one dollar in it. Everything in me wanted to be generous to this stranger but I was worried that dad wouldn't approve of me giving my dollar away. I didn't want a beating. I looked at dad as fear and apprehension got the best of me but when I looked up the man with electric blue eyes was gone. I jerked my head around in all directions trying to see where he could've gone. The parking lot was empty except for us and there was no obvious place where the man could have walked off to so quickly.

"Dad, where'd the man go?"

"What the hell?" he muttered. We drove the length of the parking lot trying to find out where the man had disappeared to, but the more we searched the more it seemed like the man had simply vanished.

That night as I lay atop my bunk bed in my parents' tiny bedroom I was lost in thought.

Did I meet an Angel?

*   *   *

I loved eccentric clothing, even as a child. When I'd go shopping with my parents I always seemed to prefer the most extravagant, and therefore most *expensive*, items. I wanted the most colorful fabrics with the softest touch and elaborate stitching. Plain shorts and T-shirts couldn't satisfy me, but I learned not to press the issue with my parents.

My parents couldn't afford much clothing. My brother and I each had five shirts and five pairs of pants. There's only so many ways you can mix and match five sets of clothing throughout the school year. When I finally did get a new shirt, other kids at school would come up to me and say something like, "Well it's about damn time!"

The first time I ever saw Sidewinder jeans I knew I had to have a pair. My Mother and I were walking by Gadzooks — a store in competition with Hot Topic — and the mannequin in the window caught my eye. My jaw hung open and I stopped in my tracks as I admired the diamond patterned stitching on the jeans, and the way they opened up at the bottom to nearly cover the shoes. I had never wanted anything in my life so badly.

Mother was in a hurry but I begged her to take me to find those jeans. She relented, and a few moments later we were being whisked down the aisles of the store by a chatty salesperson who's tattoos and piercings dazzled me as she walked. Suddenly, there they were. An entire display in the back of the store was devoted to the jeans. There was a sign announcing that the Sidewinders cost $60. I knew that was more than my parents would be willing to be spend on a single item of clothing.

"Come on," Mother grabbed my hand, "let's go." I nodded and followed her out of the store, but I vowed to return one day to purchase those jeans.

The next day I stopped eating lunch. Mother gave me a dollar and a quarter every day for lunch money but I wanted those jeans more than I wanted to eat, so I skipped lunch and saved the money. I calculated that it would take just under three months to save up enough money to buy a pair of Sidewinders. In the meantime, I started eating a huge breakfast every morning and a hefty snack as soon as I got home from school. If Mother wondered why I was so hungry all of a sudden she never let on.

A couple months later, I approached Mother while dad wasn't home and presented her with a Ziploc bag full of dollars and quarters. I had exactly $60 saved up. After starving myself every day and saving my lunch money I finally had enough to buy my coveted Sidewinder jeans.

I wasn't sure how my Mother would react when I showed her my secret savings but she actually smiled. She was impressed that I had worked so hard to save the money, not mad that I'd been deceiving her. In fact, she even offered to cover the taxes on the jeans which was something I had not factored in.

We hopped in her car and headed to the mall and I was riding high the whole way there. The moment I'd been working toward for months had finally arrived and I was about to get the jeans I so desperately desired. I don't know what I thought those jeans would do for me. I wasn't naive enough to think they would suddenly make me cool or attractive. I just wanted to know what it felt like to own them. I thought they would make me feel different about myself.

At the mall I led the way to Gadzooks, tugging at my Mother's arm up the escalator and through the aisles to the back table. Except, the Sidewinder exhibit was gone and the table was full of swimsuits.

"We sold out of those jeans," said the salesperson, noticing us looking around the table. "Won't have any in for a few weeks."

I was heartbroken. On the car ride home I fought back tears. Mother encouraged me not to cry and said we could try again soon.

* * *

The pastor's wife, Evangelist Nelson, was a central figure in the community, and she fascinated me. When she spoke at church, I could sense a powerful love behind each of her words. She wasn't just speaking words to teach us about God, but she was doing everything she could to show us how the love of God is real and always present in our lives. Most importantly, Evangelist Nelson never judged anyone.

Grandma spoke with Evangelist Nelson about the dreams I'd been having. One Sunday at church Evangelist Nelson asked me, "How would you like to start coming by my place and telling me about your dreams? I can talk to you about what they mean." I nodded and smiled. She had the kind of presence I always liked to be around.

While I was at Evangelist Nelson's house one day, she asked me if wanted to be her altar boy. She had never had an altar boy before, so I would be her very first one. I didn't hesitate to accept her offer. I didn't know why but it just felt like the right choice to make.

Being an altar boy meant sitting next to Evangelist Nelson on the pulpit during each service. I also marched in front of Evangelist Nelson as I led her up to the pulpit each Sunday. The congregation would stand as we entered the church from the back and not sit down until Evangelist Nelson had taken her seat. Once the service was over, the congregation would stand again as I led Evangelist Nelson from the pulpit to the back of the church where she would shake hands as the congregants exited the sanctuary.

Over the next few months, Evangelist Nelson became more than just an interpreter of my dreams. She started counseling me and helping me deal with hard situations in my life. I learned that I could call on her any time and she would never judge me. If I got in a fight at school, I called her and she prayed for my peace and healing. If I got called nasty names, I called her and she affirmed me with loving words. If I was feeling lonely and needed someone to talk to, I could call Evangelist Nelson and she would be my friend on the other end of the line.

Evangelist Nelson was a light in my life. When I spoke with her, I knew my physical, emotional, mental, and spiritual needs were all being cared for.

After the disappointment with the Sidewinders, I visited Evangelist Nelson. I asked her to tell me my future. She seemed so wise and gifted. I knew she would be able to tell me something about what lay in store for me. I wanted to know what I was going to be when I grew up.

She nodded thoughtfully from across the wide oak desk in her home office. Behind her, shelves of books covered the walls from floor to ceiling. The study smelled of old paper. I drummed my fingers on the arms of the black leather chair and waited.

After thirty long seconds of silence, she spoke.

"You will go into business for yourself one day," she said. For some reason, I believed her. It felt right. *Yes*, I thought. *I will have a business of my own one day!*

I didn't tell Evangelist Nelson about my obsession with the Sidewinder jeans. I told her about school, and my family drama but I kept quiet about the Sidewinders. I was embarrassed to mention them to someone as holy and wise as Evangelist Nelson though she probably wouldn't have minded.

Three weeks later Mother and I returned to the mall and shuffled through the store to that table in the back. It was filled with Sidewinders. I tried on at least ten sizing options and picked the perfect one. I tried to account for how much I would grow during the coming months.

The salesperson offered to wrap them up for us but I shook my head. I wanted to start wearing them immediately.

Walking out of the store in my new jeans I did feel different, as I'd hoped I would. I felt more confident. I felt better about myself. The jeans changed my self-perception and I loved how much they rocked with my Skechers!

* * *

The first time I saw gemstones I went into a trance. Everything else in the world ceased to exist except for the precious, shiny stones on the table in the Discovery Channel Store. Before I knew it I was over there at the table examining each rock. Some were tumbled and smooth. Others were rough and natural.

"That one is an amethyst," a man informed me. I nodded. I fell in love with the deep purple stone. I picked up the one next to it, a faded brown stone that sparkled at the right angle. I was stunned by how pretty they looked. "That's topaz," the man said. "The stone of love and good fortune." Then the woman with him began explaining the mystical properties of gemstones, and I was captivated. I couldn't help but think of the colorful jewels that covered the cross from my dream several years ago.

The man and woman said I could take a stone for free. I took the amethyst, showed it to Mother and slipped it into my pocket. Then Mother offered to buy one for me. I got the topaz, too. For the rest of the day I carried the stones around, turning them over between my fingers. When we got home I put them in a special hidden place: under my bunk bed.

In the weeks after buying me the topaz, I noticed my parents spending more money than usual. When Mother announced she was going to the mall for the second time in one week, I asked if I could tag along and she approved.

In the Discovery Channel Store there was a speaker system playing a rainforest track. Shelves of stuffed animals, toy dinosaurs, binoculars, globes, and books lined the store, but I quickly navigated to the Geology section. Onyx, opal, garnet, peridot, amber, ruby, sapphire... my eyes were alight with joy. Then I saw it: *aquamarine*. Blue and white crystallized into an electric blue fog that pulled for my fingers like a magnet. I turned around to show my Mother, and saw that she was holding a Godzilla doll.

"You still like Godzilla, De'Vannon?"

I nodded.

I returned home with two trophies to add to my collections that day. The aquamarine gemstone went in the secret spot under my bunk bed and the Godzilla doll went in the toy box in the corner of the living room.

*   *   *

I was thirteen years old the first time I saw my dad cry.

I came home from school and dad was sitting on the front step with his face in his hands. He was just sitting there staring at nothing and letting his tears fall down his face without even trying to catch them. He didn't look at me as I approached. I was afraid to say anything, so I scurried past him inside. My brother was in the living room.

"Psst. Don't go into the bedroom," he whispered to me.

"Why not?" I asked. "What's going on?"

"Mom found lipstick on dad's underwear," my brother said in a hushed voice. I wasn't sure how this was supposed to make sense, but I pretended to understand. I unloaded my schoolwork onto the couch and buried myself in my studies.

About an hour later I was distracted by bright red and white lights flashing through our windows. An ambulance had pulled up in front of our house. Two men wearing paramedic uniforms escorted my dad into the back of the vehicle and drove away.

The house held an eerie quiet that night and no one told me what was going on.

The next day Mother took me and my brother to go visit dad. We parked outside a building with a sign: "Baton Rouge General Hospital." Mother made my brother and I wait in the lobby while she went to talk to dad. When she returned, she was in tears and I saw dad running after her but the medical workers pulled him back inside.

"Mother what's going on?" I asked.

"How could he do this to me?" she sniffled as tears ran down her face, "let's go. We're going home."

The lack of information was aggravating. When we got home, Mother went straight to the bedroom and slammed the door shut. My face flushed red with anger. I wanted answers, so I turned to my brother.

"What's going on!" I screamed. "Why won't anyone tell me what's happening?"

"Dad cheated on Mom," he said bluntly. I tried to wrap my head around what my brother was saying, but I couldn't register what he meant.

Dad didn't come home that night either. The house felt like a graveyard, cold and devoid of all life. I couldn't sleep. I tried to imagine my dad with another woman, but it was impossible. I had only ever seen him with Mother. How could he be with somebody else? When would he have had the time to be with anybody else? It didn't make sense.

I went to join my grandma at her side of the duplex the next day, but grandma wasn't talking about the affair. She let me watch TV and cooked me food, but otherwise avoided the discussion. It was late in the evening when grandma told us dad had returned from the hospital and I had to go home.

Back at the house, Mother invited my brother and I into the bedroom. We stood in the doorway and looked at our parents sitting oddly, side-by-side on the edge of the bed.

"Your dad and I have come to the conclusion that we cannot stay together" my Mother stated.

When Mother looked up she asked, "Who do you want to go with?"

I felt my heart rip in two. *Can parents break up? Is that possible? What is happening?*

Tears were in my eyes. My heart had stopped working, and so had my brain.

All I could think to do was answer the question. I felt saliva stick to my lips as I said, "Mother," and I started crying.

Mother didn't look at me, but kept her gaze fixed on my brother. Out of the corner of my eye I saw him shake his head. "I'm staying with dad," he said.

I jumped back as Mother stood up from the bed and bolted past us out of the room. I heard the front door slam shut. When I turned back, dad was looking at me. My heart sank.

"Leave," he said. I obeyed.

I sat on the couch, numb. I could tell my dad was talking with my brother, but I couldn't make out what he was saying. What was I supposed to do?

Dad didn't talk to me that night. Dad never talked to me about the affair at all.

My parents never did get the divorced they promised.

One random ass day soon after all this had happened, Mother and dad gathered my brother and I into the truck and told us we were going for a ride. No explanation. The mood was ominous so I didn't dare ask. We rode through unfamiliar neighborhoods until we ended up in front of a driveway with a middle-aged woman with black hair and a medium complexion glacially sweeping away. Our truck stopped and my Mother rolled down her window and addressed the lady. "I want you to see the family you *almost* destroyed!" With not another word from any of us in the vehicle and nothing but a look of guilt from the woman standing in the driveway, we screeched off. The affair was never spoken of nor mentioned again.

* * *

"De'Vannon, congratulations. You're going to be getting a little something at the awards ceremony this year. Be sure to dress up and look nice."

"Thank you, Miss Thomas," I replied cordially. Internally, I was ecstatic. I knew exactly which award I'd be winning: the big, shiny-ass, golden trophy for maintaining a perfect 4.0, perfect attendance, and perfect discipline all throughout the 7th grade. I relished the thought of holding the trophy's cold, metal handles in my hands.

I was surprised when Mother picked me up from school instead of grandma. She had been informed of my pending award and was ready to greet me with a big smile on her face.

"Congratulations, baby!"

I was embarrassed, but it felt good. "Thanks, Mother."

On the car ride home I asked, "Would it be alright if I spent the afternoon at grandma's?" I still felt uncomfortable around my parents and preferred spending time with my grandma if I could.

"Sure, baby, but make sure you get all of your schoolwork done. This award is a big deal. Make sure you don't slack off now."

"Yes, Mother."

Grandma was delighted to see me. She congratulated me with a big hug and kiss. Her arms were warm, and I was reminded that in her presence I was always safe. I took a deep breath and relaxed. And then I did my homework.

* * *

It was shiny as *fuck!*

The golden trophy for Academic Achievement stood high above the other awards and certificates behind the podium on the school's stage. Morning sunlight angled through the gymnasium windows, giving the metallic sheen of my pending honor a special spotlight. Some years, if multiple students achieved 4.0 GPAs, there were multiple trophies for Academic Achievement, but this year there was only one. And it was going to *me!*

Grandma was the first one I spotted. She waved with a proud grin on her face from the back of the assembly where the adults sat. My heart fluttered with excitement. She had gifted me a colorful button-down shirt and black dress pants for this occasion, and I was thankful to be wearing something new. I felt fabulous.

Finally, the principal took to the podium. "Now for our very top award," he spoke calmly into the microphone. "For maintaining a perfect

4.0 GPA all year long, and for demonstrating outstanding prowess in all areas of academia, this year's Academic Achievement Award goes to…"

"De'Vannon Hubert!"

Applause erupted behind me. I rose to collect my trophy.

One kid stuck out his foot to try to trip me, but my adrenaline was on high alert. I danced over his foot and made a face at him. Then I jumped up the stairs to the stage and received my award. I was surprised by how lightweight it was. I lifted it up high like a champion boxer holding his belt over his head.

The principal concluded the ceremony and my family leapt over chairs and bodies to reach me. Mother won the race, and nearly tackled me to the ground with her hug. It was all I could manage to do to hold onto my trophy while I accepted congratulations from the rest of my family.

Then I noticed there was another man lingering right next to my dad. A white man in a tailored, navy blue suit. He had a burgundy tie and neatly combed brown hair. He held himself proudly and looked admiringly down at me. My dad motioned to introduce the man.

"De'Vannon, this is Mr. Alden Lee Ponce. He is the vice-principal at a magnet school here in Baton Rouge. He wants you to attend their school next year."

"Pleased to meet you, De'Vannon," Mr. Ponce said and stretched out his hand for a handshake. I cradled my trophy in my left arm so I could accept the gesture. "That's quite an achievement, there. I know your family's very proud of you."

"Thank you," I replied to Mr. Ponce.

My Mother interjected. "Of course, our son would be honored to attend your school, Mr. Ponce!"

My dad shot a quick, scolding glance at Mother, but she didn't notice.

"The honor is all mine, Mrs. Hubert," Mr. Ponce said. I noticed he spoke very formally. "De'Vannon, congratulations once again. I look forward to seeing what you can do at our school." And with that, he walked away.

As soon as he was out of earshot, my brother jabbed me in the arm. "Good job, bro! Hey, for every A you get at that man's school, I'll buy you a brand new CD."

More shiny trophies! I thought.

"Deal!"

*   *   *

In traffic, the drive to McKinley Middle Magnet school was ten times longer than the drive to my previous school. I remained quiet the whole ride. I could tell Mother was fatigued by the drive well before we arrived. The parking lot at this school was also ten times larger, and there were some cars parked that I had only seen in movies before. I was beginning to feel inspired.

"I'll see you later. Have a good day, baby." I could hear the nervousness in my Mother's voice. I jumped out of the car and found signs for the school office, where I got my class schedule and my picture taken for my school ID.

There was a class on my schedule called "Health & Wellness" which it turned out was just a disguise for the more accurate title: "The Safe Way to Fuck." It was Sex Ed, and my 8th grade brain was fascinated.

I had seen warnings of sexually transmitted diseases on TV commercials before, but none of those neared the horrific images we were shown in that class. As soon as we had found our seats the lights switched off and a projector was turned on. A female voice narrated the sequence of swollen dicks, boiled vaginas, and bloody urine. I felt like puking.

At the end of the video, the narrator explained to us the difference between HIV (human immunodeficiency virus) and AIDS (acquired immunodeficiency syndrome). Next, the deterioration of a man's health was chronicled after he was diagnosed with HIV. I watched helplessly as this man developed the bruises symptomatic with AIDS, lost weight, and shriveled into the corpse he was apparently destined to be. HIV seemed to be the worst STD of them all, synonymous with a "tortured to death" sentence.

As we abandoned the classroom a little paler from fright than before, I made my way to the school office again. It was lunch and I needed to pick up my ID card. Suddenly, another boy was at my side.

"Hey, what do you think of this guy?" he asked, showing me a cutout from a men's magazine of a ripped man wearing nothing but underwear.

The spray tan was obvious to me, but I replied, "I prefer him to the HIV guy in that film."

"Ha! Right?"

I looked up at this kid. He was slightly taller than me, and his skin was so golden it was practically yellow. And underneath his dirty blonde hair, he had foggy green eyes.

"What's your name?" he asked.

"De'Vannon," I replied.

"Right on, De'Vannon. I'm Dillon. Wanna grab lunch together?"

He was so kind… and *handsome*. How could I say no?

"Yes, I would love to," I responded with a smile. I just need to stop by the office first to pick up my ID card.

"Oh yes! I was wondering if you were new here. Mind if I tag along?"

"Not at all."

I loved the feel of the ID's thick plastic and the glossy sheen over my picture was nice. My smile was unacceptable, though. Dillon begged to see the picture when I walked outside, but I refused to show it to him.

Dillon led the way to a table in the courtyard where a beautiful, foreign looking girl and a white boy were sitting. I loved the racial diversity at this school! "Guys, this is De'Vannon. He's new here. De'Vannon, this is my brother, Ben, and our friend, Sasha." I smiled the smile I wish I'd given before having my picture taken. "Sasha is from Hawaii," Dillon fake-whispered in my ear.

Sasha rolled her eyes, apparently tired of a background joke I wasn't understanding.

"What music do you listen to?" Dillon asked me.

I tried to think of the most mainstream artist I could. "I like Prince."

"Yo!" Sasha nearly jumped out of her seat. "That Gold Experience album is the fucking shit! That song "Pussy Control" is fucking awesome!" She was snapping on every syllable, and before I knew it we were both singing.

Ben and Dillon blushed, but we kept going.

We were instant friends. *This school year is gonna be the fucking shit*, I thought to myself. *When I get my report card, The Gold Experience is gonna be the first CD I get.*

* * *

I don't know how Dillon knew I was gay, but within a couple of weeks it was our routine to meet in the library before classes and make out. No one ever browsed the Poetry section, so that was where we hooked up, tucked away in a windowless corner, half listening for footsteps drawing near, and half paying attention to our tongues in each other's mouths.

When it was time to go to class, Sasha would intercept me outside the library and we would sing "Pussy Control" all the way to Louisiana History.

In "The Safe Way to Fuck" class, Dillon and I negotiated with some classmates so we could sit next to each other at the back of the room.

"Alright class, today we're going to learn how to properly put a condom on."

Dillon grabbed my dick. I stomped on his foot. If anyone noticed, they pretended not to.

As the lights flicked off for the video demonstration, I whispered in Dillon's ear. "I'm getting picked up late today. Wanna study in the library?"

"Yes," he whispered back.

Our game of fondle-footsie continued into lunch.

"Would you guys stop, please," Ben asked.

"Fuck you," Dillon said. But we did stop. Our fun would have to wait. We still had pockets full of condoms from class to practice with after all.

When the final bell rang at the end of the day, I hurried to the library. My blood was pumping, and I was already hard. The library was busier after classes, but the Poetry section was still vacant. I breathed a sigh of relief and waited.

Minutes felt like hours. My parents didn't explain why I was being picked up late. All I knew was I had an extra couple of hours.

"Hurry up," I muttered under my breath.

Minutes later, Dillon stepped around the corner of the aisle and rushed to my side. Before I had a chance to whine about his tardiness, he put a finger to his lips.

"I think the librarian's onto us," he whispered.

The intensity in his voice was real. "You serious?" I didn't want to get caught any more than he did, but we were having so much fun. The fun couldn't stop, especially now that we had the perfect opportunity to experiment a bit.

Dillon glared at me with his piercing eyes. "She's practically been stalking me from the moment I walked in," he hissed. Oh, I was in love.

"Say that one more time, except this time a little raspier," I cooed.

"I'm serious," he retorted, but the hint of a smile creased at the edge of his lips. I had cracked him.

"No, no," I pressed. "Try it like this, '*I think the librarian's onto us.*'" It was a poor attempt at a low, gravelly voice, but enough to make Dillon giggle. I slipped my palm down his pants, and felt his dick reach up to say hello. *"I think the librarian's onto us,"* I said one more time, hitting the low note a bit more smoothly. I knelt down to unzip his pants. "Keep a lookout," I said. Dillon nodded.

I put the condom on the way we'd been shown to in class that morning and began giving Dillon a hand job. He tried to keep a straight face, but every time he looked down at me, smiling all sexy looking up at him, he couldn't help but break into a grin.

"Pretend your browsing," I whispered. He complied, but after a couple minutes his eyes closed, lost in a sea of pure bliss.

"Ok, your turn," Dillon said. We silently shuffled around each other, trading places.

His golden hands grasped my crotch, and I stifled a gasp.

Then I saw a shadow dart quickly down an aisle near us, too fast to be a browsing student.

"Someone's coming," I whispered to Dillon.

In a matter of seconds, the librarian stomped around the corner into our aisle. "What are you two doing?" she lashed in a whispered scream that only librarians and theater ushers could possibly master.

"Reading," I said nonchalantly, holding up a book as irrefutable evidence. *Moby Dick by Herman Melville.*

The librarian looked at Dillon, who was standing in front of me, blocking my unbuttoned pants from view and trying desperately to avoid eye-contact. She was hunched over, almost in a football stance, ready to tackle us if we made a wrong move. "I want you two to leave," she demanded. "Now!"

We cut our losses and left. On our way to the parking lot, Dillon looked at me,

"*Moby Dick*. Really?"

We laughed.

An hour later, my Mother picked me up. She looked tired, and I guessed it wasn't from the long drive.

"Hi Mother, is everything okay?" I asked as I climbed into the front seat.

"Yes, baby, don't you worry," she said, but her voice sounded a bit shaky.

As we neared home, I noticed we were taking a different route.

"Mother, where are we going?"

"You'll see, baby, don't you worry." *Why don't the adults in my family ever tell me anything?* I wondered.

I lost track of the left and right turns as Mother drove around the blocks, squinting at the signposts. I thought she was lost, but I didn't bother asking if I could help. Whatever was going on, I apparently wasn't trusted to know about it.

Finally, we turned onto a street to the sight of a big moving truck. My dad and my brother were shuttling boxes to the front door of a beautiful new house. The "JUST SOLD" sign was still posted in the grass on the front lawn. I was speechless.

"Welcome home, De'Vannon," Mother said.

I carried my backpack into the house as if it weighed as much as one of the boxes my brother was carting. When I entered, grandma greeted me with a smile in the living room as she unpacked some of her stuff. I was happy to see she would be living with us. The next thing I noticed upon entering was that the air was cool. *Central air conditioning!* My mind whirled.

I rushed to the windows. Double-paned. And the walls were thick and insulated. The carpeted floor felt soft and plush beneath my feet, and I reveled in the new sensation. A huge island commanded attention in the center of the kitchen and there was a separate dining room. Most importantly, there were multiple bedrooms!

I heard a *thud* behind me and turned to see that my brother had put a box down at my feet. "This is your stuff," he said between heavy breaths. "Our room is at the end of that hallway, next to grandma's."

Before I knew it, we were keeping up with the Joneses. Dad worked tirelessly on our front yard all week long. He welded a new iron gate, redid the stonework on the walkway to our front door, and beautiful flowers were put in neat rows along the driveway, which was quickly filled by the cool glimmer of a brand new silver Toyota Avalon.

The inside of the house was filled with flower vases and new furniture. We had new kitchenware, a full pantry, and fresh linens.

I was biding my time for an opportunity to ask for new clothes.

CHAPTER 2: CHANGES

Baton Rouge Magnet High School's colors were green and gold. I marveled at the size of the school. The class buildings reached several stories high, and green and gold banners with angry looking bulldogs waved from light posts around the front lawn. Every day, after Mother dropped me off, I ascended the massive stone steps and got lost in the sea of students as we flowed through the underpass and onto the giant campus. I didn't feel out of place, though… not until I stepped into the gym after school one day to try out for the wrestling team.

There were guys in loose hanging athletic gear who all seemed to know each other, and they were joking around.

Coach Peterson stormed in wearing a trademark scowl and a "Bulldogs Wrestling" T-shirt.

"GET DOWN AND GIIIIVE MEEEE FIFTY!" was the first thing he yelled at me and the thirty other boys in the gym. We fell to the ground and struggled through fifty pushups. Somewhere between numbers sixteen and eighteen, I made up my mind that I hated wrestling.

"NOW LIIIINE UP!" Coach Peterson yelled. His voice was hoarse, but it never cracked. One by one, he belted off our names, and we screamed back.

"MICHAEL ANDERSON!"

"HERE!"

"JORDAN GREY!"

"HERE!"
"SHANE THIBODEAUX!"
"Here!"
"SPEAK THE FUCK UP, THIBODEAUX!"
"HEEEERE!"
"JESSE BORDELONE!"

I got the gist by the time it was my turn.

"DE'VANNON HUBERT!"

"HERE!"

"HUBERT! YOUR BROTHER SET THE BAR HIGH! DON'T YOU FUCKING DISAPPOINT ME! DO YOU FUCKING HEAR ME, HUBERT?"

"SIR, YES, SIR!" I yelled back.

Some of the other boys snickered, and for a quick second I saw a grin flash across Coach Peterson's face. I hated him already.

For the rest of the afternoon, I suffered the eardrum pounding thunder of Coach Peterson's fixation on my poor form. My brother had tried to explain the rules and tactics of wrestling to me, but I never quite grasped the concept. When practice was finally over, Coach Peterson dismissed us and marched off to his office.

I was sweating as much from anger as from exhaustion. That's when Kari approached me. I had noticed her standing off to the side of the mats taking notes during practice. She wore loose black pants and a white blouse under a thin, black sweater. Her hair was long, curly, and blonde, and her eyes shone as blue as the sky, even under the yellow lights of the gym.

"Your brother was pretty good," she said. Her voice was low, and I couldn't tell if that was natural, or a purposeful fabrication. "I'm Kari, the team manager." She held out her hand and I shook it.

"Listen," she said. "Coach wants you to quit. My advice is either quit right now or prove as soon as possible that you're here to stay."

With that, she turned around and left in the direction of Coach Peterson's office.

I thought about what Kari said as I made my way to the locker room. *If I quit, I'll never hear the end of it from dad, or my brother. If I stay, I'll never hear the end of it from Coach Peterson.*

Then I entered the shower room, and to my delight it was filled with hunky, yummy high school boys washing and toweling off.

For the first time since arriving at practice, I smiled. Wrestling was starting to grow on me.

* * *

During my freshman year, every class was on the opposite side of campus from the previous one. Keeping up my perfect attendance meant running the gauntlet every day. If I stopped to chat, or lighten the load at my locker, I would be late. That means when I got to class I was usually sweating.

"You should join the cross country team," joked Marlene one day in art class. She was six feet tall and captain of the soccer team, which translated into being very popular.

I wiped the sweat from my brow and tried to laugh. "Sadly, the wrestling team has already taken me."

"Wrestling?" Marlene said, failing to hide her surprise. "I didn't take you for a contact sport kid." She was doodling snakes on a soccer field, and I was painting a sunset.

The school's speaker system cracked to life.

"Gooood moooorning, Bulldooooogs! We would like to congratulate both soccer teams on their first wins of the season against McKinley High School. Special shout out to Marlene Tuley on a four goal game!"

Everyone in the class cheered as Marlene soaked in the glory.

"We would also like to congratulate our boys wrestling team on their first place finish at the Redemptorist High School Invitational, Shane Thibodeaux coming in fourth place, and Jordan Grey in first!"

The class clapped politely.

Later that afternoon I was at a wrestling match being yelled at by Coach Peterson.

"COME ON, HUBERT! FIND THE ESCAPE!"

The clock ticked down to under a minute left in my match. The way he was yelling, it sounded as if I was losing. In fact, I was winning this match! I just had to hold on for sixty more seconds.

"COME ON, HUBERT! STAY HUNGRY! DON'T YOU EASE UP ON ME NOW, HUBERT!"

I tried to tune him out. *Just forty-five more seconds.* My opponent was all over my back, but I managed to keep my arms stiff and my shoulders up. I knew this guy wasn't strong enough to pin me. *Only thirty seconds.*

"ESCAAAAPE! COME OOOON, HUBERT!"

Fifteen seconds. I felt my opponent tug and pull in desperation, and then, I sensed a moment of weakness. I tried to pull my legs in and swing my body around, but my opponent was ready. I felt my legs give out as a crushing weight landed on my back.

The timer sounded. I had lost. Coach Peterson was silent. I stood and approached Coach Peterson tentatively.

"HUBERT!"

Here we go, I thought.

"THAT WAS SHIT! YOUR NEXT MATCH IS IN THIRTY! DO BETTER!"

As Coach Peterson walked away to scream at another one of my teammates, I absorbed what he'd said. *"Do better."* I was furious.

Thirty minutes later, I wiped the floor with my next opponent.

"What'd you score me at?" I asked Kari.

"I lost count at thirteen," she said, although I knew she was lying. She never lost track.

"Hey, where's Coach?" I asked. He hadn't watched my match.

Kari gave me a knowing smile. "Don't worry about it." And with a turn and a wave of her blonde hair, she was off to another match.

* * *

The next day in art class, I arrived on time to find Marlene in a wheelchair. She caught my eye as I entered and tried to muster a smile.

"What happened?" I asked, pulling my sunset out of my portfolio and smoothing the edges against the table.

She had a new drawing, the early sketching of a dragon hoarding a soccer ball, but she hadn't unpacked any drawing utensils. She sat pushed back from her desk. Her left foot was outstretched in a thick, white cast, already tagged with the multi-colored Sharpie signatures of a dozen illegible names.

"I went up for a header, and when I came down my foot crunched," she said with a grimace. "I'm gonna have to have surgery..." she trailed off.

I looked at the sunset in my painting. *How easy it would be to turn it into a soccer ball.* I poured out a blob of black paint and began the transformation.

When the morning announcements celebrated the wrestling team's second place finish at the meet, Marlene nodded approvingly at me as the rest of the class clapped. Then she saw the soccer ball sunset, and smiled.

* * *

After six months on the wrestling team, I walked up to Kari. "I want to be a manager," I said, "like you."

I was sick and tired of being yelled at by Coach Peterson, even when I'd been improving my performance. He couldn't help but compare me to my older brother. Still, I had learned enough about the rules of the sport that I didn't want to quit. I wasn't ready to deal with the shame my dad and brother would give me if I did that.

"Ok," Kari said, blandly. "Go tell Coach." And then turned away with another wave of her hair.

The gymnasium's corridors were a labyrinth. I nearly wandered into the girl's locker room, but managed to turn back at the distinct sound of female voices. Rounding the corner, I saw Coach Peterson at the end of the corridor.

"HUBERT! WHAT ARE YOU DOING?"

I walked straight up to him. "I want to become a team manager."

To my surprise, his face softened. "Oh." His brows pinched as he contemplated my proposal. "I suppose we'll need another manager after Kari graduates. That's fine, Hubert."

Kari put me in charge of organizing notes for each boy on the team. She taught me how to log every move of a match. Within a week I knew enough to hold my own in a conversation with my dad and my brother about the rules of wrestling. Even Marlene seemed to give me more street cred after my transition to manager.

Then came The Greater Baton Rouge City Championship. Thousands of families were packed into a large gymnasium with a dozen matches all happening at once. Kari and I split up the matches since two of our guys were often competing simultaneously.

I was dressed my best in my Sidewinder jeans, a white button-down, and Skechers. Running the gauntlet between classes had prepared me well to keep up with the matches.

Thibodeaux was in a highly contested bout with a boy from Catholic High. Every time Thibodeaux took the lead with a takedown, this boy managed to pull off a quick reversal. But as I logged the match, I noticed the judges had credited the boy from Catholic with one reversal too many.

The timer hit zero, and the boy from Catholic was ahead by one point. He began to celebrate his victory. Thibodeaux was miserable, the heartbreak painted clearly on his face.

That's when I stood up and walked over to the judges' table with my head held high. A shiver rippled across the gymnasium. All the judges in front of me were older white men, and as soon as they saw me, a 15-year-old Black kid approaching them with a clipboard, they scowled so hard I was convinced they all had unibrows.

Out of the corner of my eye, I could also see Coach Peterson staring at me, his gaze cold and desperate.

I preached from my notes. "At 1:37 of round three, Number Four from Catholic is awarded with two reversals. However, a reversal is impossible without first receiving a takedown. Either Number Four from Catholic should not be awarded a reversal at 1:37, or Number Seven from Baton Rouge High should be awarded with an additional takedown immediately prior."

The scowls darkened on the judges' faces. Their hands were tied. They couldn't deny my logic and especially not in front of Thibodeaux and Coach Peterson. They removed two points from the score for Catholic, making Thibodeaux the winner by one point.

I walked back across the mat and sat cross legged next to Coach Peterson, who stared at me, dumbfounded. Then the next match started. Unfortunately, there was nothing I could do for Anderson's heavy defeat.

* * *

Sophomore year of high school was hell. My GPA fell below a 3.0, and everywhere I went, the smell of bergamot and lavender haunted me. And when I slept, the scent became even more intense. I couldn't spit it out. I couldn't sweat it out. I couldn't cry it out. It was just always there. All of my activities suffered.

One Sunday, I entered the living room dressed up for church and encountered my father in a raggedy white T-shirt.

"Aren't we going to church?" I asked.

"Nope," he answered.

"But what about grandma?"

My dad just shrugged. "You can rake the leaves in our front yard instead."

I changed back into street clothes, dumbfounded. Grandma had stopped driving years ago so I figured I might as well get to work.

Several inches of fall leaves were piled up on our front lawn when I stepped outside. They were quite colorful, and their cold, damp smell was a nice distraction from the bergamot and lavender rooted in my nose. I grabbed our wooden rake with its red, metal fingers, and got to work.

"Be careful!" called a voice from behind me.

I jumped and turned around. He was a middle-aged Black man I'd never seen before, and he was standing at the edge of our lawn.

"Watch out for poisonous snakes under those leaves!" He pointed to the ground beneath my feet.

At that moment, with the next pull of my rake I was startled as the leaves revealed a reddish-brown snake flopping back and forth like an angry fish out of water. I immediately looked up for the man who had just warned me, but he was gone. I looked up and down our long narrow street, but it was like he had vanished into thin air.

I immediately dropped the wooden handle and ran back into the house with shaking hands and an accelerated heartbeat. I vowed to never touch a rake again so long as I live.

Did I just meet an Angel?

* * *

Parisian's was a huge department store in Baton Rouge, located inside the Mall of Louisiana. On a fabulous fall Saturday, I saw a poster at the mall advertising Parisian's Teen Board modeling program. "Tryouts today," it announced. "Do you have what it takes?" This opportunity was one I couldn't afford to miss.

The large room was packed with sexy young men and women when I arrived. I was one of at least six hundred other teens vying for one of ten spots. When my number was called I stood up and strutted the full length of the room, sashaying my hips and pouting my lips as I made eye contact with everyone sitting at the judges' table.

On Friday, I came home to a letter in the mail from Parisian's. They wanted me to join their modeling team! It was like getting a golden ticket from Willy Wonka's Chocolate Factory!

My work modeling at the mall was everything I could have dreamed and more. I was given a schedule of appearances, competitions, and community service projects. I even got to choreograph dance routines to go along with our runway shows. I also got a hefty discount at Parisian's. Within a week, I had completely upgraded my wardrobe.

One afternoon after a rehearsal, I wandered into the shoe section. My Skechers were running up against the end of their clock, and my feet were in desperate need of some new flare.

"Hi there, how can I help you?" The young man behind the counter smiled at me. His white button-down looked spectacular tucked into the vest of his black business suit. His name tag read "Chase," and he was twiddling his thumbs with nervous, nerdy energy. His platinum hair and gray eyes were majestically framed by silver square-frame glasses, his face was firm, and his jawline was chiseled for days!

"Hi," I said, lighting up my smile. "My feet need to feel hugged."

Chase laughed. "I think I can help you with that." Then his expression changed to one of intense curiosity. "Hey, sorry, do I know you? You look extremely familiar for some reason?"

I gave a knowing smile to put him at ease. "You've probably seen me on the billboard ads around this place."

I loved the look of shock that followed on Chase's face. "Oh, no shit! That's right!"

I spent the entire afternoon trying on new shoes and talking it up with Chase. It didn't take long for us to get on the same wavelength, and soon he was spilling all the gay tea.

"If you want to experience the real gay life," he said, "you have to go to the Boots Bar down in New Orleans. Forget Baton Rouge. New Orleans is where the party's at! Just look for the rainbow flags on Bourbon St."

"How old do you have to be to get in there?" I asked.

"You just have to be confident," he winked.

"Will you go with me?"

Chase's face fell. "I'm afraid I don't have the time these days, but don't let me hold you back!"

I was sold. The next morning I asked my parents if I could borrow their car to go "hang out" with friends but I didn't tell them we were headed to New Orleans. Then I called up my girlfriends and we hit the road.

True to Chase's word, the Boots Bar was unmissable. A large rainbow banner framed the door and bumping club music pounded from within, along with the smell of spilled cocktails and cigarette smoke. *Eureka!*

A muscled stud in a tight pink neon tee that read "Security" stood at the door. I smiled as confidently as I could and flashed my driver's permit in front of his face. Behind the plastic card, I could see the man's eyes narrow, and a smirk creep across his face. He gave an exaggerated check over his shoulder, and then looked up and down the block before reaching in his pocket and pulling out four bright orange wristbands.

"Drinks on me. You guys be safe."

Hell yes!

The bar was packed with the most eclectic cast of outfits (or lack of outfits) I had ever seen. Depending on where I looked, I saw cowboys, devils, angels, ripped men in nothing but speedos, and women looking wild in cat suits. The dress code was: *anything goes!* These were my people.

I walked up to the bar with my girlfriends. They ordered some cocktails, while I asked for a couple shots of vodka. I heard a snort off to the side and turned to find a couple of mostly naked men lining up what I assumed was cocaine on the bar counter and inhaling it with a twenty dollar bill.

We enjoyed our drinks and took in the scene. There were several VIP booths with bottles of champagne on ice, hookah pipes, bongs, cigars, and other substances I couldn't identify. The DJ on stage was bouncing to his beats, and I gazed longingly at the dance floor.

"Come on!" I shouted to the girls, and then b-lined it for the epicenter of the party without waiting. The alcohol hit me just in time for the beat to drop. Chase was right. This was the place to be.

A flash of white rippled across my periphery, and I turned to see a shirtless man wearing bright flowing pants with a partner in tow. As soon as he had my attention, he knelt down and pulled out his partner's dick and sucked I like he like was trying to win an Olympic gold medal. I felt my face flush red. *People can do this in public?* I marveled. Sexy, very sexy.

The Boots Bar won me over. From now on, this was to be my home base.

After dropping the girls off, I returned home around 3:30am and crashed. I was sure I would pay for the late night in some way in the morning, but I didn't care as I dizzied off to sleep.

* * *

"DE'VANNON!" Coach Peterson screamed at me, loud enough for all the other coaches and managers to hear, "WHAT THE FUCK DO YOU THINK YOU'RE DOING?"

I was snacking in the break room while I waited for the next wrestling match to start. Being allowed into the coaches' break room at tournaments was one of the few perks of being a team manager. Ever since Kari graduated, however, Coach Peterson had been taking more cheap shots at me. "I'm eating some crackers," I said matter-of-factly.

"YOU FAT, LAZY, SON-OF-A-BITCH!" He grabbed me by the back of my neck and shoved me out the door. "GET THE FUCK OUT OF HERE!"

All the other coaches and managers pretended not to notice. I dropped the plate I was holding, and marched away, fuming.

"WHAT THE HELL ARE YOU DOING, DE'VANNON?"

I nearly dropped my pencil in shock, for the voice shouting at me from across the gymnasium wasn't that of Coach Peterson, but my dad. The whole building, filled with at least a thousand people, had hushed in the wake of his heckle.

"WHAT THE HELL ARE YOU DOING JUST SITTING THERE, TAKING NOTES, YOU COWARD! PUT ON A WRESTLING UNIFORM AND MAN UP!"

My face was red with anger and embarrassment. Everyone in the entire gymnasium was staring. I turned around and walked out.

Outside the gymnasium, my dad caught up with me. "Where do you think you're going!"

"Why would you do that?" I pleaded with him.

"Excuse me?"

"Why would you yell at me like that in front of everybody?"

My dad smacked me across the face. "You ain't doing shit! All you care about is looking good and feeling good," he said with disgust. "You don't deserve the things you have. Why don't you stop being a coward, man the fuck up, play a real sport, and get a real job?" I shook my head. I couldn't believe what I was hearing. Tears welled up in my eyes and I began to cry. My dad walked away, unable to stand in my presence any longer. I hated my dad now more than ever. *You're a terrible fucking parent and you always have been!*

I never went back to wrestling. The managerial position was volunteer, and I had no obligation to stay. Quitting in the middle of the season was the best *Fuck you!* I could think of giving to Coach Peterson and my dad that wouldn't get me beaten.

* * *

"Mother," I asked one day, "can I take dance lessons?"
We were in the car on the way to church. We were becoming a rare Sunday presence. "Dance?" my Mother echoed, doubtfully.

"Yes," I said. "I think I can make a career out of it."

"De'Vannon," my Mother looked at me in the rearview mirror. It was just the two of us in the car. "Isn't the men's modeling work close enough?"

"Modeling pairs well with dancing," I countered.

"Do you know how much money dancers make?" my Mother asked. Before I could respond she answered her own question. "Not much."

"So what?" I questioned. "I enjoy it, I'm good at it, I think I can make it work."

"If dancing makes you happy, then fine, I'll pay for your dance lessons" my Mother replied, "But don't be fooled into thinking it's a career."

That was good enough for now.

* * *

Grandma rushed around the house from room to room, she told me and my brother that she loved us and then went into my parents' room and spoke to them as well. Eventually she turned for the bathroom. "Move!", she said as she forcefully pushed me out of the way and squeezed past me. I was amazed at how much strength was still left in her bones.

It was a long time before she left the bathroom, and when she did she went straight to her room and closed the door. She was quiet for the rest of the night.

In the morning, I woke to a sound I had never heard my Mother make before. At first I thought I'd imagined it as my brain transitioned to groggy wakefulness. Then I realized the sound had come from grandma's bedroom. Mother was wailing.

"No, God, no! Wake her up, please! Call Pastor Nelson! Call 911!" She continued to moan as my dad made the phone calls. Then he came to tell me and my brother, but we already knew.

The last thing I saw before the paramedics took my grandma away was her blue eyes, still and deep as an ocean that had finally found its rest.

* * *

One month after grandma died, we moved back to our old house. My parents couldn't afford the new house anymore. And similarly to how we moved the first time, we left without warning. I got home from school one day and was told that we had lost the house. Everything was already packed up and overnight I was thrust back into poverty.

The gossip of my family's move travelled fast.

Kids I didn't even know came up to me at school asking, "Where did you move to?"

I was too embarrassed to reveal the truth. "Just a little ways south," I responded cryptically.

"How's the new house? Does it have central air conditioning?"

"Yes," I lied. "Of course it does."

My grades began to slide again senior year. The tension at home was unbearable, and the close quarters that came with living back in the hood made it impossible to focus and be productive. I was suffocating. Then came the ultimate pop-quiz.

The Armed Services Vocational Aptitude Battery, or ASVAB, was a mandatory test for all seniors. There was no time to study, as the time between finding out about the test and taking it was about ten minutes. No sooner had the morning bell sounded were all seniors marched off to the assembly hall.

Men and women in camouflage military uniforms greeted us as we entered. The tests were already placed face down on prepositioned tables.

"This is a test to determine if you've got what it takes to join the military," one man proudly stated after we had all taken our seats. "Each section will be timed. Good luck, and Godspeed."

I breezed through each section with time to spare, giving bullshit answers most of the way.

Two months later my Mother passed me the telephone. "There's a call for you from a… Staff Sergeant Powell?"

Curiously, I took the phone. "Hello?"

"Is this Mr. De'Vannon Hubert?"

"Yes."

"Hi there Mr. Hubert, my name is Staff Sergeant Powell, and I'm calling because I am incredibly impressed with your ASVAB test results."

"Really?" I asked. "What did I get?"

"81 out of 99, scoring consistently high in every subject. Frankly, anything over 70 is impressive."

Fuck, I thought to myself. *Does this mean I'm military material?*

"Mr. Hubert, have you considered what a future might look like in the Air Force? I think you'd do well, and I'd love to tell you more about it. Would you have time for a meeting?"

"Oh, thanks," I stuttered. "That's very kind of you. I will consider it."

"Very well, Mr. Hubert. I look forward to following up with you."

I hung up the phone and smiled. It felt good to have someone pursuing me.

After that, recruiters started to call every night, begging my parents to sign me up for the Army, Navy, Marines, or Air Force. I was flattered, but I didn't see myself as the military type. Then one afternoon as I was leaving my job at the mall I saw a train of recruiter tables in the main walkway.

The man behind the Air Force table was in the middle of a speech. "At the Air Force, every individual who passes our training is unique and gifted. We invest in you. You'll learn from the best instructors, with the best equipment, and in the best country in the world!"

As he went on, I inched my way closer to the table and nabbed a handful of Skittles packets from the candy jar that served as the centerpiece. "Sgt. Powell," his nametag said.

When his speech was done, I introduced myself. "Hey, I spoke with you on the phone some time ago. I like what you're saying," I said. "I just have one question."

"What's that, son?"

"Are you gonna send me someplace cold?"

Sgt. Powell laughed. "Boot camp is in Texas, then you can go anywhere you want."

I nodded.

"If you sign up today I'll throw in a $6,000 bonus," he said, cocking an eyebrow.

I enrolled in the Air Force on the spot and signed up to be an Electronic Warfare Systems Apprentice.

My parents were happy when they found out about my enrollment because it meant I was on the path to a real career that didn't involve dancing. At the end of my senior year, they surprised me by funding my senior trip to London and Paris. I was torn at first because the trip meant I would miss my dance school's recital, but I was going to the military. I wasn't going to be a dancer. So I travelled with a handful of other graduates to Europe. I saw Big Ben, the London Eye, the Louvre, the Mona Lisa, and the Palace of Versailles.

It was the most relaxing two weeks of my life… and it was quickly followed by the most hellish six weeks of my life: boot camp.

PART II
(2000-2006)

CHAPTER 3: BASIC TRAINING

SUMMER 2000 – LACKLAND AIR FORCE BASE, SAN ANTONIO, TX

"Stand up, you weak fucking dick suckers!" screamed Drill Sergeant Stafford, a six-foot-eight, bald head man with a permanent frown hung under a badly crooked nose. Veins bulged out of his neck as he stepped onto the bus to cordially welcome us to Basic Military Training. "God gave you two legs, didn't he? Use them, dammit! Up!"

One recruit near the front yelled back, "Sir, yes, sir!"

Sgt. Stafford continued, "You maggots are nothing to me! I have more respect for the concrete under your feet than you assholes! I walk on it and it holds me up! So when you leave this bus, you're going to kiss the concrete like you kissed your mama goodbye! And if you think you're here to become a man, you're wrong! You're here to become a dog! I'm gonna tear you down and then build you back up again! Do you understand me, you little fucks!?"

"Get off this bus and start kissing dirt like the fucking worm you are! Now!"

After we kissed the concrete, Sgt. Stafford lined us up and chewed us out one by one. I figured it was his way of doing roll call. Like Coach

Peterson, his voice sounded pained, but it didn't crack. I had never heard a man yell so loud for so long other than my dad.

When he was finally done, another drill sergeant stood in his place with a clipboard. It was after midnight and too dark for me to see the name on his badge. "Anyone feel like quitting?"

One boy keeled over and barfed. I heard a sniffle from someone else.

"If you're quitting," the officer said, "the bus is right behind you."

To my amazement, a handful of boys slumped off and boarded the bus.

When it was clear the rest of us were staying, the officer assigned us to our Flights. I was in Flight 515.

As we gathered our bags to go to our quarters, another recruit alongside me gestured to the group of quitters back on the bus. "Them white boys can't handle a little yelling?" he muttered.

I snickered, "At home I woulda got a beating to go along with the yelling," I joked. "Stafford is a walk in the park compared to my old man."

* * *

"HAVE YOU EVER PUT YOUR DICK INSIDE OF ME?"

"Uuuh, no–" said a startled recruit.

"THEN DON'T YOU EVER CALL ME BY MY FIRST NAME! I AM YOUR FLIGHT CHIEF! NOT YOUR FUCKING GIRLFRIEND!"

Flight Chief Olga Dominguez was five feet flat, but she had the loudest, meanest voice on base.

She also had the meanest car. Each morning at 4:45am, the trumpet alarm called *Réveille* sounded and we had fifteen minutes to get our barracks in order before the headlights of her sleek, black Mercedes Benz flashed through our windows signaling her arrival.

When Sergeant Dominguez arrived, everything had to be perfect.

"SHOW ME YOUR LOCKER, SAMUELS! YOU CALL THOSE CLOTHES FOLDED? THIS AIN'T A FUCKING PAPER AIRPLANE CONTEST, DAMMIT, THIS IS THE AIR FORCE! FOLD YOUR DAMN CLOTHES!"

"HUBERT! YOUR BED SHOULD BE AS STRAIGHT AS A BRICK! DO IT RIGHT!"

"LEE, DO YOU LIKE JEWELRY? YOU LAME FUCK! YOUR DOG

TAGS ARE NOT JEWELRY! THEY ARE YOUR IDENTITY! TUCK THEM UNDER YOUR SHIRT BEFORE I SHOVE THEM DOWN YOUR THROAT!"

"NOW LISTEN UP YOU SACKS OF SHIT! WHEN YOU GO TO THE MESS HALL, THERE WILL BE NO DESSERT! THERE WILL BE NO! DAMNED! DESSERT! THERE WILL NOT EVEN BE SODA! LIFE IS A LIVING FUCKING HELL! GET USED TO IT! IF YOU WANT YOUR PRIVILEGES BACK, EITHER LEARN TO FIGHT FOR THEM, OR GET THE FUCK OUT OF THE AIR FORCE! YOU ARE HERE TO STARVE FOR THE ORDINARY COMFORTS OF THE AMERICAN DREAM, SO YOU'LL FIGHT YOUR FUCKING ASS OFF WHEN THE SCUM OF THIS EARTH TRY TO TAKE THEM AWAY! SO IF I HEAR ONE COMPLAINT FROM ANY OF YOUR FUCKING MOUTHS, I WILL PULL A 341 ON YOUR ASS SO FAST YOUR DICK WON'T HAVE TIME TO GET HARD!"

A 341 is a small form all recruits in BMT carry containing identifying information. Any drill instructor on base can pull them from any recruit if they feel like a rule has been broken. If I got too many pulled from me I could get recycled and have to stay in BMT even longer. The drill sergeants were good at their job. Day after day, to my continued shock, recruits were leaving the base. Hardly a few hours went by without another person packing up and heading home. I admired the systemic weeding out of the weak, as long as I didn't incur too much wrath.

"Two hands on the fucking tray, dammit!" Stafford grabbed my tray of food and flung it to the floor. "We don't want any fucking messes around here! Now clean that shit up! And gimmie a 341!"

I went hungry for the rest of the day.

* * *

After three days the sergeants escorted us new recruits to the telephone stations and allowed us each a short call home to our parents. I could see some guys holding back tears as if this was the longest they'd ever been away from home. After this first call we were allowed to make phone calls whenever we had free time... which was never.

I was assigned to the laundry room with a guy who was also in Flight 515 named Adam, and we were quickly becoming best friends. "There are a lot of gay guys on base," I said.

"What makes you say that?" he asked. I could tell he was being genuine.

"Oh honey, it's obvious. I'm not the only one stealing glances in the shower. One guy even showed me a picture of his boyfriend! And we're surrounded by sexy dudes all the time. It's a gay paradise!"

"I can see that," Adam admitted. The dryer finished spinning and he started pulling out the shirts. "Is Samuels gay?"

"No," I said, playing along with his effort to be insightful. "Samuels is just a scaredy-cat trying to pretend he's a lion. He's not gay, though."

"What about Borris?"

"No, Borris really *is* straight. Who is *trying* to be straight?"

"Lee," Adam said confidently.

"Bingo!" My boy was learning. "That bitch, mmhmm." Adam laughed, and I dove into my rant. "Okay week one, he's a mess. Week two, he's got his shit together like, 'fool can't be playin' no more!' Then he sees me one bunk over actually being perfect, and he's like, 'shit, if I'm like De'Vannon, everybody's gonna find out.' Week three, he's back to being a mess again."

My washer finished up, and I got to work hauling Air Force sweat shorts into the dryer. "And check this out," I continued, "yesterday we passed each other on the stairs, and I saw he had his dog tags out again, so I tried to point it out to him but he jumped back like I'm some sexual predator or something! I mean, shit! Can you be more obvious?"

The following morning the trumpet sounded Réveille and Flight 515 scrambled to get our shit together for Sgt. Dominguez. Lee dawdled. His bed still looked like a bird's nest when Sgt. Dominguez stormed through the door.

"WHAT THE FUCK IS THIS! DAMMIT, LEE, WERE YOU DREAMING OF YOUR GIRLFRIEND? OR IS HUBERT GIVING YOU A HARD ON? PULL YOUR SHIT TOGETHER AND GIMMIE A 341! WE'RE RUNNING A 10-MILE!"

The air froze with stifled groans, but I breathed happily. I felt vindicated.

After a few weeks we were all getting used to the drill sergeants' verbal abuse and the high standards for appearance and performance. As my nerves eased, I realized I had not taken a shit or jerked off since the moment we'd arrived three weeks prior. I'd been too tense!

At the end of the 10-mile run we showered off, and a sense of comradery fell over the group. I basked in the sight of fit young men finally at ease, naked together in the shower.

"Holy shit," Adam said as we toweled off. "We're doing this."

Then I slipped into a bathroom stall to relieve my bowels and give myself a hand job that would make a porn star jealous.

* * *

It was the fifth week of basic training, also known as Warrior Week, and I had thirty pounds of gear strapped on my back. I lined up with the rest of Flight 515 as Flight Chief Olga Dominguez blew her whistle and led us marching into the desert.

As the sun rose high in the noon sky beating down 120° rays of heat on us, a pair of buses passed us. Other flights' drill sergeants allowed them to take the bus into the desert but not ours. We all gazed longingly at the taillights as the buses passed ahead of us, and Sgt. Dominguez laughed.

There were strict rules about hydrating. The Air Force didn't want anyone dying of thirst, but they also didn't want us feeling too comfortable. The desert was over a hundred degrees, and within a few hours my dry mouth could barely swallow as I watched the flight chiefs dump gallons of water over the dirt of an obstacle course. Barbed wire stretched ominously over a pit of mud.

I felt the stinging cut of the metal wire against my shoulders as I dove underneath, mud clogging my mouth, nose, and ears. We climbed rope walls, dangled across monkey bars, and jumped from twelve-foot mounds, forcing our tired feet to tuck-and-roll.

Later that afternoon, with mud still crusted over our sinuses, we gawked as our drill sergeant pointed to a rock where she said a rattlesnake was hiding. "...in the wilderness, it's kill or be killed..." She held out a long, metal rod and lifted the rattlesnake by the middle of its body.

In a blur, the snake's head whipped around and it bit its own ass. Seconds later it died from its own poison.

At night, we slept in tents and rotated shifts to keep watch, simulating the vigilance of a warzone. The drill sergeants loved that word: "vigilance." Everything was a matter of life and death. It didn't help that it was the year 2000, "Y2K," and my watch-partner, Jerry, was hooked on every conspiracy theory known to man.

"Just because the world didn't end exactly on New Year's doesn't mean it won't end *this year*," he kept trying to convince me.

"Hush!" I hissed back. It was 2am, and we were supposed to be staying *vigilant*. Slacking off on watch was a heavily punishable offense.

Jerry managed to shut up for a minute, but then, "I hear the military's recruiting twice as hard this year in anticipation of an alien invasion."

"Shut the fuck up, Jerry! Save it for the morning."

He fell quiet again, but I could sense he was just biding his time.

Suddenly, the night seemed to get darker. I looked up, but there were no clouds in the sky. In fact, the stars above me were quite beautiful. I could see more of the Milky Way than I'd ever known existed. On the horizon, a full moon rose. It was blood red.

I braced myself for more of Jerry's conspiracies, but he kept his mouth shut. He saved his antics for the morning… when Sgt. Dominguez told him to "SHUT THE FUCK UP! YOU WANNA SEE A BLOOD MOON? BEND OVER AND I'LL WHIP YOUR ASS!"

* * *

The final week of BMT was the best. After surviving Warrior Week, everyone in my flight got to wear our Air Force Blues. I found Adam, and we walked around base like hot shit. We landed in line at the telephones.

Now that we were within a week of graduating, we could call home and invite our families to come to our graduation.

"Hello?"

"Hello Mother."

"De'Vannon! How are you?"

"I'm good, Mother. I'm in the last week, and I'm on track to graduate on Friday. Family's invited."

"Godzilla's growing wings! Yes, we'll be there!"

* * *

Graduation was a sea of blue. Flights from all across the base filled a grassy stadium, standing patiently on the parade field through the course of the hour long ceremony. Parents and military officials looked on from the seats in the stadium. A wave of warmth bubbled through me. I had survived a grueling six weeks, and I was fitter, healthier, and prouder for it.

Adam put an arm around me. "Shit, man. I'm looking forward to getting to Keesler Air Force Base over in Biloxi for our tech schools. We won't have much time together though cuz my program will have me out of there in a quarter the time as yours. Just wanted to say, it's been an honor doing the laundry together."

I laughed.

"De'Vannon!" I heard my Mother call. I ran over and gave her a big hug.

"Look at my handsome son!" she beamed.

Then my dad stuck out his hand. "Congratulations, De'Vannon."

I stood up straight and shook his hand.

CHAPTER 4: RANK 'N' FILE

SPRING 2001 – DAVIS-MONTHAN AIR FORCE BASE, TUCSON, AZ

"Suck my dick, you faggot!" The insult echoed from an Airman standing outside his dorm which was across the street from mine.

I tensed my arms and slammed my door in frustration. Sid was a shorter, uglier looking version of Keanu Reeves, and he'd pounced on my flamboyance from the day I arrived in Arizona. The nightly catcall from across the street was getting on my nerves.

"Easy, friend," said Idris, my new, sexy ass roommate, picking up on my tension.

I turned to Idris. "This motherfucker–"

"Look, I know, it's cowardly, but–"

"I swear, next time he calls me a fag, I'm reporting him."

Idris was silent.

"Fuck!" I screamed.

I'd heard the term, "Don't Ask, Don't Tell," and I already knew reporting Sid would accomplish absolutely nothing except getting me kicked out of the Air Force.

After a minute, Idris tried to calm me down again. "Look, I don't give a shit whether you're gay or not. Sid's a dumb fuck for harassing you like that."

I collapsed on my bed and tried to steady my breath.

"Look," Idris continued, "this may not be what you want to hear, but you gotta keep it cool so you don't sacrifice your enlistment. Alright?"

I nodded. "As soon as possible, I'm getting the fuck out of these dorms."

"Amen to that, brother."

* * *

I was assigned to the 355th Component Repair Squadron which was a unit consisting of over three hundred Airmen and officers. This squadron was the second largest at Davis-Monthan AFB. This base held over 6,000 Airmen and officers in total, not counting military families, retirees, etc., which raised the tally to well over 40,000 people. This gargantuan base had offices, dorms, flight lines, base housing, a golf course, and so much more, plus it even had its own zip code. I was an Electronic Warfare Systems Apprentice responsible for the maintenance of line-replaceable units from a number of C-130 Hercules aircraft. This maintenance was conducted in our "Back Shop" which was located in an isolated office near the flight line. The best thing about this job was that I rarely had to go outside as most of the maintenance was done on aircraft parts brought into our office.

One day at work I waited for Aldo to stop by my station. He was a Filipino refugee who'd moved to America to escape a gang that was trying to kill him. He had a barcode tattooed on the back of his neck, and his shadow seemed to darken any workspace more than it should. No one fucked with Aldo, and he didn't fuck with sub-perfect work. We had one year to become proficient in the Back Shop, and he had no pity for anyone who wasn't cutting it. The seven months I had spent in tech school had prepared me well, but none of my instructors had been as tough as Aldo was.

I had a broken circuit board assembly in front of me. It was a small piece, but if I couldn't get it to function then a C-130 Hercules pilot would not be taking off.

"Alright, De'Vannon. Begin," Aldo said as he approached my station.

I narrated my troubleshooting process, following a step-by-step procedure printed out for this specific piece. If I skipped any step, my work would be deemed an automatic failure.

"First, I'm examining the circuitry for foreign, invasive matter." I looked for any specs of dirt and anything that was not a part of the circuit board. I already knew the problem was a bent connector on the output, but I couldn't skip a step. The task took me 2 minutes and 44 seconds to complete.

"You're getting there," Aldo said, "but I still want you to get below 2:30." He moved on. It was the best any of us in the Back Shop could ask for. Aldo never missed a teaching opportunity, and never said anyone was perfect until he signed off at the end of the year. *If* he signed off.

* * *

I was an Airman First Class (E-3) and on track to become a "Senior Airman Below the Zone," which meant I could rise to the rank of Senior Airman (E-4) in less than three years. It would also make me a high enough rank to be able to move off base, plus I would get a raise. Until then, I went after the Military Outstanding Volunteer Service Medal. It seemed easy compared to other medals, but it was highly applauded because no one ever went for it. The squadron administration explained to me that there wasn't a set number of volunteer hours required for this medal. They said it had to be a "significant" amount and it was suggested to me that I aim for at least 500 hours to be on the safe side. I needed a shit ton of volunteer hours, so I applied to volunteer at the Tucson Food Bank and at a local Big Buddy program.

Then I applied for a military Star Credit Card. I was approved for all three! That Saturday, before my first day volunteering with Big Buddy, I drove to the Base Exchange which was a lot like Walmart. Everything there was tax free. I put my $500 worth of credit to use and bought a few packs of Calvin Klein underwear and a fresh pair of Timberlands.

Drake was a quiet African American kid wearing a Cardinals baseball cap and sketching in a journal.

"What are you drawing?" I asked as I sat down across the peach-colored table from him.

"This is me kicking a Super Bowl-winning field goal," he said, eyes lighting up.

I looked at the colored pencil drawing of a flat green football field with two massive yellow goal posts shooting up to the top of the page.

"Do you play?" I asked.

"I was going to, but then the coach at my school got fired," Drake explained. "Now we don't have a football program."

"He got fired?"

The supervisor spoke up over my shoulder. I hadn't even noticed she was still there. "There was a bit of a... *scandal*."

My chest tightened and I remembered the scent of bergamot and lavender. My knuckles went white on the handles of the chair. I shook my head. *Focus*. I wanted to make a difference for Drake. "So, is there a football game tomorrow?" I asked.

"Yes," he replied.

"How would you like to go together?"

Drake stopped drawing to look at me. "Seriously?"

"Of course! When is it?"

"1pm."

I paused while my brain converted that to 1300 hours military time. "We can grab lunch at Burger King and then head to the game after."

Drake was smiling from ear to ear, and it made my heart burn with joy.

* * *

When I arrived back at my dorm on base, something was off. The lights were on, and I could see shadows moving across the bottom of the door. My vigilance was about to take a U-turn into paranoia when I heard the unmistakable purr of Madonna's voice. I opened the door.

"HAPPY BIRTHDAY!" yelled Idris and two other friends, Jacob and Yoshi.

I stepped in to see Madonna's "Immaculate Collection" on VHS, tied in a blue ribbon. One of the tapes was playing on the television. I screamed, and then bear hugged the guys.

Idris passed me a bottle of Jack Daniels. "To keeping your shit together," he said.

"Amen!" I agreed.

Then came the echo of Sid's voice from outside. "You gay ass bitch! Suck my dick you–"

"FUCK YOU, SID! YOU DICKSUCKER!" Yoshi yelled back.

"You're all a bunch of faggots!"

Jacob and Yoshi stormed out the door. "You're the one screaming like a pussy! You wanna play big mouth? Come here, motherfucker!" Their voices faded away and Idris and I were left laughing in sweet harmony with Madonna.

When they came back, they dragged me out of the room. "Okay, let's go!"

"Where?" I asked.

"You're 18, you son-of-a-bitch! To the strip club!"

"We're buying you a lap dance!" Idris teased.

* * *

"The timing of the snap is everything," Drake was saying. He'd finished naming off all the starting players for the Arizona Cardinals between bites of his hamburger, and I tried to listen as he went on to explain his take on the mindset of the quarterback. But I was distracted. Images from the previous night flashed on repeat through my mind: the stripper grinding on me; the warm feel of her pussy as she let me finger her; the chorus of cheers from the guys afterward.

After dropping Drake off at his house, I drove to the Base Exchange and bought a leather jacket, some new jeans, and some camo underwear. Then I hurried back to my dorm to shower and change clothes.

I jumped in the front seat of my silver Chevy Cavalier which my parents had purchased for me during tech school in Biloxi. As I started the engine I thought, *I wonder if there's a bar I can get into.* I headed toward Downtown.

Neon lights bled through the front doors of Tucson's nightclubs, and trance music pulsed through their walls. I found a parking spot and started to try my luck at the bars. DV8 was the only bar I was old enough to get into, and as soon as I saw that I had club access, I paid the cover fee and dove the fuck in.

A merchandise stand was selling glow sticks, and I bought two orange ones. Everyone's eyes seemed to be rolled toward the back of their heads. People were jumping and moving their bodies in the weirdest ways, and I loved it. I started to shake my body, too.

The bass was heavy, and I could feel my heartbeat sync up with it. Soon I was waving my glow sticks in a sea of neon, and I felt like I was bouncing on a trampoline in heaven.

One guy with a white-haired mullet bounced up to me. "Duuuude! You want some blow?"

I smiled politely and screamed back, "No! I want to dance!"

"Alright! Have fun!" And he bounced away.

I danced until close (which turned out to be 0200 hours). As I stepped out of the club my heart and mind were racing. I felt like my night was just beginning.

Even at 0200 hours, the Tucson strip had its fair share of lights. I turned right onto N. 4th Ave. and saw a huge rainbow flag. *Eureka!* I slowed my car to a crawl as I tried to get a look at the sign on the place. "IBT's" it said, and there was something underneath it, but I had to stop the car to get a better look. "It's 'Bout Time!"

Suddenly my view was cut off by a short, petite Latino man in a black T-shirt. "You cruising?" he asked.

"Yeah!" I said excitedly, not sure what he was referring to.

"Right on, brother!" He opened my passenger door and slipped in. "How are you?"

A little stunned, I replied cordially, "I'm good."

"Fun night?" he asked.

"Yes," I couldn't lie.

"Want to have some more fun?" The man reached into his pockets and pulled out a handful of XXL condoms. I looked doubtfully at my little new friend. Seeing the look in my eyes, he stared back at me confidently. "Want to see it?" he asked.

How often do you get to see a XXL dick?

"Show me."

The man unzipped his pants and... boom! Out popped a MONSTER DICK!!!

I swear, this thing fell past his kneecaps.

"Go ahead," Monster Dick encouraged. "Touch it."

I couldn't *not* touch it. It looked like it was at least 14 inches long. I reached across the center console and stroked it gently. I couldn't even wrap my hand all the way around the thing. I shuddered.

"So, do you need a ride or something?" I asked Monster Dick. I still wasn't sure why he'd invited himself into my car.

"You could drive me back to my place."

"Show me the way."

Twenty minutes later we arrived at a house with several cars in the driveway and all the lights on. I could faintly hear Top 40's music resonating from inside.

"Come on," Monster Dick beckoned. "Come meet my friends."

"I don't know. Isn't it late?"

"It's never too late for fun." It was hard to argue with Monster Dick.

Inside, several drag queens and trans girls in sparkling drag were beginning to collect empty port glasses.

"Well hello! Who's this?" one of the ladies asked. She wore a bright blue scarf draped around her neck and approached me like she was walking on water.

"I'm De'Vannon," I replied.

"De'Vannon!" she cooed, trying out the name. "That's lovely!"

"Aw, it's even better when you say it," I replied.

"You're sweet." She bopped me on the nose. "My name is Faye, and, well, these are the girls," she waved to the other girls who were pouring another round of drinks. "I see you've met our little champion, here."

Faye made it so easy to laugh.

"Yes, we were just going up–" Monster Dick started, but Faye cut him off.

"Oh, don't steal De'Vannon so quickly! I'm just getting to know the sweet thing!"

Monster Dick looked at me. "I'll be upstairs." He left.

"What's it like being a Drag Queen?" I asked Faye.

"Being a Drag Queen is a lot to handle, especially once one has reached the status that I have." Faye replied, suddenly seeming a bit less energetic than a moment ago. Faye continued, "The world wants more of me and yet it's hard for me to share myself with another. Being an entertainer and not being able to balance a romantic relationship with another is the worst part of it all. It sucks but at the same time I've been able to experience moments I wouldn't trade for the world. I absolutely live for this my dear."

Emotions of pity and intrigue mixed together inside of me and rendered me unable to speak.

Faye put her hand on my shoulder. "Listen, if you want to go upstairs and have fun, don't let me stop you, but if you want to bide your time, or if you need an alibi, I could sure use a ride home."

"Will he be okay?" I asked.

"Oh, he'll probably swing his dick and smash something, then jerk off and blow something else up. Then he'll crash and tomorrow he'll be fine. Don't you worry."

"Where do you live?" I asked. A car ride with friendly Faye at any hour was better than the thought of succumbing to Monster Dick.

"I'll lead the way," she assured me, "but if we're going, we should leave *now*."

Timing is everything after all."

* * *

I stared out of my dusty dorm window at the construction workers shuffling in and out of the building across the street. As I watched, a man set up a ladder and began positioning a neon sign above the entrance: "Stormy's Cyber Café."

On my lap was a yellow piece of legal paper with dates and numbers. Listed on the page were the hours I'd been volunteering the past month with Drake and at the food bank. It added up to a hundred hours, which was leagues below the numbers I needed to be hitting to earn the medal for volunteering. I had to get more involved.

The plywood door to Stormy's Cyber Café creaked noisily as I entered. A short woman was scribbling away at the front counter, her head adorned with California bleached blonde hair. Long, pink nails slammed the pen down as she looked up to address me.

"Good morning! Computers are set up in the back. Unfortunately, the coffee machine doesn't get here until tomorrow, and our boys are repainting the lounge today."

She looked tired, and I was astonished by how much energy she mustered up to greet me. I approached her to state my intentions. "Thank you, but I'm not here for the computers, or the coffee. I'm wondering if you need anybody to help out–"

"You can apply for work when we open, dear, but I'm afraid that won't be for another month at least."

"Oh, excuse me, let me clarify. I'm not looking for paid work. I'm trying to get more volunteer hours. So, if there's any way I can help out–"

"Oh!" She perked up, "Volunteer? That would be great! Wow! Uh, yes. ELLEEEEN!"

There was a sharp *clang* from the back room followed by a grouchy, "DAMMIT! WHAAAAT?"

"THERE'S A MAN HERE WHO WANTS TO VOLUNTEER!"

"WHAAAAT?"

"A MAN WANTS TO–"

"DAMMIT! FUCK! ONE SECOND, SHIT!"

I cringed at their shouting, but there was something humorous about their dynamic. They weren't hostile.

From the back room emerged a tall, slender woman with jet black hair and a leather jacket. She looked angry, but I also got "resting bitch face" vibes.

"What the fuck do you want?" Ellen asked the shorter woman, completely disregarding me.

Unfazed, the shorter woman explained once again my intention for volunteering. Ellen looked at me. "Did Nash send you?"

"No, I'm here on–"

"Did Morales send you?" Ellen asked again with one sharp eyebrow raised.

"No, I'm here on my own accord. I'm trying to get more volunteer hours and want to know if I can help."

Ellen looked back at the shorter women. Everything about them was yin and yang. "Is this guy for real?"

The shorter woman shrugged.

"Alright." Ellen said. "Yeah, put him to work. And tell him which parking spot is mine. Don't be stealing my fucking space!" With that she hurried back to the room she came from.

The shorter lady looked up at me, grinning. "You catch all that?"

"Yes," I said, trying not to roll my eyes at the absurdity of this duo.

"Don't worry about her. My name's Florence, by the way. Flo for short. What's yours?"

* * *

The subject line of the email read, "Seeking Master Sergeants for Volunteer Opportunity."

I was not a Master Sergeant (E-7), but I read the email anyway. It was from the Booster Club. *Maybe this can bolster my volunteer hours,* I thought. But then

I shrugged the notion away. I was already feeling overwhelmed between the food bank, the Big Buddy program, and Stormy's Cyber Café. And I needed to keep up with learning the parts of the C-130 Hercules aircraft. If I wasn't proficient by the end of the year, I'd be thrown out of the Air Force.

I closed the email and went to work.

At the end of the day there was a new email. "Seeking Tech Sergeants for Volunteer Opportunity."

I felt a pull in my heart that this was important. I was not a Tech Sergeant (E-6), but I could already see the trajectory. They would go down the ranks until people finally volunteered. *This is your opportunity,* I thought, but then shoved the idea down again. I was overworking myself. There was no way I could take on more volunteer hours at the Booster Club!

But I did need more hours. As much as I was committing myself, I was still falling short of the numbers needed to earn my coveted medal. I went to bed with my mind racing, and when I woke up there was another email.

"Seeking Staff Sergeants for Volunteer Opportunity."

I felt my heart skip a beat. I was not a Staff Sergeant (E-5), but they were getting closer to my rank. And as I read the body of the email I saw that all positions were still open. It seemed no one wanted anything to do with this. And yet, I had a good feeling.

Two more days went by, until finally, "Booster Club Seeking Volunteers, Any Rank."

I was an Airman First Class (E-3). I hit "Register" for the meeting that night.

There were no windows in the meeting room, and the lighting cast dim shadows over me and a handful of other Airmen of various ranks who seemed to be just as curious as I was. 1st Lieutenant Skylar Millie's hair glowed bright, fiery red. She marched up to the front of the room, turned sharply on a dime, and got right down to business. "Airmen! This Booster Club needs a president. Any volunteers?"

There was a stunned silence. No one raised their hand. I cautiously put my arm up to see whether anyone would follow suit. No sooner had my elbow twitched did Lt. Millie point at me and declare, "You! You're president of the Booster Club! Now, any volunteers for vice president?"

A sea of hands went up. Two minutes later, I had my cabinet of volunteers.

The next day I was approached by my squadron commander, Lieutenant Colonel Nash, with marching orders for the Booster Club: "The big task this year is to expand our annual Christmas party so everyone rank E-4 and under can attend for free. This means fundraising to ensure no one in those ranks has to pay for admission. Also, the generals are requesting an open bar. We have $500 committed to the effort so far. You will be judged solely based on the Christmas party. Any questions?"

Col. Nash was a tall, walking daydream, with the most perfectly gelled black hair I had ever seen.

I had a million questions, but they all got backed up in my throat.

"Good!" he said before marching away, leaving me in stunned silence.

I ran the numbers along with my new cabinet. In order to provide an open bar and free admission for the majority of over three hundred people, we were going to need to raise at least $8,000. We had less than five months.

How was I going to raise that much money with my rag-tag team of volunteers who I'd only met yesterday? *Why did I join this stupid club?*

Evangelist Nelson's wise words echoed in my head: *"Child, some things you just know. You won't know why you know, but you know. When those times come and you find yourself just knowing things, don't get caught up wondering why you know. Understand that God is letting you know for a reason, and then get a move on. You hear?"*

I lingered on the thought of Evangelist Nelson and our private counseling sessions.

I didn't know why volunteering for the Booster Club was important, but it was. I could feel it. And although I'd been given an impossible task, I was going to complete it.

CHAPTER 5: INTO THE AURORA SEA

"Zachary, what did you find?" I asked. "Should we invest our $500 in a car wash or bake sale first?"

"Oh, um. Car wash. For sure."

Zachary, my treasurer, was shit. He was the hardest worker in my cabinet, but only because he pretended to do the work. The rest didn't even bother with pretense.

"Ok, car wash it is." I sighed. "Neil, which weekend is looking best for us?"

Neil shrugged. He was supposed to be my secretary, but I would have preferred a rock.

"Ok, next weekend it is," I decided. "Let's call it a day."

"Thank God," said Tom, my vice president. He was in his late thirties, the oldest person in the room, and he hated taking orders from me.

I was 18, about as fresh as it gets in the military, and I was the youngest in the room by far. None of the other guys enjoyed taking my directions, but Tom was the most bitter about it.

That night, I complained to Idris. "If they wanted to be president, they should've raised their fucking hands! They don't have to sabotage our work just to take their bitchy attitudes out on me!"

"Why don't you ask Kevin?" Idris said. "I hear he's looking for volunteer hours to go for Senior Airman Below the Zone, too."

I thought about it. "Shit. That's perfect! I'll hire a bunch of assistants who actually give a fuck. Then it won't matter if these motherfuckers keep sucking ass!"

Within forty-eight hours, everyone in my cabinet had their own personal assistant, and we were on track to have a kickass Christmas party!

"Hey De'Vannon, I just got the lineup for "The Big One" concert at Tucson Electric Park," said Dino, my secretary's assistant. "They're gonna have Smash Mouth, Jessica Simpson, and Mandy Moore! We should definitely be there, and then I've got a list of baseball games for our free dates in September. What do you think?"

"That's great!" I replied. "Let's try to sell popcorn balls and hot dogs at all the events we can possibly be at. What's our return on those at the Diamondbacks games?"

Ned, my treasurer's assistant spoke up. "We're gaining traction. Returns are up twelve percent from August to about five hundred bucks per game. And the weekly car wash is overperforming by a margin of three hundred percent! Last week we made over seven hundred bucks."

I clapped in delight. At this rate, we would make $8,000 easily, even after covering expenses. Our Christmas party was going to be LIT.

As I exited the room at the end of the meeting, Lt. Millie intercepted me in the hallway. "Hubert! Col. Nash would like a word with you!"

I followed Lt. Millie's flaming hair around several corners to an office where Col. Nash was waiting for me. He was sitting at a huge oak desk looking as delicious as ever. I breathed deeply to prevent myself from breaking into a cold sweat as he asked Lt. Millie to close the door.

"De'Vannon," he started in a deep, raspy voice. "I've received some complaints."

My heart sank.

Col. Nash continued, "Some Booster Club and squadron members do not appreciate that you have been assigning roles and responsibilities to your friends. They do not appreciate that there has been no electoral process."

I looked back in disbelief. "Col. Nash, I received this position because

I raised my hand. I was not elected to this position. Why would that be different for anyone else in my cabinet? Besides, we're accomplishing so much! I'm on track to surpass our budget goal."

Col. Nash was not judging me. In fact, there was a hint of bemusement behind his eyes. "I don't expect you to do anything," he said. "I am just telling you, as is my responsibility, that I have received some complaints." Then, Col. Nash winked at me.

"Yes, sir," I said. "Understood, sir!"

I left Col. Nash's office with my head held high. The members of my cabinet could eat shit. They had tried to pull a Brutus on me. But they didn't realize that I'm no emperor. I'm a motherfucking Queen!

* * *

After a few months, my volunteer time at Stormy's Cyber Café had turned into a paid job, which was great because it meant I had some extra money. Except, now I needed another source of volunteer hours.

The brochure of volunteer opportunities I'd picked up at City Hall folded out to a four-foot square map of Tucson and the surrounding area. I stared in awe at the dizzying array of lines and labels. There were so many parts of the city I had yet to discover. The chance to have new experiences and connect with new people excited the fuck out of me.

I picked up the phone and started dialing.

After leaving several voicemails, my stomach was rumbling. And I felt like treating myself. My first check from Stormy's Cyber Café was burning a hole in my pocket and I wanted to get out of the city. Looking up at my map, I quickly identified the foothills of Tucson as the place to go for a good view and a 5-star meal. Then something caught my eye: the Loews Ventana Canyon Resort.

I hurried to dress myself up and hop in my car.

The mountains offered the most glorious backdrop under the setting sun, an amber crown under a blush-colored sky, and the air blowing in from the golf course smelled of wildflowers and cut grass. I was tempted to ask for a wine menu but decided not to push my luck. The odor of food wafting my way from the other tables was making me salivate like I hadn't eaten all week.

I ordered a handful of appetizers, some pasta with shellfish, and a caramel waffle dessert. It was the most decadent meal I'd ever eaten in my life. And with each new course, a new phase of the evening sky put on a show for me. Then I heard the distant sound of a horse whinnying, and I felt my heart pull toward it.

I promptly asked for the check, paid, and made my way to the information desk.

"Excuse me," I said to the concierge. "Where might I go for horseback riding?"

She pulled out a map and circled a location a short drive from the hotel. When I got home, the same circle was duplicated on my map, next to a star where the restaurant was. I vowed once a month to go horseback riding followed by a meal at that resort.

As I turned the lights out to go to bed that night, my laptop remained open. The light on the screen was captivating, and I did not want my day to end. Besides, as fabulous as my evening had been, I hadn't socialized at all, and of all the sensory delights I was indulging in, one was missing.

My hands shook as I opened the browser and typed for the very first time. G-A-Y-.-C-O-M.

* * *

The next morning, my phone rang.

"Hello. Is this Mr. De'Vannon Hubert?" asked a lady's squeaky voice.

"Yes, it is. Who's calling?"

"My name is Kate and I'm calling from the Sun Scouts Girls' Club. We received your call yesterday about volunteering and it sounds like you have some incredible dance experience. I have 15 girls between 8 to 10 years of age who I could use some help with. Would you be free to come in for an interview?"

The Sun Scouts Girls' Club was housed in a cramped room with a single office in the back. When I entered, a petite woman in a red Sun Scouts shirt greeted me eagerly. "So, this year the girls want to learn hip-hop, and I'm trained in ballet. Based on your resume, it looks like you have experience choreographing and performing. Can you get the girls ready to put on a recital for their families in about six weeks?"

I blushed. This was the best volunteer opportunity I could ask for.

"Absolutely." Kate's face lit up. "I do have to ask, though," I continued, "is this the only space you have to practice in?"

She bit her lip. "Well, we do use a ballet studio, but the people there wouldn't want a hip-hop routine going on in their space." She looked away, embarrassed. "I know this room isn't much, but do you think we could make it work?"

There was no way I could teach a full routine in that tiny space. "I have an idea." I said. "I work at a café with a lounge area in the back, and I'm going to ask if we can reserve it a couple nights per week so we can practice." I knew Flo would love the idea, but I didn't know how Ellen might react to such a proposal. Still, I had to try. I couldn't think of any alternative.

Kate was in shock. "That would be amazing! Wow!"

"There is one thing I need to know," I said.

"What's that?"

"Who is the girls' favorite artist?"

Kate's smile stretched from ear to ear. "Madonna!"

* * *

As I saw Ellen's blue Mustang pull up across the street, I ran over to Stormy's Cyber Café. I was in such a hurry that I damn near ran into a cactus before almost tripping over a cute little roadrunner dashing across the street like Wile E. Coyote was after his ass. Ellen and Flo were already going over the new year's expenses in the lounge. Flo jumped as I entered.

"Whoa! What's got you excited, tiger?"

I explained the opportunity about the dance recital for the Sun Scouts Girls' Club, and asked about using the lounge space twice per week. When I finished, Flo looked at Ellen.

"That sounds lovely, wouldn't you say, Ellen?"

Ellen pursed her lips. "The Sun Scouts are doing hip-hop?" I was worried Ellen was going to give me some grief about the idea, so I pleaded with puppy dog eyes. She shrugged. "Okay, that's fine with me. You can use the space."

Thirty minutes later, I was in the break room in my dorm, sorting through the Booster Club's schedule for the rest of the year. I had to map the next six weeks out to pull off this dance routine. Suddenly, siren alerts for DEFCON 3 sounded. I rolled my eyes. These drills were all too common.

But then Lt. Millie came running in, wide-eyed and out of breath. "Let's go, Hubert! Move your car! This ain't a fucking drill!"

Adrenaline shot through my veins as I scrambled to my room to find my keys. In a DEFCON 3 scenario, the Air Force must be ready to mobilize within fifteen minutes. The first order of business was to move my car to a different parking area, across the street from my usual one. During major emergencies on an Air Force base, cars need to be moved at least one hundred feet from all buildings, in case terrorists attempt to use them as bombs. Once our cars were safely distanced from the buildings, a small cadre of tractors emerged and positioned massive blockades to all parking lot entrances.

After parking my car, I ran to the briefing room and witnessed a sight I'll never forget.

The North Tower of the World Trade Center was up in flames. All around me people were whispering the word 'terrorists.' A spark ignited in my chest. There were good, hard working people in that building. They didn't deserve the violence that had been inflicted on them. Whoever did this had to pay, and everyone else in the room watching the screen with me felt the same way.

"What happened?" someone asked. "What kind of bomb could do that?"

The black streak flying across the sky was way too slow to be a missile. I tried to deny the truth, but when the second plane hit the South Tower, I didn't cry, I howled.

"NOOOOOOO!" I slammed my hands down on the table in front of me.

My head was spinning. Our nation was under attack, and it was coming from the sky I had sworn to protect. How could this be happening? I felt defeated, ashamed, and angry.

We waited for orders to be issued, but nothing happened. We remained alert and ready, and the stillness itched under my skin worse than a mosquito bite.

And then the towers fell.

The room was silent. We worked so hard every day in the military to be prepared for anything, but nothing could have prepared us for the helplessness we felt in that room on 9/11.

* * *

Three weeks later I received an email inviting me to an awards ceremony at the Air Force base. "Where dress blues," the invitation said.

Dress blues are the Air Force's version of a tuxedo so I figured this awards ceremony was a big deal, and I was surprised to receive an invitation. I was nearing the minimum number of volunteer hours needed for the Military Outstanding Volunteer Service Medal, but I didn't expect to receive it until later. *Is that what they're awarding me?* I wondered.

I didn't have to wait very long, because the ceremony was that Friday night.

Thanks for the fucking heads up, I thought.

There were many Airmen and officers receiving awards, and the banquet hall was packed. I easily lost myself in the crowd. The colonels really stood out, with their ornate ribbons and badges, but they also appeared to be having the least amount of fun. Though they socialized, they remained stiff and held a steadfast, neutral demeanor. The sight of them made me tense.

Throughout the ceremony, numerous Airmen walked on stage to receive awards for their achievements. Finally, Col. Nash took the stage and locked his dreamy eyes with mine.

"It is my privilege to welcome to the stage to receive the Military Outstanding Volunteer Service Medal, Airman First Class, De'Vannon Hubert!"

Col. Nash stopped. There were no other names. It was just me!

I stood to a round of cordial applause and walked on stage. Col. Nash pinned a medal attached to a blue and yellow ribbon on my chest, and then extended his arm for a handshake. When I shook his hand, I felt something metallic touch my skin. He was passing me something. The colonel's smile and firm clasp encouraged me to take it.

When I returned to my seat, I looked down at what he had pressed into my palm. It was a gold service coin which had *Outstanding Volunteer Service* embossed on it much like my medal did! I couldn't believe it. In that moment the little object meant everything to me. I'd done it! My hand started to sweat, and I quickly pocketed the coin. I could not lose it. Such awards were irreplaceable.

When the awards ceremony was complete, a DJ took to the stage, the lights dimmed, and the party started. I swarmed the dance floor with the other Airmen who had just received their awards.

As I danced, I noticed only one officer on the dance floor. I couldn't see the name on his badge, but I could tell he was a lieutenant. Suddenly, Col. Nash entered the dance floor, grabbed the lieutenant by the arm, and pulled him back to the perimeter of the party. I watched as the two talked, and the face of the lieutenant who had been enjoying the party slowly fell. After the chat, he went over to the bar, grabbed a drink, and stood to the side while the party went on.

Even the lieutenants are not allowed to let loose? The thought was unfathomable. I decided then that I didn't want to rise to the ranks of a lieutenant. Not if it meant never having fun. In fact, I wondered, *when I become a Senior Airman, will I be able to let loose?*

* * *

In the weeks that followed, I continued my work with the Sun Scouts Girls. They were fantastic. I created a mashup of Madonna's best hip-hop songs, which my girls already knew backwards and forwards. All I had to do was teach them the choreography and how to avoid running into one another on stage.

To my delight, Kate was able to rent an assembly hall on base to use for the recital. When the day of the recital finally arrived I could hardly keep still.

The synthesizer faded in, the curtains raised, and my girls cat-walked proudly to the center of the stage, taking formation. Then the beat hit.

DUN! DUN-DUN! DUN! DUN-DUN! DUN!

The room lit up. *"OW-OWWWW!"* the mothers cheered and whistled from the audience, and even the dads who had come along smiled. The girls nailed every beat and moved in perfect synchronicity. I lost myself in the melodies of Madonna's songs, moving along with my girls in my little space backstage.

The song ended and the girls all shouted, "SUN SCOUTS! SUN

SCOUTS! SUN SCOUTS!" with their fists in the air.

The room erupted in celebration, and the girls bowed. Then they all went jumping into the arms of their proud parents. Before the lights had even faded back up, I was mobbed by a swarm of eager moms and dads wanting to shake my hand. As I received their praises, I noticed a few of the dads wearing military uniforms.

I panicked and excused myself. Then I made my way toward the exit. When I reached the door, no one stopped me from running to my car and speeding home, where I collapsed on my bed, buried my face in my pillows, and screamed. *How could I have been so naive?*

My thoughts raced. I'd been foolish to think I could teach dance lessons on the base without anyone from the Air Force finding out. *Did they see me dancing off to the side?* I thought with horror. *If word gets around about this I'll never get awarded with Senior Airman Below the Zone.*

I shuddered at the thought of losing my coveted award because of my sexuality. I needed a distraction. I needed to get drunk.

"Hello?" came Idris' thick voice on the other end of the phone. I wondered whether he was already drinking. Idris loved to party almost as much as I did, and he was over twenty-one.

"Idris, hey, what are you doing tonight?"

"I'm on my way back to base. I was grabbing a new outfit for a big rave out in the desert next week. You should come!"

A rave? I'd never been to a rave before. "That sounds great! Why don't you come over and tell me about it over some drinks?"

"Yeah, sure. I'll pick up beer on the way."

"Mmm. How about vodka?" I suggested.

"Ha! If you say so, frat boy."

I certainly wasn't an alcohol virgin, but I'd never gotten legitimately wasted before. Tonight, I felt like letting loose. As soon as Idris cracked open the bottle of Smirnoff and poured a glass I downed the entire thing, wincing as the burn ignited my chest. Idris gave me an inquisitive look, then told me about the rave in the desert as he poured another.

"There'll be thousands of people there, but it's hush-hush. The biggest DJs of the underground are playing, so the music is guaranteed to hit hard. I'm talking DJ Irene, Mix Master Mike, and even fucking Pharel!"

I downed the second glass of vodka as Idris kept talking. I wanted to get drunk, but I wasn't feeling anything. Idris raised his eyebrow and poured me another glass.

"This rave is not for pussies," he continued. "This is the fucking Liquid Lotus Festival! We'll party all night until the sun is high the next day. You need to eat well before going. We'll buy glow sticks and bubbles. You know how to tie glow sticks into your shoes?"

I shook my head. I was trying to follow the conversation, but my brain was focused on getting fucked up. *When is this alcohol going to hit?* I wondered.

"Ok, I'll teach you how. Last thing, it's $40, cash only. So bring money." I downed the third glass of vodka.

"Hey, hey, hey," Idris said, pouring me a fourth. "What are you doing?"

"I'm trying to get drunk," I shrugged.

"What, with no music?" Idris asked with exaggerated disapproval. Then he wagged a finger at me in mock seriousness and said, "Nobody gets drunk on my watch without a party! Finish your drink. We're going out."

I downed my drink and we jumped into Idris' car to head Downtown. As we neared N. 4th Ave., my vision started to blur, and my head was suddenly light. I felt great.

Idris led me into an underground bar. I tried to catch the name on the sign, but the letters kept dodging my gaze. Idris said something to the bouncer, who opened the door and waved us in. The music hit me so hard even my vision vibrated. It was time to dance.

Then cigarette smoke swirled around me, and my stomach felt sick. I grabbed Idris' shoulder. "Where are the... Um..." I couldn't think of the word. "Piss rooms?"

"Oh, shit," Idris groaned. "Here, come with me!"

He pulled me to the bathrooms and threw me into an open stall. The smell of shit filled my nostrils, and I puked. Then I blacked-out.

The next morning I woke up face down in my bed. I was still wearing my clothes. A big glass of water sat on my bedside dresser. My mouth tasted bitter, so I sat up and downed the whole glass. Water never tasted so good.

My stomach growled. Eggs and chorizo sounded amazing. I got up and started cooking breakfast. The savory smells hit me, and my head cleared. I was awake. I was alive. I felt great.

* * *

My Christmas party kicked ass.

My team raised over $10,000 and we were ahead of schedule. Even with the open bar, we had money left over. We held a raffle, and there were so many prizes that we ended up throwing piles of free stuff into the crowd at the end of the night! The only thing that sucked was that I wasn't old enough to drink at my own party.

As the room celebrated, Lt. Millie caught my eye from across the room. Her red hair was done up in a bun that reached almost a whole foot above her head. She gave me a thumbs up and winked. *Job well done, Airman,* I imagined her saying.

I was flushed. I felt like my cheeks were blushing redder than her hair. Christmas carols boomed over the loudspeakers. I danced away the rest of the party and did my best to not get caught ogling Col. Nash.

When the party was finally finished and I was back in my dorm, I couldn't sleep. Everything was moving so fast. I didn't want the rush to end. I swung my feet stealthily from my covers, and in two deft strides reached my computer. It was only me in my dorm, but I couldn't help the feeling that I had to be secretive about what I intended to do. I quickly dimmed the brightness as I woke the machine from its sleep. And then I opened the browser.

GAY.com was waiting for me, and I had a message to respond to.

JoyBoy69 - *what's your favorite condom flavor?*

I had finally accustomed myself to the terms used on GAY.com. Tops, Bottoms, and Vers were obvious. That was just who was giving dick, who was taking it, and who were equally good at doing both. Similarly, hosts invited dick over to their places, and travelers drove to the dick. Finally, there were requests and boundaries... "basic fucking," "blow job only," "BDSM," "bareback," "will do anything…"

The possibilities of what two (or more) men could do with their dicks was apparently endless. My fingers sprang into action to answer the message.

KuriousKitty - *caramel. You?*

JoyBoy69 - *I like your picture. Want to meet up?*

KuriousKitty - *And do what?*

JoyBoy69 - *how about some taste testing?*
KuriousKitty - *hmm. Let me think about it...*

* * *

My Mother was happy to have me home in Baton Rouge, even if only for two weeks of leave before I shipped back out to Tucson. If I had the choice between two more weeks of boot camp and two weeks back in the hood, I would have chosen boot camp.

The Air Force had structure and order. At boot camp we worked and suffered for a purpose, and even though I didn't like it, it made sense. But the hood sapped the life out of me. There was no comradery. It was boring and monotonous. The resentment I held toward the people around me couldn't be suppressed in light of a higher purpose.

I missed the guys from the military. Dammit, I missed being around sexy men! The sudden and complete loss of that masculine energy burned in my chest. And in the boredom of the hood, I had nothing to distract me from it. I had to scratch my itch.

I pulled up my laptop and opened a web browser. I typed...
GAY.com

It was exactly what I was looking for. An entire universe of men, desiring to scratch the same itch I felt, opened its door wide and welcomed me. And its gravity was strong. My heart rate quickened, and my hands shivered on the keyboard. I wasn't ready to do anything crazy since I was still a virgin, but I had access to a car, so I updated my profile to say I was a "traveler" and "blow jobs only."

Then I browsed for someone in Baton Rouge whose requests lined up with mine. Eventually, I found him. *"ElSinnator; host; 10 inches; looking to receive a blow job; may NOT spend the night."* I clicked his chat bubble and sent a message.

Within a couple minutes, I heard back.

* * *

Everything about the Pentagon Barracks Hotel was colonial era posh. A perfectly flat brick walkway led up to a layered fountain that was showing its age with small cracks along its rims. White pillars dwarfed the doors to the rooms that waited discreetly in the shadows underneath white balconies. *What kind of hotel is this?* I thought to myself. It felt more like Napoleon's fuck house than the Baton Rouge I was used to. *Who fucking cares! This is fabulous!*

I knocked on the door of Room 204 and a very fit, white man with firm features and foggy hair opened it. He was in a white shirt, fine gray slacks, and on the back of a golden chair rested a gray jacket with fabric woven way too precise not to be custom made. *Who is this man?*

"Hey, can I get you anything?" he asked, "Or do you wanna just get right to it?"

I was tempted to ask for a bubble bath with rose petals but thought better of it. *I don't know what I'm doing! I've never sucked a dick before!* I panicked. *I'm still a virgin!* "Let's get to it," I said before I psyched myself out.

ElSinnator unzipped his gray slacks, dropped his bleach-white briefs, and presented me with his large, erect dick. The look of bewildered hesitation on my face must have been obvious, because ElSinnator pointed down at his dick as if I needed instructions on what to do next. He didn't sit or lie down, so I knelt down in front of his crotch and leaned in. Suddenly I felt the man's hand grip the back of my head and push me forcefully toward his dick. I barely had time to grab his dick with my hand and direct it into my mouth.

The strong hand on the back of my head guided my movements. His huge dick hurt my mouth and my throat as ElSinnator seemed to want the whole thing to fit in my face. Eventually the man started thrusting, too. My lip caught on my tooth and I winced, but ElSinnator didn't seem to notice because at that moment he ejaculated. I swallowed every drop of his cum. It was warm, salty, and delicious.

ElSinnator pulled away from me, turned his back, and zipped up his pants. I took my cue to get up and leave. I never asked for his name.

After leaving the hotel, I stood on the waterfront of the Mississippi River and watched the quiet vessels bobbing in the night. As I turned around, my gaze fell upon the unmissable structure of the Louisiana State Capitol. It was right across the street from the hotel. *Did I just suck a senator's dick,* I wondered?

I got my answer the next day when I caught a glance at the front page of the newspaper. "Legislature in Session," read the headline. Below was a photo of several distinguished looking white dudes standing on the steps of the capitol building.

One of them looked eerily familiar, with foggy hair and a custom gray suit...

* * *

The only people in Tucson who were waking up earlier than me worked at the post office. I didn't receive a lot of mail, but I loved the ritual of stepping out of my dorm early in the morning to check my mailbox. One morning I received a letter postmarked from *The Sun Scouts Girls' Club of Tucson, AZ*. I hurried back to my dorm to open it.

When I did, I screamed.

> *Dear Mr. Amazing, De'Vannon Hubert,*
>
> *We are so honored that you were willing to volunteer so much time to help us pursue our dreams. We had so much fun learning, laughing, and of course, dancing. It was the most amazing 6 weeks any of us could have asked for! Please keep in touch! We miss you!*
>
> *Love,*
>
> *The Sun Scouts Girls and Kate* ☺
>
> *P.S. We know you said you were doing this for volunteer hours, but because you went above and beyond all of our expectations in creating such an otherworldly experience, please accept this payment for your time, talent, and energy. We do hope to collaborate with you again soon!*

Inside the letter was a check for $80. I had to push the note away to avoid sobbing messy tears all over it.

A celebration was in order, and when my shift at the Back Shop ended that day I met up with Idris to attend my first rave.

We packed everything we needed into my car and were about twenty minutes into the desert when Idris started to panic.

"Shit! Shit! Shit! Turn around!"

"Turn around? No! What the fuck? Why?" I couldn't believe what I was hearing.

"I forgot my contacts. I can't dance without my contacts!"

"Yes, you can!" I reassured him, not wanting to go all the way back and miss an hour of the party. "You don't need contacts to dance! You can dance with your eyes closed!"

"Fuck you! Come on, De'Vannon, I can't see. Turn this fucking car around!"

I slammed on the brakes and made a U-turn. The only thing worse than being late to the show would be Idris cussing me out the entire night.

By the time we made it back to the base, retrieved his contacts, and got back on the road, the sun had gone down and the moon was rising. Anxiously, I sped back to the highway and out into the desert, pushing my car's engine as hard as I could.

We could hear the rumble of the music even before we pulled into the parking area on the perimeter of the event. Before we left the car Idris insisted on stringing glow sticks into our shoelaces. I was impatient to get to the party, but I waited while he wove the colorful neon strips onto the tops of our feet. A moment later we hurried past rows of cars and tents, toward the waves of the aurora sea of neon lights, which we could see in the distance. As we neared the front entrance, we saw a check-in table and a few staff members. Strangely, they were all lying on the ground with their hands behind their heads. Beneath the pounding of the music, we could hear someone crying.

"Hey!" I smiled. "We're here for the party. What's going on?"

"Some jackasses just fucking robbed us at gunpoint!" said one of the staff members, standing up and dusting himself off.

I turned to Idris. "Holy shit! Just now?"

"Yes! Just fucking now!"

I clasped my head in disbelief. If we hadn't waited to tie the glow sticks into our shoes we would have been caught in the middle of an armed robbery.

Idris and I paid our $40 each and headed into the party.

We walked past a couple of security guards standing near a rather large saguaro cactus, talking to some girls.

"Hey, just so you know," said Idris, "y'all just got robbed."

Then two men rushed past us yelling into their walkie-talkies.

"We've heard reports of a robbery. How many fuckers were there?"

"Four or five!"

"Fuck! And how much did they take?"

"All of it! Forty-thousand fucking dollars!"

"Fuck!"

I looked wide-eyed at Idris. He shrugged. "Fuck it! Let's party!"

For a second, I wanted to help find the criminals or something. But there was nothing we could do. The money was gone. Then the DJ yelled out, "MAKE SOME NOOOOIIIISE!"

I shook my head. "Alright! Fuck it!" And into the aurora sea of endless glow sticks, colors, and electric lights we dove.

Inside, people were dancing like nothing was happening. They hadn't even realized a holdup had taken place. Helicopters hovered in circles overhead, their spotlights scraping the perimeter of the rave. But the dancing continued below.

I was starstruck by the waves of people. The desert air was cool on my sweaty skin as I danced all through the night. DJs took turns blowing sounds of awe and wonder into the pulsating crowd, and at that moment I was delighted to be a drop in the ocean.

* * *

I was awarded Senior Airman Below the Zone and was finally able to move into an apartment off base. But all the boys in the Back Shop on the day shift I was assigned to hated me for my promotion, so I transferred to the night shift. I was still working for the Booster Club and volunteering with my teenage buddy, Drake. I was lucky to get four hours of sleep each night, but I didn't care.

Idris did research to find weekend raves which seemed to be happening less frequently. I got friendly with the workers at Hot Topic, who helped me pick out new outfits for each rave that he was able to find. But Idris was over 21, which meant that there were only so many places we could hang out together. I loved hanging out with Idris, but still... I craved meaningful, masculine attention. All of the male relationships in my life felt unfulfilled. The "Don't Ask Don't Tell" culture of the Air Force didn't help, but the bigger problem I knew was that if I stayed in the military long enough, I would eventually be relocated. The prospect of a long-term relationship seemed out of reach.

I was lonely.

And GAY.com was an awfully good band aid.

JoyBoy69 - *what's taking you so long? Wanna hook up?*

KuriousKitty - *I'm still thinking…*

JoyBoy69 - *what are you afraid of?*

KuriousKitty - *I don't know…*

JoyBoy69 - *R U A VIRGIN!?!?!?*

KuriousKitty - *yeah, so?*

JoyBoy69 - *So… r u gonna keep pulling my chains? Or r u gonna pop that cherry!?*

I closed my computer. Why was it such a big deal if I was a virgin? For some reason, I wasn't ready to change that yet.

* * *

Soon after my move to the nightshift, work in the Back Shop stopped completely.

Our jobs at the Back Shop were outsourced to our contracting company, Raytheon, which made sense. Civilian workers were experts coming from a manufacturing background, and they knew every part on the C-130 Hercules aircraft inside and out. Plus, they were cheaper. I couldn't argue.

The higher-ups moved everyone from inside the Back Shop out to the Flight Line office to perform routine maintenance and upkeep on the C-130s. After a few days the reality of my new position set in. This job was *booooring!* And the worst part was that we were outside in the cold all day working to keep the planes mission-ready at all times.

My least favorite task was the flight walk. During takeoff military planes are at risk of engine failure if any type of debris gets swept up into the engines. This means someone has to examine the entire flight line for nuts and bolts and any little thing that might have wandered onto the runway. I could barely see past my own eyelids as they watered in the cold wind. Winter in the desert was unforgiveable. This was not the weather I expected in Arizona.

"Airman! This is the third time in a row you've come back from a flight walk empty handed! Do you want our planes to break down? You can spend the rest of the afternoon taking inventory!"

I looked over to see a short Crew Chief berating one of my subordinates who had transferred with me from the Back Shop. My worker looked over in my direction and caught my eye. I saw the desperation in his gaze and a motherly fury awoke within me. I was the same rank as the Crew Chief, and we outranked everyone else out there, so I broke lines and confronted him.

"Hey, fuck off! You can't make him do that!"

"Excuse me?" The Crew Chief looked at me, ready to bite back, but I raged on.

"I said you can't make him fucking do that! He hasn't done any-fucking-thing wrong, and you are not in charge of him… I am! So leave him the fuck alone!"

The Crew Chief recoiled, scowling in hatred as he tried to calculate his retort, but after a few seconds I knew he had nothing, so I returned to the line and continued my sweep.

That night, I started browsing other opportunities. I had been in the military long enough to start applying for special duties. Unfortunately, changing a career isn't as easy as putting in a simple request. Any new job I applied for was going to require months of additional training. All except one, which involved just forty-five days of school back in San Antonio. And it was a job I knew I would be good at.

I was going to become a recruiter.

* * *

The dildos were unsatisfying. I tried playing with them while watching porn, but that only seemed to disappoint me even more. I needed the real deal, but it was getting late.

My hands shivered as I navigated my way through GAY.com; the sight was familiar, but the conviction was so foreign. I was suddenly ready to have *sex*! I was 19 years old and that being a virgin shit had run its course.

"Spikey-Mikey. 4-5 inches. Very average. Top. Host."

"Host." That meant I would go to his place. It was past 0100 in the morning when I arrived at an inconspicuous one-story house in a clean neighborhood. A skinny, small-framed, dark-haired white man opened the door. We stood there for a few awkward seconds. *Do we have a conversation?*

Apparently, we do.

"Hi there. Come on in." Spikey-Mikey was cordial. "Can I get you anything to drink? How are you feeling?"

"To be honest," I said, "I've never done this before and I'm kind of freaking out about it so… Can we just get to fucking and talk after or something?" My host was happy to oblige.

It hurt. Spikey-Mikey informed me that I have a very tight asshole. Who knew? I had to ask him to slow down a couple times, and thankfully he listened. He turned out to be quite the gentleman and invited me to stay the night and leave in the morning. I accepted his offer at first, but when he took out a pipe and offered me meth, I politely refused and left. I wasn't trying to get kicked out of the Air Force for drug use.

I replayed the experience in my head as I slowly fell asleep. I was glad he was only five inches. I thought back to Monster Dick who had jumped in my car a while back and shuddered. I could *not* have handled a 14-inch dick.

As soon as I woke up the next morning, I logged on to GAY.com again. Less than an hour later I had a man at my door ready to fuck. He was rougher, and it still hurt, but something about the experience was more enjoyable. He was firm and energetic. I wanted more.

I messaged all of the most dominant, powerful, masculine men I could find on GAY.com. And when the third guy arrived at my doorway, there was no doubt. I was in my zone.

I let him fuck me hard, and he even thanked me afterward. That felt good. I didn't know I could satisfy a man like that.

I quickly fell into a rhythm, filling all of my free time with sex. I tried keeping a notebook with a tally of all the guys I slept with, but eventually I was sleeping around so much that it was difficult to keep track. GAY.com was my new social life and it was addictive as fuck.

A few weeks went by. Then a few more. And then a few more… Until finally my transfer to Recruiter School was approved. I had a bittersweet farewell party with Idris. I had always found him attractive and now that I was no longer a virgin, I had serious thoughts about how I could get him to stick his dick in me. But he wasn't gay, and I had no idea how to even begin such a conversation with somebody unless I met them online. By the time I left Tucson for San Antonio, I'd fucked *over 180 guys.*

CHAPTER 6: CURIOSITY

Recruiter School was forty-five days in San Antonio, and I was so busy I didn't have sex once during the entire time.

The curriculum was a collection of sales courses that the Air Force had licensed from Fortune 500 companies. My job was to *sell* the Air Force. I learned marketing techniques. I also learned how to give speeches, keep a meticulous schedule, do research, paperwork, and outreach.

The only thing that sucked was that I was once again the youngest person in the room and the lowest ranked, but at least I was 20 by now. The other recruiters in training commented on my age incessantly and I looked forward to never seeing any of them again.

The most important thing I learned was to never give up control of the conversation. It was our job to control the sale from introduction to close, and we learned how to overcome every barrier to enlistment that parents and prospective recruits might have. I passed with flying colors and was assigned to an office at a strip mall in San Bernardino, California. I would be recruiting in the Inland Empire, which included both San Bernardino and Riverside Counties.

On the long road to California, I felt a tickle in my pants that made me cringe. Something was oozing out of my dick, and it was painful. Five minutes later I pulled into a gas station, hustled to the grimy bathroom stall, and frantically locked the door. Then I pulled down my pants to inspect my dick and discovered that my underwear was moist. My dick was slowly dripping a thick yellow secretion that looked like puss.

I stuffed a bunch of toilet paper in my underwear over my crotch and went back to my car. I didn't want to think about what the strange yellow goo could be. Maybe it would just go away on its own. But for the rest of the drive, the dripping sensation didn't go away.

That night I stayed at a hotel and the next morning I felt like I was pissing fire. What was once a yellow discharge was now pale green, and my dick was swollen and red. When I was finally done relieving myself in the bathroom, I packed up and got back on the road.

After arriving at my new apartment in San Bernardino, I immediately went to urgent care.

"Are you sexually active?" the doctor asked, eyeing me judgmentally.

"Not for over a month!" I exclaimed. "And I always use condoms!" The doctor sharpened his gaze on me. "Okay, I *almost* always use condoms," I confessed. There had been one or two instances where I'd let a guy fuck me raw and a few occasions where I had experimented with topping as well. Sometimes with a condom. Sometimes without.

"Mr. Hubert," he said with a condescending tone, "chlamydia and gonorrhea can take up to four weeks or more to manifest with symptoms. And condoms do not guarantee protection though they do reduce risk of disease significantly. It's a good thing you haven't been having sex for the past month, as you would have been spreading this infection around. And it's a good thing you called right away because such an infection can backtrack to your kidneys and cause serious harm."

I sat in stunned, bewildered silence. It was as if God had intervened in my sex life by sending me to Recruiter School to prevent me from spreading this disease around to other people. I didn't want to think about how many guys I could have infected if I had stayed in Arizona for the past forty-five days.

The doctor took a blood test to check for any other STDs, prescribed me some antibiotics for the chlamydia and gonorrhea, and sent me on my way. After taking the pills, my dick stopped hurting, and within five days it was back to normal. Thank God for modern medicine!

* * *

When I walked into my new office for the first time I was wearing a red, long-sleeve GAP tee with the number nine on it, a brown leather baseball cap turned backwards on my head, a magnetic earring on my left ear, skinny jeans that were also from the GAP, and brown flip-flops. I met my new Flight Chief, Sgt. Howard, and the rest of the team of recruiters. Per usual, I was the youngest person in the room... and the lowest ranked.

Sgt. Howard introduced me to the team. "This here is Brock, Lane, Marco, Timothy, and Lisa. Lisa is your office partner, so you two will be spending quite a bit of time together. Everyone else has offices scattered all across Southern California so won't be seeing them near as much. My office is close to this one so I might pop in from time to time. Now listen, before you go thinking that these people here are your competition and that you're the new hot shot in town, just hear me out. The only person who answers to the numbers is me, and I need all of you working together in order to make the numbers that'll make me look good. These people here are your friends, not your enemies. There may come a time in the future when you need them. Remember that."

Brock looked at me as if I were his ex-wife, but didn't say anything.

"Yes, sir." I said. "Understood."

My first day on the job I had three appointments. When I arrived in my recruitment office at the strip mall in San Bernardino, Lisa pulled me off to the side.

"Hey, quick tip. I know you just spent forty-five days in Recruiter School learning how to spin a fancy lie, but listen. You're young and you're new. Don't lie. Just tell these kids and their parents the truth. Last year, one parent came into one of the offices upstate wanting to shoot the recruiter who had shipped their kid off to some military job he hadn't signed up for. And trust me, the gangs here in California don't fuck around."

I nodded. "Tell the truth. Easy enough."

By lunch, I was two-for-two on my appointments; both of the kids I met with had decided to sign up. I knew from the moment my third appointment walked in, though, that I was not destined for a perfect first day. This young woman had tattoos, piercings, and a swollen belly. She was everything the military rejected, and my heart sank.

If someone was serious about enlisting, the piercings could be abandoned and tattoos could be painfully removed, but pregnant women were an automatic "No."

In this case, I did refer to my scripted rejection speech. "I'm sorry, Miss Gutierrez, but unfortunately pregnant women cannot enlist in the military." That was it. That was the easy let-down I was equipped with.

From across my desk, she looked at me inquisitively. "How old are you?" she asked.

I told the truth. "Twenty."

"Oh, thank God! I was afraid you were going to say, like, twelve, or some fucking stupid shit like that."

I smiled. I immediately liked her.

She waved her hand. "I tell you what, forget this whole idea. This was stupid of me. Do you like piercings?"

I was caught off guard. "I, uh, don't know. I mean I wear a magnetic earring but I've never had a real piercing before."

"Well fucking hell! Why don't you try one out! For free, on me. You're young, you should experiment with some things!"

I loved her energy. For some reason, I loosened up a bit and gave in. "Sure. What the hell."

"Great! I own a shop in Yucaipa. Will you come see me when you're ready to explore?"

"How late are you open?"

"As late as you need."

My spirits were lifted as she left, but before the door closed behind her Sgt. Howard walked in with a grim look on his face.

"What's the matter?" I asked as he made sure the door was closed behind him. When he turned to face me he got straight to the point.

"De'Vannon, it's my job to make sure this team runs smoothly. Unfortunately, that means it's my job to settle disputes. I'm here to tell you that," he paused and took an exasperated breath, "*the team* doesn't like the way you're carrying yourself. They do not approve of your backwards ball caps, skinny jeans, flip-flops, and your overall laid back style."

"The team?" I echoed inquisitively. It was clear by the way he said it that it wasn't the whole team. *It's just fucking Brock,* I figured. Plus, *the team* had only seen me that one time when I first came to my office to get everything set up. I wasn't even on the clock!

"Look, just take it for what it is, okay?" Sgt. Howard said, urging me not to escalate the issue, and without waiting for my response, he left.

* * *

Kase was a walk-in.

I wasn't a fan of walk-ins because they usually showed up with demanding parents and expected immediate service, as if I had nothing fucking better to do than drop everything and tell their little boy or girl all about the military. My job involved a lot of research and paperwork, and walk-ins added extra stress to my already packed schedule. But Kase came in by himself, and was patient with me as I finished up my tasks and prepared myself for an impromptu appointment.

Kase was wearing a Lakers jersey, a Lakers sweatband, and rhinestone earrings. His shiny black hair seemed to wave "hello" to me. I accurately placed him at 6' 2," Latino, and to my dismay, straight.

"So, boot camp?" he asked.

"Fucking sucks," I answered.

"Right. And the girls?"

"If you wanna fuck 'em, you can fuck 'em, just don't fuck with 'em."

This got a laugh out of him. "Right. And if I want to be a pilot?"

"You're going to have to work your fucking ass off, starting from the bottom and working your way up. I suggest maybe becoming an Aircraft Mechanic to get familiar with planes and flight line operations. You can use the Air Force to pay for college then you can apply to Officer Training School. You can also apply to the Air Force Academy and earn your degree and commission there. Either way, a four year degree is necessary in order to become an officer, go to flight school, and then become a pilot. The road won't be easy but you can do it, providing you don't have any medical conditions like pre-existing heart or lung complications."

"So if I have asthma–"

I pretended to cough obnoxiously, cutting him off. "Uh-hem, sorry. Something in my throat. As I was saying, if you have *any* heart or lung complications, for instance, asthma, I cannot enlist you. Now, tell me, do you have any heart or lung complications?"

Kase raised an eyebrow. "No," he said.

"Good," I smiled. "You're going to go far in the Air Force. Now, normally this would be the part when the recruiter schedules you for a physical and gives you a bus pass to take the Greyhound to the processing station in Los Angeles and wish you luck, but that's honestly some fucking bullshit. What you're doing is very brave and I'm going to be with you every step of the way. I'll drive you down there myself once I get you on the schedule."

"Cool," he said. "Being an Aircraft Mechanic sounds like a great place to start. Wanna grab a drink later?"

I considered this. I absolutely did. "Do you know a place that doesn't card?"

Kase raised his eyebrow again and smiled deviously.

A few minutes later we were stepping into a nearby bar and Kase was acting differently from how he did in my office. Here he was relaxed and talkative.

"Yo, so what made you want to go into the Air Force?" he asked me.

"It just seemed like a good opportunity," I shrugged. "It was a way to get free education, a job with benefits, and do some good for the world. Overall, though, when the opportunity presented itself, it just felt right."

"I hear that," he nodded.

"Plus, my recruiter gave me free Skittles," I smiled. "What about you?"

"Didn't you already ask me that in the office?"

"Yeah, but like, *for real*," I said. "Why do you really want to go into the Air Force?"

That trademark grin came across Kase's face again as he looked at me and said, "Top Gun."

I sucked my teeth teasingly as Kase persisted.

"Yo, girls dig that shit, man! Especially here in California. You see, Cali girls, they ain't like other girls. Something in the water maybe, but man when you see some sexy ass worth chasing you better hope you have a fast car! And there ain't nothing faster than a fighter pilot! I mean, come on! Don't tell me you haven't been eating ass since the first day you wore those blues!"

It was my turn to give Kase a wry smile. For some reason, I didn't want to tell him I was gay. I really liked talking about girls and straight stuff with him.

* * *

"Hey Larry, how are you today?"

Larry was the maintenance guy for the strip mall. He was an old guy with a chronic hunch and silver hair, but he was one of the friendliest people I knew at the mall.

"Hanging in there, De'Vannon," he replied. "How are you?"

"I'm good! I'm almost 21!"

"Hey, it's the big blackjack! Try to survive it without busting."

"Thanks, Larry!"

In my office, Lisa was picking candy out of my candy bowl. "Are you driving up to the MEPS tomorrow?" she asked. By MEPS she meant, "Military Entrance Processing Station."

"Yes, of course."

"Would you mind giving one of my recruits a ride back after?"

"Sure!"

"Great. Oh, and don't be surprised if Brock asks the same thing for one of his recruits."

I didn't mind the long drives to the MEPS in Los Angeles, and the more recruits the merrier. Driving recruits home meant more time on the road, and I loved listening to the radio. My favorite stations were KIIS FM 102.7 and 94.7 The Wave, and extra hours of flipping between stations and singing along to their playlists actually sounded relaxing.

At the MEPS, most of the recruits looked miserable. Fear and doubt were painted on their faces as they went through the motions of filling out their remaining paperwork and lining up for their physical examinations.

Throughout the day I checked on Kase and other recruits from my team. This helped relieve the tension for them.

I saw some other recruits look on enviously, apparently wishing their own recruiters were there with them. But I figured if they were willing to suffer through a little envy on their way to boot camp, then maybe they stood a chance alongside my recruits.

"Hey De'Vannon, how's work at the strip mall?" Sgt. Jenkins asked. I had built a strong rapport with her at the MEPS, which helped push my recruits through the system if there were ever any complications.

"Oh, it's good," I said, taking a seat by her desk. "Everyone's feeling the Christmas cheer."

"How's Larry?" she asked.

"Larry's hanging in there."

"That's good. I like that old bastard."

"We all do."

"Hey, listen. One of your recruits, Kase, he's scored excellently on all the tests and could feasibly do anything he wanted, but we're in more need of security guards than mechanics right now. Higher-ups have already transitioned his processing from aviation to security. Do you think you can sway him to take the job?"

I couldn't believe what I was hearing. They were asking me to lie to one of my recruits, my friend, about his future. And I knew Kase was dead set on working on planes. I was ready to fight, but I knew that in order to do that I had to first look like I tried to convince Kase.

"I'll give Kase a call," I said cordially. If I was going to fight, I didn't want to start with Sgt. Jenkins. She would probably be the best chance I had at reversing the decision, so I had to be patient. I was tense, though, as I turned back to my recruits.

After driving all the recruits home that night, I swung by Juanita's tattoo and piercing shop. She was still pregnant and overjoyed to see me. She insisted that my first piercings be free. I didn't argue.

I asked about covering up my brand new eyebrow piercing for work, and Juanita gave me a pair of plugs for the piercing holes that matched the color of my skin. I thanked her graciously.

"Come back soon, okay?" she said encouragingly as I made my way out the door.

"I will," I promised, and I wasn't lying. I liked her, and I liked the look of a real piercing on my face. The next week I got two more piercings in each ear, and one in my nose.

* * *

"Yo, Kase!" I spoke into my phone.

"What's up?"

"The higher-ups in my recruiting division want to know what you'd think of being a security officer."

Kase laughed. *"Security officer? Nah, fuck that, bro."*

"That's what I figured. I'll let them know."

"Thanks, brother. Peace."

The higher-ups were just gonna have to fuck off.

* * *

After hanging up, I made my way to a house party that I had been invited to in Riverside and met a guy named Guido. Guido was cute and curvy with big, hooped earrings, and his black hair with blonde highlights was fucking perfection. Like many people in Southern California, he was Latino and incredibly gorgeous. His demeanor was very girly and his hug was warm and soft. He reminded me a bit of Lisa.

I started the formalities. "So, where are you from?"

"I've lived in SoCal my whole life. I grew up in a trailer park, actually. What about you?"

"I'm from Baton Rouge, Louisiana originally. I came here from Tucson, and it feels like I just moved here yesterday. I mean, I've been here for months, but I still haven't figured out the L.A. culture. I mean, I turn 21 soon and I want to explore more, but I don't know how to dress for these clubs. What do you think?"

Guido's face lit up with excitement. He took half a second and scanned me up and down, "No, this outfit is not going to work. Not that shirt, not those pants, and definitely not those shoes! You're not going to be able to get in anywhere." Guido sighed, but then he pointed to my black, silver studded Wilson's Leather bracelet. *"That* is L.A. Everything else needs to go."

My heart ached with the pain and thrill of finally hearing the truth. I was from the country and needed help. Ever since leaving Baton Rouge, the military had chosen my uniform for me. And now that I was about to be old enough to have a real social life, I needed to make some serious changes. While I didn't like hearing Guido's brutal assessment, the excitement of finally having some direction struck an emotional chord deep within me. I was ready to evolve.

* * *

"Hi! Welcome to The Rail at Nordstrom. My name is Kylo, how can I help you?"

Kylo was easily a foot shorter than me, but he commanded his space with unrelenting prowess. Somehow, I felt like while I was looking down at him, I was also looking up at him.

"I need you to make this country ass look Californian," I said.

Kylo looked me up and down, similar to how Guido did the night before, and gave me his assessment: "Alright, we'll need to get you boots, T-shirts, and designer jeans. Lose the polo. I'm also going to encourage more accessories, like that bracelet." Then we got to work.

"We'll start at the bottom and work our way up," Kylo said. "Here is our collection of Kenneth Cole boots. These are going to be about $700 per pair, but if I'm being honest, you can try them on here and then get the same look at a country western store for half the price. Cowboy boots work well because when you're wearing jeans over them they look pretty much the same as high fashion boots."

I loved the boots. They were pointy and the heels gave me an extra couple of inches.

"Now, speaking of jeans, though, let's get you fitted!"

I didn't realize it, but getting designer jeans meant having them tailored after purchase, and then later shipped to my house. My first designer jeans were a pair of True Religions for $400. Each of the T-shirts Kylo recommended were priced in the $70-$80 range. I bought it all, regardless of whether it was on sale or not. I loved the feel of paying for expensive outfits. The confidence boost surged through my veins and I was ready to tackle any club in L.A.

To finish my makeover, I stopped to see Juanita on the way home and got another free piercing on my bottom lip.

* * *

The Sunset Strip in West Hollywood was more vibrant and electric than I'd ever seen it as we strolled up to the first club of the night. There was a line out the door and I gawked at the beautiful people, who looked like they'd been cut straight from the pages of a magazine. *You're fabulous*, I told myself, glancing down at my designer T-shirt, True Religion jeans, and brand new black cowboy boots. Of course, I was wearing my black leather bracelet.

"My boy here just turned 21 *today*," said Kase, skipping the line and dragging me straight up to the bouncer at the door. The man frowned and crossed his arms. "Show him your ID, De'Vannon," Kase commanded. I did as I was told, and the guard squinted at it in the darkness. Finally, he nodded, winked at me, and waved us into the club.

"Happy birthday," he said, handing me back my ID.

The same pattern played out every single place we went. We bounced around from one upscale club to another all night. We spotted TV stars, actors, directors, and singers. Kase bought me drinks everywhere we went and I marveled at the fact that they were $15 each. *I guess that's L.A. prices*, I told myself.

If the other clubs had been posh, Lure was opulent. Stepping inside, we found ourselves in a tasteful patio with two bars and an outdoor dance floor where people smoked cigars and held martinis as they bounced to house music. Kase's eyes were wide as he scanned the room from left to right, pointing out the most attractive women to me.

As we passed into the main room of Lure my jaw fell open. It was massive. I looked from the gigantic bar to the towering stage at the front of the room. Colorful LED screens on all of the walls were pulsing hypnotically to the music.

Everything happened quickly from that point on. I remember Kase pointing out a man who I realized was Snoop Dogg. Then I glanced into the VIP area and saw Owen Wilson toasting champagne with Charlie Sheen. Next, Kase was sliding a drink into my hand. Then we were back out on the patio with a couple of girls he'd met inside, and he was lighting up a joint.

"I'm joining the Air Force," he said to the ladies, leaning coolly against the wall. "But I'm not sure when I'm getting shipped out. So, I'm chillin' with my boy De'Vannon and this dude just turned 21 today." He smirked. "How can we show him a good time?"

The women turned to me and one of them handed me the joint. I froze. Drug use wasn't allowed in the Air Force and I could be tested at any time. She placed the joint into my fingers and her hand caressed my skin lightly. There was something about the way she looked at me, with soft hazel eyes and bouncy brunette hair, that I couldn't resist. I slowly brought the joint to my lips and breathed a puff of smoke into my mouth, making sure not to fully inhale.

Kase winked at me.

*   *   *

"Have you ever stuffed a goose up your ass?" someone asked. After a moment of silence, we heard a penny clank into the bucket. In the darkness, everyone started laughing and chuckling all at once.

"I guess we have a freak in our midst," came a voice from off to my left.

"Someone up in here is nastaaayyy," said someone else.

I giggled. My brother's friends were a bit strange, but I appreciated him organizing this party to celebrate my 21st birthday during a quick visit back to Baton Rouge. I squeezed the pennies in my hand, feeling the alcohol work its way through my system.

"Does anyone want to sleep with someone in this room?" came the next question. I tossed a penny into the darkness. *Clank.* A couple of my brother's friends were hot. To my surprise, a second clank followed close behind mine. There was someone besides me in this group of masculine southern men who wanted to sleep with someone in the room. A few groaned, but nobody made any comments.

After an awkward moment someone else asked a question: "Has anyone been with two chicks at the same time?" No pennies clanked into the bucket.

Later, after the lights had come back on, I looked over each of the men closely, intrigued to discover which of these alpha males was secretly harboring homosexual urges.

I didn't have to wait long to find out.

Soon the alcohol started catching up with me and my vision blurred. My hands and feet were no longer cooperating like they usually did, and I felt clumsy and slow.

One of my brother's long-time friends, Cairo, grabbed me by the arm and marched me toward the bathroom.

"You're about to spew, De'Vannon," he said knowingly.

A moment later I was hunched over the toilet, puking my guts out. I heaved for what seemed like ages, until my stomach felt completely empty.

When I pulled my head out of the toilet to wipe the spew from my lips I came face to face with Cairo's dick. He was leaning against the bathroom wall and his pants were down around his knees.

Suddenly, I realized what was going on. Cairo nodded as it dawned on me. It was his penny I'd heard earlier!

Cairo placed his hand behind my head and moved my mouth toward his dick. *I guess he doesn't care that I still have vomit dripping from my lips*, I thought. *This guy is a freak!!!*

I sucked Cairo off on the spot. His head rolled back in ecstasy, and I could feel his muscles tense as he came in my mouth. Just then, someone knocked on the door.

"Hey, Cai?" it was my brother's voice. "Are you in there with De'Vannon? Everything OK?"

"All good," Cairo said. "He's just puking his brains out."

As if on cue, I felt another wave of vomit rising inside of me and I plunged my head back into the toilet as it flowed out of me.

"Wow, thanks man," my brother was saying. "That's nice of you to take care of him like that."

We sat in silence for a moment as my brother's footsteps padded away down the hall. Cairo's dick was so hard I could see veins bulging out on the sides. It looked like a beautiful caramel lollipop, and I decided I had to have more.

I glanced up at him, mischievously, and licked the tip of his dick.

"Ask me for it," I whispered. "Beg me to make you cum again."

He was already begging with his eyes, but I wanted to hear him say it.

"Please," he whispered back. "I want it so bad. I'm begging you."

"For what?" I asked, luxuriating in the feeling of absolute power.

"To suck my dick," he finally said.

I got right back to work, keeping him just on the edge of cumming for as long as I could. Every muscle in his body tensed up and he tried desperately not to make a sound, but he was gasping in pleasure when he deposited a load of cum in my mouth for the second time.

CHAPTER 7: MONEY

Even though I had been attending a Pentecostal church in SoCal, something in my heart told me I needed to start hearing a broader sampling of preachers so I could expand my perspective on the Word of God. That's how I found myself sucked into The Word Network (TWN), a 24-hour TV station dedicated to the Bible. On TWN I could watch preachers from all over the country delivering sermons to all kinds of different congregations.

There were some preachers on TWN who screamed and yelled about all sorts of rules about why it's not okay to have fun.

"Masturbation is having sex with demons," one proclaimed, shaking his finger sternly at the audience.

"Dancing at nightclubs is a sin!" shouted another preacher. "You might as well be dancing with the devil."

But for all the fiery rebukes there were also some preachers who were more positive and upbeat.

"Jesus is love," said one. "When we treat each other with love, we build the Kingdom of God right here on earth."

"You are good just as Jesus made you," preached another. "Your urges and desires aren't evil, they are a natural part of you."

My favorite preacher was named Joel Osteen at Lakewood Church in Houston, Texas. I loved the way he talked about the Word of God. His sermons left me feeling good about myself, as opposed to the hellfire and brimstone sermons of other preachers, which filled me with fear and confusion. Joel's church was gigantic. His congregation had purchased an old basketball stadium in Houston and turned it into a mega church, with thousands of seats. The band was incredible, and the choir was hypnotic. His services felt like one big life-affirming party.

* * *

"Hey, did you just have an appointment with a guy named Jensen?" Lisa asked as she reached deep into my candy bowl for a pink Jolly Rancher.

"Yes," I answered. "Why? You wanna poach him?

"No," Lisa said, peeling off the candy wrapper. "But the guy from the Marines next door just might."

She popped the candy in her mouth and watched me, expectantly. I didn't make her wait long. I bolted up from my chair and marched out the door. It was twenty steps to the Marine recruiter's office. I didn't knock or say a word as I opened the door and walked in. Sure enough, Jensen was sitting at the desk listening to the recruiter drone on about the Marines. I grabbed Jensen by the ear, yanked him out of his chair, and dragged him back to my office.

The Marine recruiter watched me with his mouth hanging open and looking dumb, and I knew his sorry ass couldn't say anything. Jensen was my recruit, and I wasn't going to let him fall prey to someone's scripted bullshit propaganda. I dragged Jensen, whimpering, back to my office. Lisa was grinning with delight.

I sat Jensen down and said, "If you're gonna cheat on my ass, don't be stupid enough to do it with the man next door!"

Lisa burst into laughter, and Jensen blushed.

"You know what, fuck it," I said. "Let's go to In-N-Out Burger and forget about it. We can't go wrong at that blessed establishment."

* * *

I fought back a wave of emotion as I dialed Kase's number. It had been a year and a half since we first met, and he had become like an older brother to me. We'd gotten laid together. He'd introduced me to weed. He taught me about Cali women and helped me make friends. With Kase I'd been able to get a glimpse of what life was like as a straight man. The church had always told me being gay would land me in hell and I honestly thought I could become un-gay by praying and doing the things that straight guys do. It didn't work. But in a strange way, this had been one of the closest friendships of my life.

"De'Vannon," he said, "what's up my man? Are we partying this weekend homie?"

"Hell yeah we are!" I said excitedly. "You've been approved to be an Aircraft Mechanic. You ship out next week for BMT so we gotta send your ass off in style! Congratulations, Kase!"

"Hey, that's awesome!" he screamed. "Then we really need to celebrate! I've got some ladies looking to hang. I'll set it up."

Kase and I had grown to be close friends, and knowing I was going to lose him felt terrible.

"Yes," I said, "let's celebrate."

* * *

"Sorry, your card's been declined," said the bartender. "Is there a different card I could put this on?"

"That's impossible," I said, embarrassed. "Run it again."

"I already did," she said, "three times."

Kase reached for his wallet but I stopped him.

"There's no way you're paying for drinks," I said. "This is your going away party."

I flipped through my wallet and handed her another credit card and a debit card.

"Try these," I muttered.

She eyed me with a look of pity mixed with annoyance as she took the cards from me.

"All set," she said, returning a moment later. "I was able to put $8 on the debit card and the rest on the credit card. Don't worry about a tip, honey. You always take care of us here."

I handed Kase his beer and grabbed my lemon drop martini.

"To your last weekend of freedom!" I called out.

He smiled.

"I got a couple of great girls meeting us later," he said.

"Nice!" I downed the rest of my drink. "Let me run across the street to the ATM and grab some more cash."

A moment later I was walking through the cool evening air toward the neon sign a few buildings down from the club: Payday Loans.

"No, you're maxed out," the man told me when I slid my ID across the counter. "You've got three loans out, that's the limit."

"This can't be right." I was desperate. "They told me last time that I could still get one more loan since I only took out $1,000 each, not the maximum of $1,500. My paychecks are $1,500 twice a month. Please, I need this."

He sighed.

"I can give you $500," he said. "That's it."

Relief washed over me.

"Thank you so much," I said, and headed back to the bar where Kase was waiting.

* * *

"I'd like to take out a personal loan, please," I said, sitting up straight on the hard plastic chair, trying to look as professional and trustworthy as possible.

"Alright, I can help you with that," said the banker from behind his desk. "How much would you like?"

"Ten thousand dollars," I replied with as much confidence as I could muster.

"Do you have a job?" he asked.

"Yes sir," I said, "I'm a recruiter for the Air Force."

He smiled and jumped up to pull a few papers from a row of cubbies at the back of his cubicle.

"Perfect," he told me, "government jobs are a slam dunk. I can get you approved for that within an hour. I just need to ask you a few more questions."

Forty-five minutes later I walked out of the bank with $10,000 in cash.

I'm going to use this responsibly, I told myself. *I'm not going to blow it on frivolous things.*

But even as I made myself this promise I hopped in my car and headed toward Nordstrom. There were some new accessories in stock I wanted to check out. And I really needed a new pair of True Religion jeans. The only ones I had were a dark wash. *A light wash will really go nice with my green T-shirt*, I thought.

Now that Kase was gone there was a hole in my weekend schedule, and in my heart. I missed having a partner to show me the ropes and introduce me to people.

I decided to fill that hole with my latest addiction: shopping.

* * *

"Cash this for me, please" I slid a check across the counter.

"No problem," said the teller. "Just a moment."

She took the check and headed into the back. I silently thanked the Lord for this money. The previous week I'd learned that I could write myself a check at the Exchange on the nearest Air Force base and they would cash it for me. Then the best part was the check didn't clear my account for a few days. So, I had written myself a check every day for the past few days and deposited the cash into my account to cover the previous checks while I waited for payday.

I just need to make it 'til the 1st of the month, I told myself.

Suddenly, I felt a firm hand on my shoulder.

"Sir, please come with me," came a deep voice. I spun around to find myself face to face with a man wearing jeans and a black shirt, and holding a badge that read "Security Officer" on it.

"What's the problem, sir?" I asked as we stepped away from the counter.

"Are you aware that it's a felony to write a check that you don't have funds in your account to actually cover?" he asked.

Oh, shit!

"Um…" I scrambled. "Is that so?"

"Come with me," he growled again.

I gulped and did as he commanded. *At least he didn't cuff me,* I thought, as he ushered me to a backdoor that opened up into a room that was empty except for a bench.

"Wait here," the officer said before closing and locking the door behind me.

Oh, shit. Is he calling the police? If I go to jail, I could get kicked out of the Air Force! I started to panic. Thankfully I still had my cell phone on me, so I quickly called Evangelist Nelson.

"De'Vannon? What's going on, child?"

"Evangelist Nelson, I think I'm in big trouble. I tried to cash a check at the Base Exchange, and an undercover store cop took me away to this back room. I think he's calling the police."

"Okay, I'm with you. Don't panic. I'll handle it."

"Yes, okay. Thank you, Evangelist Nelson." She hung up.

This is how Evangelist Nelson would often handle my situations whenever I called her with some stupid bullshit I would've gotten myself into. I don't know what she told God, or how she approached Him, but this woman defined what it means to be a true Pastor and a true Prophetess. She stood in the gap and shielded me from much danger and this time was no different.

Slowly, I calmed down. I no longer felt alone. The peace of her loving spirit extended to me in that holding room, and I could sense that everything was going to be alright.

Soon after we hung up the phone, the security officer returned.

"You can go," he grumbled. "We did have the police on the line but they suddenly had a rush of urgent calls come in so there is no one available who can come arrest you."

"Thank you, Jesus!" I muttered under my breath and hurried out of the room.

* * *

Jude looked nothing like the typical recruit. He stepped into my office wearing Tommy Bahama loafers, a high-end button-down shirt, khaki shorts, and Ray Ban glasses. His short black hair was carelessly tousled, and his white skin was tanned and weathered, like he'd come straight from a yacht.

This guy was a total stud.

What the fuck was he doing applying for the Air Force?

"You've already had quite a successful career," I noted, glancing through his file.

He nodded.

"I've had all the success I could want," he said. His voice was deep and dreamy. "I've sailed around the world, eaten at the finest restaurants, studied with the most brilliant minds, and gazed upon the most beautiful sights."

"I don't get it," I raised an eyebrow. "Why do you want to join the Air Force then? You don't need free education. You don't need to see the world. You don't need a place to start your career. Those are generally the reasons why people find themselves in my office. What is it you think we can offer you here?"

Jude sat back in his chair and pondered this.

"I guess what I'm looking for is a sense of meaning," he said finally. "I want to be a part of something bigger than myself."

Long after he left my office, Jude's words stuck with me. Something fascinated me about his life. He was charming, attractive, and accomplished but he was still searching for meaning. For the first time, I begin to understand that having money doesn't guarantee fulfillment.

* * *

Three new silver rings hung from my lower lip as I sorted paperwork into their appropriate folders in my office at the strip mall on a sunny Saturday afternoon. I also wore ripped skinny jeans and a tight red tee. I didn't have any appointments scheduled for the day, so I felt like I could let loose. Lisa knew I wore the piercings at the office and didn't care, even though it was against Air Force uniform regulations. *And why should anyone care? I have the best recruiting numbers in the whole motherfucking region!*

"Excuse me, is this the Air Force recruiting office? May I speak to your supervisor?"

I looked up from my desk. A large, dark haired white man in a white polo shirt and khaki shorts stood a prideful foot taller than a teenage boy with a skinny baseball build who I assumed was his son.

"Yes, you're in the right place," I said cordially. "How may I help you?"

The prideful exuberance slowly faded from the man's face. "No," he said, nearly gasping. "You're not the one in charge here. You can't be."

"I am," I said as dismissively as I could manage. *I know my appearance is probably well below his standards, but this is fine. I'll manage. He'll get over it. And we'll get his boy off to the military.*

"THIS IS UNACCEPTABLE!" he shouted. "You? Representing the Air Force? Looking like... THIS? Your jeans look like you've stepped on a landmine and your face has more holes in it than a fucking Taliban insurgent after I've gotten my hands on him! And you have the *audacity* to be representing the AIR FORCE? THIS IS UNACCEPTABLE!"

Spittle spewed aggressively from his mouth as he yelled. Under his chin, his son looked at me with pinched brows as if he was still deciding whether to judge me or not. Suddenly the boy turned around as his dad steered him toward the door. As the pair exited the dad yelled back, "I'll have you reported! You have my word!"

Fuck him, I thought to myself as the door to my office closed. *Even if he does report me, it's not like my commander is gonna discipline me over one complaint. Not with the way I've been performing.*

* * *

Next Friday morning during my drive into work, I got a call to visit my commander's office. *This is either going to be really bad or really good*, I thought to myself. The incident with the angry dad came to my mind, but so did my recruiting numbers.

My commander, Col. Hooper, eyed me levelly as I stood at attention in front of his desk.

"You've fucked up, Hubert!" Col. Hooper barked. "We received a complaint from the dad of a promising young recruit, and I can see clearly from the brown fucking stubs in your face that he was telling the truth. Fucking disgraceful! For no reason do you ever get to break the rules, Hubert! No reason! I don't care how fucking good your numbers are! Being the best damn recruiter in the region does *not* put you above the rules! That's child's thinking, and if BMT didn't train that shit out of you then I'll be sure to right now! The uniform code exists for a reason! To protect the face of the Air Force for respectable recruits such as the family you disappointed on Saturday! That kid could've gone far in the Air Force! You ought to be ashamed of yourself, Hubert! I'm ashamed of you! That's why I'm issuing you an Article 15! And if you put one more toe out of line you'll be out of the Air Force with a dishonorable discharge! Do I make myself clear, Hubert?"

I thought about reminding Col. Hooper that I was being productive for the Air Force presently, in real time. That kid may not even pass the physical or make it through Basic Training. My commander was giving this kid a hell of a lot of credit upfront, before he had even earned it.

I looked back in shock and gulped. "Sir, yes, sir!"

* * *

I felt like a Rockstar as I stepped into the awards banquet and sat down at my table. The room was filled with other recruiters from the entire region, which included Southern California and the entire state of Arizona. And everyone in the room knew I was about to win the Recruiter of the Year award. It was no secret that my numbers were more than double Brock's numbers, and he was the next best performing recruiter after me. I recruited 4-10 people each month whereas Brock was only recruiting about 2-3 people per month. The numbers were sent around by email to all the recruiters in the region each month to keep the spirit of competition strong between us.

"Hey man," said Lisa as I sat down. "Congratulations!"

I beamed. I'd worked my ass off for this award. Not only did I have the largest territory of anyone in the room, I also drove all the way to L.A. multiple times each week to accompany my recruits to the MEPS. Plus I went the extra mile to get waivers and exceptions for my recruits as well.

Tonight, I was finally going to be recognized for my efforts.

"Thank you all for coming," Col. Hooper took the mic as we dug into our meals. "While the purpose of this event is to honor all of you for your hard work, there's one person in particular we want to bring up on stage for some special recognition. This recruiter has been putting up stellar numbers every month and he always goes above and beyond. Please put your hands together for Brock Bellingham!"

The room was silent. Nobody moved. Had he misspoken?

Everyone looked from me to Brock and then back to me.

"Come on up Brock," said Col. Hooper. "Get up here and take your plaque. Can we get a round of applause for this man's hard work this year?"

There was polite clapping as Brock sheepishly made his way up to the podium. He looked confused and embarrassed as he accepted the award and then sat back down.

I was furious. I knew exactly what had happened. The fucking Air Force couldn't handle my style. They didn't like my piercings. They hated my flamboyance. They snubbed me!

"For what it's worth," said Brock after the ceremony had ended, "you earned this award De'Vannon. That was some bullshit. Everyone knows what just happened."

"Thank you," I nodded. As much as I hated Brock, his words meant a lot.

* * *

"Will you stay for another six years?" the officer asked hopefully. "We're prepared to offer you a bonus of $3,000 if you sign on again."

"Absolutely not," I said. "I am done with the bullshit here. No fucking thank you. Just tell me where to sign and I'm out of here."

"Certainly," he nodded and slid a stack of papers over to me. "I'll make sure you're issued an Out Date for the near future. In the meantime, if you really need a break, you have a month of leave saved up. You can still use that."

"Fine."

In my hotel room that night I took off my uniform for what would be the very last time. I carefully removed my flight cap, shirt, and slacks, and I folded them into a neat pile. On top of that I placed the shoes. I had all of my uniforms with me as I was still deciding what I was going to do with them now that I was leaving the Air Force.

On the way to my car the next morning I chucked my uniforms into a dumpster, and I felt some of the resentment I held for the Air Force lighten a bit. The only one I kept was my Air Force dress blues because they were like a tuxedo and too nice to let go of. It was one of the most satisfying feelings I've ever experienced.

My Cavalier was packed with all of my essential belongings. I'd already moved out of my apartment and there was a new one waiting for me a thousand miles away.

I was heading to Houston, Texas.

PART III
(2006-2012)

DREAM

The house was ragged and run down. It was in the middle of an abandoned lot and there were no other houses around it. White paint flaked from the walls and piled up in chips. The wood was a rotten mess. The whole place looked like it might collapse at any moment. The house scared me. But, like a magnet, I was drawn to it.

In the foggy glass pane of the front door I caught the moonlit reflection of my altar boy uniform: a white shirt and black pants, ironed to the perfect crease. A tingle ran up my arm and down my spine as I twisted the rusty door handle and begin to cautiously open the door. Thick, damp smells of mold and mildew wafted toward me from the doorway. The air crackled with foreboding, but I was too curious to turn away. I swung the door open and stared inside.

There was a single hallway with three or four doors on either side. Each room had a face poking out of it through a creaked open door, inviting me silently to come join them. This house had vacancies. All I had to do was step inside. Those faces were made of black static, but none of them made a sound. None of them moved an inch. They waited for me as I looked down the long narrow hallway. They waited for me to make a move. They waited… and waited.

I lingered at the entrance for a long time, but my feet did not move. I longed to inch forward, the way a mouse must long to sniff the cheese on a mousetrap. But I knew it wasn't a good idea to step forward. The desire was pungent, and it tasted like sweat on my tongue. I wanted to go inside. I wanted to so badly.

My silent stand-still with temptation yawned into the night. There was a palpable darkness that desired to prevail over me. It pulled gently, delicately, at my heart, but I pulled back.

Adrenaline sent a rush of blood through my face as I realized the trap. My mouth was suddenly dry, so I waved my hands frantically to swat away the darkness. The faces poking out from behind the doors watched as I turned and walked away. The moonlight caressed me, and I continued to wave my hands as I walked across the abandoned lot. The darkness lingering around my body haunted me.

When I woke up, it was still dark. I did not go back to sleep that night.

CHAPTER 8: WELCOME TO HOUSTON

SPRING 2006 – HOUSTON, TX

The building was impossible to miss. If it weren't for the *Lakewood Church* signage across the front I would have guessed I was arriving at the most extravagant conference center on earth—or a Madonna concert. I had high expectations from watching the church's services on TV for the past few years, and my wildest dreams were immediately surpassed. Sleek silver rails directed attendees up a wide staircase to the second floor, which was a bit like Disneyland. There were massive wall posters featuring inspirational quotes and colorful cardboard cutouts of Bible characters. There was also a whole team of ushers ready to greet us with warm smiles and show us to our seats.

The plush blue and gold carpet of the wide halls gave way to the soft darkness of the sanctuary, which was jaw-droppingly massive. It had been converted from an old basketball stadium and held over 16,000 churchgoers. My eyes swept over the sea of congregants as I walked down the aisle. At the bottom of the bowl was the stage, polished and shiny, bathed in blue theater lights. I found the most central seat that was available and waited.

I leafed through a blue and white brochure and noted some of the upcoming events: worship nights, Sunday services, and singles ministry. On one page I saw a picture of the youth pastor and my dick instantly went hard. This guy looked like an Abercrombie model. He had a tall, muscular football physique, gelled hair, and skinny jeans. *Fuck me*, was all I could think. I was hot for the fucking preacher.

The photo faded into darkness as the lights dimmed and the band ascended from a platform beneath the stage. I always knew from watching on TV that the music was good, but being there in person, amongst a sea of worshippers, was extrasensory. The vibrations of the speaker system pulsated through me as I raised my voice with thousands of others to meet the sound.

Am I in heaven?

After hearing an array of angelic songs, I felt as if the music had ripped open my chest cavity and forced my heart to receive true beauty. I was nearly brought to tears with ecstasy. Then Joel Osteen took to the stage and began to preach.

After the service I made my way over to Lakewood's corner bookstore (meaning it took up the whole corner of the block). It featured books from Joel Osteen as well as some other pastors I had seen on The Word Network, but I was drawn to the music section.

Rows of CDs lined the music section of the shop. I didn't know where to begin. I started in the Pop section, but after browsing some cover art, I couldn't imagine anyone singing about Jesus in the way Madonna sang about sex. I moved over to the Rock section.

I didn't know any of the artists, but one CD jumped out at me: Building 429. The cover art was a simple photo of four white guys with edgy, short haircuts sitting on a couch in front of a white wall and staring blankly into the camera. I purchased the CD.

* * *

I was singing at the top of my lungs along with my favorite Building 429 song, "No One Else Knows." In fact, I had already purchased the sheet music online and was planning to teach myself the song on my keyboard.

Something about the song resonated deep within me. I sang it every morning and afternoon as I drove to and from my new job at the GAP. The best part about working there was the 50 percent discount. In just a few weeks I'd stacked up a very nice wardrobe for myself. As I clocked in one morning, Stacey, my supervisor, reminded me we were having a quick staff meeting after work that day.

I hadn't made any friends at the GAP. Everyone kept to themselves and saved up their social energy for the customers. Keeping the store neat and tidy was calming, and I loved helping customers pick out clothes when they came in. It felt like repaying all the kind workers from the past, like Kylo, who had helped me get my shit together when I was having a fashion crisis.

Stacey had sent out an email the day before letting everyone know about the meeting. It seemed important because even off duty assistant managers were scheduled to come in.

At the end of the day I gathered with the rest of the employees in the center of the store. It was after 9pm, the store was closed, and we were all tired. Stacey and the assistant managers were all present. I noticed that the assistant managers were all wearing sweatpants, though.

"Alright, y'all," Stacey started, clasping her hands together, "thanks for sticking around, because we are having *a folding party!* We have a regional manager visiting tomorrow so it just needs to get done. So go, go, go!"

We all looked around at each other. *Is she serious? Is this a joke? After a whole fucking day of work, they're gonna make us do more work? This is the fucking "quick meeting" she was talking about?*

As angry as I was, I got to work folding clothes. There wasn't any use complaining and compared to boot camp a few hours of folding clothes was nothing. Still, I watched in distant sorrow as my coworkers, who didn't have military endurance, broke their backs as they attempted to shoulder this extra burden. Stacey wasn't taking any shit.

"Come on, y'all, don't let up! Move faster! Let's get it looking good in here!"

I felt my blood burn hot. Why did Stacey think she could pull a fast one on us like this? She was a dubious, disrespectful, and treacherous bitch.

"Come on, De'Vannon," Stacey urged, "fold like your hands are on fire!"

I dropped the black shirt I was folding and glared at Stacey. "Excuse me?" I snapped. My hands were on fire because all the fucking folding had my hands aching like a motherfucker. "I did not sign up to be in the military all over again!"

Stacey looked at me, stunned. Her mouth hung agape, the way Miss Piggy looks when Kermit the Frog makes a bacon joke. Her response was cold and resolute. "Well, you can clock out, but I can't guarantee you'll have a job the next time you try to clock in."

Without saying anything, I turned around and walked the fuck out.

* * *

I was proud of the foot-high stack of shiny Lakewood Church brochures riding home with me in my passenger seat. There were new printouts available every two weeks, and I loved passing them out to people I met in public. The services at Lakewood helped me experience God in ways no other church had before.

Suddenly, "No One Else Knows" came on the radio. The song seemed to get better every time I heard it. I sang along, belting my heart out.

My heart was filled with joy as I felt like God was looking out for me through music. I was sad when the song ended, but then the station's DJ spoke.

"What is up, Houston!? This is Emmy from KSBJ God Listens Radio, and that was 'No One Else Knows,' by the incredibly talented band, Building 429. I hope you liked that. And if you have songs that you would like to hear played right here on this station, we are now accepting submissions for listener playlists! Go on our website and submit a one hour playlist of your favorite music, and if we like it we might just give you a call and let you run the show for an hour! How does that sound?"

My jaw hung limp in shock. I *had* to enter this contest. But first, I had already promised myself I was going to sign up for volunteer opportunities at church. I looked over once again in anticipation at the shimmering pile of polished brochures riding shotgun. *One thing at a time*, I told myself.

When I got home, I opened the top brochure to the volunteer opportunities, and I saw it: Lakewood KidsLife. The next day I drove by Lakewood to pick up the application form and drove back to my apartment to complete it. It was more paperwork than I'd ever been asked to complete for any other volunteer opportunity in my entire life. They were asking for various forms of identification, permission to perform background checks, and if I was lucky there would be an interview. I scoffed at the volume of scrutiny, but I wanted to serve the church. Lakewood was so *extra*, but I couldn't *not* be a part of it. So, I got to work.

Name and Date-of-Birth. No problem.

Have you volunteered with kids before? Yes!

Have you ever been convicted of a crime? No.

The form went on and on like a formal job application until I ran into one particular question that stopped me.

Are you gay, or homosexual? (We cannot allow people who identify as gay or homosexual to serve with KidsLife.)

I was stunned by how forward they were about disqualifying people on the basis of sexual orientation. But I knew I didn't pose any threat, so I lied. *No.*

"Besides," I muttered, "I'm technically bisexual after the experiences I shared with Kase."

I moved on with the application and submitted it. I didn't linger on the question of my sexuality. The Air Force had prepared me to operate in a "Don't Ask, Don't Tell" environment.

My phone rang.

"Hello?"

"De'Vannon! How are you doing?" It was my brother.

"Hey! I'm doing good. What's up?"

"What's up is your birthday is this week! And as long as we're sharing the same city, I'm gonna make sure you ain't bored on your birthday. Do you have any plans?"

"Well, I've made some friends at church, and they say they like to take each other out to their favorite restaurants on their birthdays."

"Okay if your brother comes and celebrates with you?"

"Sure thing! I'm thinking of inviting people to The Oceanaire."

"Damn! That place is fancy. Let me know when you've got the reservation set so I can put it in my calendar."

"Ok, I'll let you know."

After we hung up, I made a note to invite my new church friends to dinner at The Oceanaire. Next, I opened a new window in my web browser and went to the KSBJ God Listens Radio website. Sure enough, there was a button in the top menu bar for submitting playlists. I got to work.

* * *

The following Sunday, I finally managed to get a good parking spot on the lower level of Lakewood Church's parking garage only to be delayed entry at the front door by a protest.

"Lakewood Lies!" "Osteen is a Hypocrite!" "Down with the Prosperity Gospel!"

Picket signs rose up above the angry crowd like multicolored speech bubbles. Security guards barred the entrances to the building from the protesters. I tried not to get mixed up with the angry crowd. *There's got to be a way in.*

Sure enough, a small pathway had been carved out by metal barriers, and after confirming with a security guard that I was there for the service, I was able to enter.

Inside, everything was back to normal. It was quiet, the ushers on the second floor were happy to greet me, and I made my way to the side of the theater.

I'd learned the side seats had a better view of the choir during service. The more connected I felt with the choir, the more connected I felt to God during worship.

I already knew the words to all the songs, and I joined passionately with the choir as they swayed from side-to-side along with the music. My heart yearned to be up on stage singing with them. Finally, Joel took the stage for his sermon.

But someone in the center section stood up and started yelling, "How hard it is for the rich to enter the Kingdom of God!"

In an instant, security converged on the man, who continued to shout as he was escorted out of the sanctuary.

"Your money can't save you, Joel! Money can't save any of you!!!"

After the man was gone from the building, Joel continued with the service as if nothing had happened. He spoke passionately and with a smile, and after a few minutes, there may as well have been no interruption at all.

In this same service I saw a woman catch the Holy Ghost during worship. I was happy to see the Spirit move this woman, but as soon as she had gotten up out of her seat, the ushers escorted her right out of the sanctuary. I was confused because any expression of God should be allowed in a church of all places. It seemed as though this church made quick work of anyone perceived to be a disruption no matter what. This did not sit well with me, but I also understood that no church is going to be perfect.

When the service ended, there were small groups taking place in several conference rooms throughout the building. I made my way to the singles group, looking forward to catching up with my newest friend, Brianna.

"Happy birthday to you! Happy birthday to you! Happy birthday dear De'Vannon! Happy birthday to you!"

My face lit up. I had no idea how the whole group of forty people had arrived in the room before me to sing for me, but I didn't care. I felt so loved and welcomed.

Brianna walked up to me, smirking.

"If you think I'm paying for your bill tonight at The Oceanaire, you got another thing coming."

"Aw, not even one drink?" I asked teasingly.

"I'll pay for the water, if I can afford it," she retorted. "Who else is coming, anyway?"

"Janine from choir, who can hopefully help get this beautiful voice on that stage. And some people from KidsLife, who I'm trying to befriend so I can volunteer there. Oh, and my brother!"

"Oh, what's his purpose, to pick up the tab?"

"Y'all can fight over that honor amongst yourselves."

"Yeah, yeah," she waved me off. "Why are you always trying to get into so many church groups anyway? Don't you ever get tired of all this bullshit?"

"Tired?" I asked, shocked. "How could I? This is the best church I've ever been

to! Why would I serve it any less than all the others I've attended in the past?"

* * *

Before going out to dinner at The Oceanaire I needed to buy a new outfit, so I made my way to the Galleria shopping mall. I found a good middle-of-the-line store and walked in. I didn't take more than three steps before stopping in my tracks.

There amongst the racks of clothes, browsing for what looked like a new sweater, was Victoria Osteen, the Lakewood pastor's wife. She often spoke for several minutes during the weekend services, and I always felt more spiritually uplifted during those minutes than during the twenty to thirty minutes that Joel would speak. Now in the same store as me, she was no longer sporting the six-inch heel spikes she'd worn on stage at church earlier that day and had slipped into some flats, but her diva style was still admirable. Even without theater lights shining down on her, her golden hair hung in perfect waves. I was starstruck. I had to talk to her, even if only for a moment. I couldn't let this opportunity pass.

"Hi, Victoria?" I stuck out my hand. "I'm sorry to bother you. My name is De'Vannon. I go to Lakewood, and I just want to say how thankful I am to you and Joel for everything you do to make our church what it is. I also really like what you said earlier this morning."

She looked at me with tired eyes. I remembered the protesters and the man who had interrupted the church service. I could see that the day had taken its toll. I felt bad for interrupting what was probably a momentary escape from the turmoil for her.

Victoria closed her eyes, took a deep breath, and then placed her hand on my forearm. My heart jumped at her gentle touch, and my whole body stiffened. When she opened her eyes, there was a new energy there. I felt as though God's Spirit was rejuvenating her from within. In the corner of my vision, her mother smiled, knowingly.

"De'Vannon," Victoria spoke, calmly and with intention. "Thank you for those kind words. I want you to know that God sees you. No matter what storm is chasing you, God is with you, and you don't need to worry about the storm catching up to you. He knows how scary the storm is, but no storm lasts forever. His presence, however, *is* everlasting."

I focused all my energy on breathing normally, but I knew that I was shaking. Her words echoed in my head.

I held back tears as she finished speaking. "God bless you, De'Vannon."

"Thank you," I managed to respond, before leaving the store and retreating straight back to my car. I sat in the parking lot, shivering, and replayed the encounter in my head. Gratitude filled my heart. And then anger.

I thought about the protesters at Lakewood. How could people judge her and Joel without getting to know them? Sure they were wealthy, but since when are pastors not allowed to have money? Especially when their fortune is amassed outside of church donations. I decided that people are just jealous. They are envious of the Osteen's money and beauty.

This first-hand interaction with Victoria made me want to serve the church even more and so that is exactly what I did.

* * *

The Oceanaire was even better than I had imagined it would be. We walked past a 10-foot table with beautiful cuts of salmon laid out on a marble slab, filleted down the middle and topped with capers, cream cheese, lemon, and rosemary. In the next room, there was a long table for my party of ten, and once we were all seated the servers brought out bowls of cubed fish soaked in citrus sauce, on the house. They placed menus in front of us, specially printed with my name embossed on the top of each. They offered us oysters and champagne, and we accepted. Everything was *extra*, just the way I like it.

Brianna gave me a sideways look to playfully judge my extravagant taste. I didn't care. The evening was turning out to be quite fabulous. Then she looked down at the bag I'd brought with me. She probably expected to see a gift from my brother, but at the sight of the polished pages of Lakewood Church brochures her eyes shot back up at me.

"What are you doing with all of those?" she questioned.

"I bring a stack with me everywhere I go," I said. "Even on my birthday. At restaurants I like to pass them out to servers and invite them to come to church."

On cue, a team of servers returned to deliver our oysters and champagne flutes. Brianna didn't let the subject go, though.

"I think you give our little church too much credit."

Then a different voice spoke up. "You guys go to Lakewood?" It was one of our servers. He was a tall, lanky man with carefully gelled black hair.

"Yes," I replied, "do you?"

"No," the server said. "I find the Osteen's ministry to be quite distasteful, actually. The Jesus I know preaches good news and blessings to the poor, not to the rich."

"I thought Jesus lived and died for all people," I said defensively.

"He did," the server said calmly. "And then he commanded us to lay down our lives as he did. I don't see how the Osteens can be doing that when they're wearing expensive outfits every Sunday and spending ridiculous amounts of money when they go out to eat in places like this."

"Well, I strongly encourage you to reconsider," I said, and turned back to my champagne flute. I sensed the server leave, but I felt Brianna's cold eyes remain on me. I looked at her. "What?"

"He has a point," she said.

"He's just jealous. Doesn't Jesus say a thing or two about envy?"

Brianna rolled her eyes and turned back to the oysters sitting in front of her.

"Now how the hell do you eat these?" she asked, mercifully changing the subject.

The rest of the night was filled with bubbling champagne, laughter, and the best seafood of my life. When the server placed the tab in front of me at the end of the night, I waited for someone to take it and offer to pay. Everyone pretended to ignore the fact that the bill had been placed on the table. Finally, I looked down at the paper in front of me. The four digits made my heart skip a beat.

I gulped and looked back at my friends, trying to scheme out how to broach this topic. Then I felt a hand on my shoulder. It was my brother.

"I got it," he said, and took the check.

I breathed a big sigh of relief and rejoined my friends in the pretense that the bill was no real issue.

That night on the drive home, I heard the familiar sound of my favorite Building 429 song begin to play on the radio.

I felt God reminding me of his presence, and I was comforted.

CHAPTER 9: ASPIRATIONS

The last thing I had done before departing the military was to take out a loan and buy myself a second car to go along with the Chevy Cavalier I already owned. It was a candy-apple red 1984 Corvette with a V8 engine and a removable top. As if the engine wasn't loud enough, I took it to a sound shop and had Crunch amps, new speakers, and a retractable DVD player installed. This car was a work of art. I had it shipped to Houston from California as I figured it would be best to put miles on my Chevy rather than on an old school car.

In the months after moving to Houston I worked four jobs, and none lasted more than a couple months. On the bright side, my application to volunteer with Lakewood's KidsLife ministry was approved.

For my first day volunteering with the kids, I dressed my best. I showed up with my California cowboy boots and the top off my Corvette. It was a Wednesday night, I was thirty minutes early, and I felt like a Rockstar. A woman named Molly was there to meet me, but if she noticed my Corvette and cowboy boots, she didn't show it.

"Hi, De'Vannon, thanks for being on time. We're really excited to have your help."

Molly was nice, but she didn't waste time on pleasantries. She got right down to work showing me how to set up, which was a rather extensive process.

"So, pay attention, because normally you're going to be doing all of this setup on your own," Molly said as she escorted me to one of the larger meeting rooms on the third floor of the building. "There's going to be twenty groups of boys and twenty groups of girls. We need to partition the room up for all of those groups and set up their signs."

She walked over to a large, tan purse in the corner and pulled out a handful of manilla folders. "These are the teaching packets. We'll have new ones printed out for you each week. I'll start setting these out. You check the closet for a blue bin that should be full of snacks. That will also be restocked for you each week."

As we finished up, Molly addressed me one more time, sounding nearly out of breath. "Now, do you know which group you'll be teaching?"

"Yes," I answered. "The third grade boys."

"Great," she said. "Here's your teaching packet." She passed me a pile of white papers with colored images of animals reenacting stories from the Bible. "Oh, and one more thing. You'll need to wear this whenever you're here from now on."

Molly reached into the bottom of her purse and pulled out a bright red jersey. "KidsLife" it said in big, bold, white letters. A surge of pride filled my chest as I received the uniform and pulled it over my shirt.

"Great," Molly said. "Now let's make sure the registration kiosks are ready to go outside so we can get this show on the road!"

Within five minutes, the room was flooded with the joy and laughter of kids. I welcomed the boys in my group with glee, and when it was time to start, we got down to reading our animal Bible stories and talking about God and Jesus. They laughed as I made different voices for each of the animal characters. I felt like they loved me, and at the end of the evening I was sad to see them go.

As I waved goodbye to the boys, I saw some of the parents (fresh out of the adult service which happened simultaneously) casting curious glances at my cowboy boots. I felt a knot tighten in my stomach as the thought of them complaining about me crossed my mind, but then I relaxed. *Let the parents complain,* I thought. *I'm having fun and providing a good service. So, what if they can't take my Cali style?*

After everyone left, I put the place neatly back in order. I pushed myself to get it done in under thirty minutes by myself and succeeded. It was just like mornings in boot camp when everything had to be in order before the

Flight Chief arrived. When I was done, it was 10pm and the December sun was already well below the horizon. I should have been tired, but I was more energized than I'd been all year.

I jumped over the door of my Corvette into the driver's seat, gunned the engine, and drove Downtown to the clubs.

* * *

"Please!" I begged.

"Why would I want to sit with your ass and wait for your car's oil to get changed?" Brianna was being stubborn, as usual.

"What if they find a bigger problem with the car and I need a ride?"

"Then you can use your damn cell phone and call me. Or hell, call a taxi!"

"Brianna!"

"Stop acting like I ain't got shit to do."

"I'll buy you lunch, just please go with me."

"Excuse me? What kind of friendship do you think we have? If you want to buy me lunch, you can buy me lunch, but I am not promising you any favors in return."

"Ugh, fine!" I groaned. Brianna could be aggravating, but her headstrong attitude was also one of the reasons we were friends. I liked the banter, even if it meant losing most arguments.

Before stopping at the Chevrolet dealership, I swung by a liquor store and grabbed a six pack of beer. I was not looking forward to the boring wait while my car got fixed up.

I was wearing black nail polish, pinstripe rave party pants, and a black "CAN'T SLEEP... CLOWNS WILL EAT ME" T-shirt from Hot Topic. The brown beer bottle in my hand was really just the cherry on top of my emo girly look. The Mexican street vendor selling fruit near the dealership gave me several odd looks, but I didn't care. She was eventually distracted by a tall, slender guy in jeans and sandals making a purchase.

After buying the fruit, the man in the sandals walked right over to me.

"Mango?" He offered me some. Without saying anything, I picked a slice out of the bag. "My name's Juan. What's yours?"

"De'Vannon," I answered, taking a nervous swig from my beer. *What does this guy want?*

"I'm going to the beach in Galveston this weekend," he said. "Do you want to come with me?"

My mind started to race. *I've only just met this guy and he's already asking me to go out of town with him! Would I be safe? What would my friends at church think? What would God think?* I looked down at his sandals and nearly puked. His toes were dry, bruised, and beat up. *Dealbreaker.*

I grimaced as I took another sip of my beer. "Um, thanks for the offer, Juan. That sounds nice, but I'm gonna pass."

Juan nodded understandingly. "Ok, no problem. But if you change your mind, here's my number." He passed me a business card with his name, number, and a construction company's logo on it.

"Thanks," I said as Juan walked away.

I twirled the card between my fingers. *Was this guy serious? There's no way all that chivalry was legit. He had to be bullshiting me, right?*

A dealership worker came outside and called my name. *Finally!*

I pulled into a gas station on my way home. The fuel tank was almost empty, and I hadn't thought to fill it earlier on my way to the dealership. But as I slipped my card into the gas machine, the screen went red: "DECLINED."

I tried again. "DECLINED."

I went inside the gas station and tried my ATM card. "INSUFFICIENT FUNDS."

"No, no, no, no, no," I muttered to myself. I checked my wallet for cash, but there was nothing but dust bunnies dancing around in there. I put my hands on my head, trying not to panic. *Think. Think. Think.*

I pulled out my damn cell phone and dialed. "Brianna? I'm at the gas station and all of my cards are getting declined. I need some help."

"*Ha! And you were gonna buy me lunch.*"

Ten minutes later, Brianna arrived and paid for my tank of gas.

* * *

I wasn't technically a member of the Lakewood Choir yet as Janine had explained that I had to attend roughly a month of practice before I could become official. It felt like a formality because I already knew all the music by heart, and I was confident in my singing, but this was part of the application process.

On the way home from practice, my phone rang.

"Hello?"

"Hi! Is this De'Vannon Hubert?"

"Yes it is, who's calling?"

"This is Emmy from KSBJ God Listens Radio, and I'm calling to say CONGRATULATIONS! Your setlist has been selected to air for one hour this week!"

I screamed. "Whaaaat! This is so exciting! Oh my! Whaaaat?"

"Yes! Congratulations! I love what you submitted, and would like to schedule a one hour interview with you sometime in the next couple of days to talk about the songs you chose, as well as a little bit about yourself."

"This sounds fabulous! Yes! Anytime! You name the time, and I will make it happen! Yes!"

I screamed again. "Aaaaah! Thank you, Jesus!"

This was all too good to be true. I needed to celebrate. I needed to keep the high going.

When I got home, I opened up my web browser and was about to type in GAY.com when I stopped. That was an old high. I needed something new. I entered, "Gay district, Houston."

Immediately, one word popped up: Montrose. I lived in West Houston and Montrose was further into Houston than I felt like driving. I needed some local hookups, so I redid my search: "Gay dating sites."

The results offered an array of options. Craigslist, Adam4Adam, and Scruff were the top three. Out of curiosity, I clicked on Scruff.

I realized the site was meant for men who fetishized hairy men. I laughed as I recalled a line from a joke I heard somewhere, "Don't pluck it! Fuck it!" I hit the back button. *Hot, but too intense for me.* Next, I clicked on Craigslist.

Houston, Men for Men. It was surprisingly simple to find the ads of other gay guys in Houston looking to hook up. *"Looking for a dance buddy!"* read one. I clicked on his ad, and immediately felt my dick get hard. His picture was gorgeous. I sent an email to the address he provided.

The response was almost instantaneous. Twenty minutes later I was dressed in a new party outfit and in my car on the way to the clubs… in

Montrose. And the drive was totally worth it.

I danced the night away with this mysteriously gorgeous man. We never traded names. After a few hours we ended up back at his place, and we were unfastening each other's belts even before the door to the bedroom had closed. He turned me around and shoved me down onto the bed. I moaned as he pressed his dick into me. The first thrust hurt. My fingertips dug into the mattress, and I arched my back, my asshole burning from the rough force. He pulled out and I gasped for air. Then he was back inside of me, working hard to get the job done. When he came, the warmth of his semen felt sublime, exploding deep inside of me. I could feel his sticky, hot cum and it was glorious.

After we fucked, he finally sparked up a conversation.

"Man, what a fun night. And I haven't even tapped into my Tina, yet."

His words made me uncomfortable. I knew Tina was code for crystal meth on the streets. "Uh, yeah. This has been really fun but I don't do drugs." We didn't talk for the rest of the night.

* * *

When the hour of my KSBJ radio appearance came, I got in my Corvette and drove.

"What's up, you lovely listeners! This is Emmy from KSBJ God Listens Radio, and I'm about to step down for an hour to make room for the incredible winner of our setlist competition, who is going to DJ with some really upbeat hits! It's gonna be a rockin' hour!"

Then I heard my own voice.

"Hello, Houston! My name is De'Vannon Hubert, and I love Jesus because of the way he meets me through music. I go to Lakewood Church, and if you've been there or seen it on TV then a lot of these songs might sound familiar to you. And if you haven't then you're in for a special hour of discovery!"

I rocked out to my setlist as I drove around the city. In between every song the producers had edited in portions of my interview that I had with Emmy. I heard my story of growing up in Baton Rouge, enlisting in the Air Force, living in Arizona and California, and how God had been reaching out to me through music ever since I arrived in Houston.

Then, finally, after an hour of Lakewood Church worship songs, music from My Brother's Keeper, and Israel Houghton, the end came.

"Alright, Houston, I hope you've had a fun time listening to my setlist. Before I leave, though, I want to leave you with one last song. It's not as upbeat as all the others, but it's my favorite song in the world because God keeps meeting me over and over again, in different circumstances through this track. I love the lyrics, and I love the band, and I hope you love this song too! This is 'No One Else Knows,' by Building 429."

It was so surreal to hear my voice on the radio introducing my favorite song. I let the awesomeness of the experience wash over me as I pulled back into my apartment complex. As the song faded out, I turned off my car. In the silence, I cried tears of joy. Could life get any better?

* * *

One Wednesday evening after the parents had collected their kids from KidsLife, Molly stayed to help me clean up.

"Listen, De'Vannon, the work you're doing is incredible. I've spoken with the other staff members, and if you're okay with more responsibility, we're making you Volunteer Supervisor."

I stopped and looked up. "Volunteer Supervisor?"

"You'd be in charge of scheduling and managing all the other volunteer teachers as well as the kiosk workers for KidsLife. You'd also be in charge of handling problems between any kids, parents, and teachers. You still get to teach your own group, of course. We would also need you to be here on Saturday nights as well as Wednesday nights."

I was smiling and nodding with excitement before Molly finished talking. Her face lit up at my agreement, and she breathed a big sigh of relief. "Oh, good! Thank you, I was worried it might be too much."

"No!" I insisted. "I love working with you and my fellow volunteers! I'm honored!"

"Wow! Awesome," she said. "I'll let the others know."

They like what I'm doing here! The thought warmed my heart, and suddenly I pictured myself working on staff at Lakewood Church. I loved the idea, and since I had an interest in ministry, I reasoned that in order to be on staff I would probably need some sort of degree in theology. Just about every minister on every church website I had ever visited had some sort of degree from a seminary.

That night I went straight home instead of heading out to the clubs. I pulled up my laptop to research seminary schools. By midnight I had applied to the Houston Graduate School of Theology.

*   *   *

The military paid for my tuition at HGST, but I also took out a $6,000 student loan. Because… why not? It felt like free money, so I went for it.

I loved driving up to the square buildings of the seminary in my little red Corvette. I also loved the look of my license plates which sported brand new frames around both of them with the words, *CHAMPION IN LIFE… THE NEW LAKEWOOD CHURCH,* engraved into them. The red bricks of the school might as well have been gray next to my bright candy-apple red car. I recognized a few other vehicles in the parking lot that I'd also seen at Lakewood. Degrees in theology meant a lot in the church world, so I was excited to find out what seminary was all about.

The first week of classes blew my mind. I learned the difference between an interpretation and a transliteration of the Bible's original Hebrew, Greek, and Aramaic languages. It turns out most of the Bibles I'd been reading my whole life were interpretations rather than transliterations, which are known to be a bit more accurate.

A new curiosity came to life within me and I went to the HGST library and found some transliterations of the Bible. Then I looked up all the passages I'd ever heard referenced with regard to homosexuality. The first thing I noticed was that the words "gay" and "homosexual" didn't even appear in any of the original texts. It turns out the words in the original texts more accurately condemned pedophilia ("boy molester"), and that the change in translations from "man shall not lie with young boys as he does a woman" to "man shall not lie with man" (Leviticus 18:22) didn't occur until 1946![1] For my entire life I had accepted what others told me about the meaning of the Bible. But now I realized the meaning was complex and that people's interpretations tended to be very subjective.

---

1   The Forge Online. (2019, October 14). *Has 'Homosexual' always been in the Bible?* United Methodist Insight. Retrieved September 21, 2021, from https://um-insight.net/perspectives/has-%E2%80%9Chomosexual%E2%80%9D-always-been-in-the-bible/.

As I further examined the transliterations, I noticed that all the other passages I had been taught to believe condemned homosexuality actually did nothing of the sort. The Bible's original text did not say being homosexual was bad.

Why have church leaders been lying to me my whole life?

I checked out all the books, walked out to my car, and sat in the driver's seat. My face felt fuzzy and numb. Questions flooded my head. And anger. *Didn't Jesus die because of the lies of religious leaders?* I felt stupid.

Thankfully there was one spiritual leader I knew I could trust.

When I got home, I called Evangelist Nelson. "How do I know who I can trust?" I asked.

"Child," her voice was calm and comforting on the other end of the line. I missed hearing her voice on Sundays. She never spoke anything that wasn't out of the pure love of the Spirit. *"The first and foremost voice of authority in your life will always be the voice of God. He may use other people to speak to you sometimes, but even then, a human voice is an imperfect voice. You must know how to consult the truth of God directly, by the power of the Spirit. Have you been having any dreams?"*

"Yes, mostly music," I answered truthfully. Since arriving in Houston and joining Lakewood Church, most of my dreams had been filled with original worship songs given to me by God.

"You keep paying attention and studying. And concerning the new music you're receiving in your sleep, just hold onto those songs for now. Write them down. God will use those songs to touch people one day."

"Evangelist Nelson?"

"Yes, De'Vannon?"

"Did you ever practice what you were going to say before preaching at church? Were any of your messages ever scripted?"

"Never needed to, child. I just let the Spirit speak through me. Why do you ask?"

"At Lakewood, every word spoken during a sermon is scripted and previewed in advance."

"And how do you feel about that?"

"I don't know. I was wondering what you thought."

"De'Vannon, God either is or isn't speaking through these people. Whether the words are chosen in advance or in the moment doesn't matter."

"It's just so much easier to trust what's being said when it isn't scripted.

It feels more honest."

"Well, if you truly are doubting the honesty of what's being said, you now have the power to check it yourself."

She was right. With what I was learning at HGST, I could fact-check everything the preachers said.

* * *

Law was my least favorite class at HGST. I had a C, which was way beneath my standards, but I didn't care. I was losing interest in the lists of rules spelled out for the Israelites in the Old Testament. I knew it all ultimately boiled down to a strict system of requirements designed to keep the subjects healthy and orderly, but the rules didn't apply to modern day Christians.

Suddenly, during one of those pointless Law lectures, I wondered, *What does the transliteration say about money?* I paged through my books. The class was small, only about ten people, but the professor didn't seem to notice me not paying attention. He just went on rambling away.

I quickly discovered that Jesus talked a lot about money, and that we were all supposed to pay taxes. *Dang.*

"...and that's how we control people's minds in the church."

My attention shot back into focus. *What?* I looked around the small classroom. The other students were nodding along as if the professor had just said "the sky is blue." The professor continued plodding along in monotone with his lecture.

"Excuse me," I interjected. "I think I misheard something there. Did you just say that's how we control people's minds in the church?"

"That's right," he nodded, matter-of-factly. Then he continued along with his lecture, as if controlling people's minds was so obviously the goal of a preacher that it needed no further explanation or discussion.

He's actually serious! I couldn't believe it.

That night I went to the clubs and partied until they closed at 4am. I racked up a bar tab in excess of $400 and used my student loan money to pay for it. I got completely shit faced and somehow managed to drive myself home without wrecking my Corvette. The next day I slept for as long as I could. I tried to avoid thinking about my Law professor at HGST.

I'm never going back to that place.

CHAPTER 10: DEBTORS & COLLECTORS

A song came to me in a dream.

> *"I will worship You while I live!*
> *I will worship You while I live!*
> *I will worship You while I live,*
> *and beyond!!!"*

In the dream, it was as though I heard a full choir singing this song with strength and passion. It was so vivid that when I woke up I pulled out my laptop, wrote out the rest of the song, and recorded it with my keyboard and microphone. Then I called Evangelist Nelson.

"What do I do? It was so vivid and real!"

"Easy, child. Take it easy. If God didn't tell you what to do with it, then just hold onto it. I know I've told you this before, so just be patient. Don't get yourself stirred up into a panic over nothing."

As usual, Evangelist Nelson was right. I needed to stop stressing myself out, relax, and stop getting ahead of God. But for me that was more easily said than done.

SEX, DRUGS & JESUS

* * *

It was a Sunday, and I felt more uncomfortable at Lakewood Church than I had in a long time. Even in my bright red KidsLife volunteer jersey, I felt self-conscious of the parents.

"Do you have a girlfriend?" Molly had asked me earlier in the week after KidsLife.

"No," I said. "Why?" *Was she asking for herself, or for someone else?*

She had fidgeted uncomfortably, but not in the embarrassed way she might have if she were expressing her own feelings. "It's just that," she said slowly, picking her words carefully, "Some of the parents have shared with me that they feel uncomfortable with you around their children."

"Is there something I'm doing wrong?" I asked, startled by the revelation.

"No!" Molly insisted, "I'm just telling you what some parents have told me."

I walked among the congregants that Sunday confused. *God, am I really supposed to be at this church?* As I settled into my seat in one of the side sections of the sanctuary I opened the glossy brochure and browsed, trying to distract myself. But then I saw it.

On the page where there was usually a picture of the youth pastor and information about KidsLife, there was a picture of me.

"Our KidsLife Volunteer of the Year Award goes to De'Vannon Hubert!"

I couldn't believe it. I wanted to feel pride, but I only felt more confused. How could the staff and leadership of the church be so grateful for my work and the parents be so ungrateful at the same time. I buried my face in my hands and waited for the service to start.

When the choir finally took to the stage and worship began, I was thankful to lose myself in the music. Worship was where I felt closest to God, and in the echo of a thousand voices I felt the most heard by him. Tears started to fill my eyes as the music simmered down to a faint, background melody. I immediately felt better the moment I saw Victoria Osteen take the stage.

* * *

"De'Vannon Hubert, you have outstanding debt! If you do not pay now, we will escalate matters to the next level! This could mean a serious court case. Pay your dues immediately!"

Click.

Debt collectors were calling me ten to twenty times per day. My money problems had been accumulating ever since my military income went away after my enlistment had ended, and I didn't know what to do. So, I did nothing... Well, I at least got another job. This one was with the Texas Workforce Commission.

The work was similar to military recruiting. I helped people get jobs, and I had to hit a monthly quota of twenty people hired. We were located on Westheimer Rd., just down from The Galleria mall, and because it was December the area was packed.

The woman working next to me smiled as I settled in. "Hey, sweetie, good morning! What's your name?"

"I'm De'Vannon," I said.

"De'Vannon!" she marveled at my name. "Well I like the sound of that! I'm Mallory. If you have any questions, just ask."

I smiled in response. I liked Mallory already.

Slowly, the day picked up. At first there was just a trickle of people coming to the kiosks, signing up, and receiving service. Then there was a wave. By lunch we were servicing a storm of people searching for employment.

The waitlist stretched and accrued.

When we broke for lunch, Mallory could see I was flustered by the masses of people. "Don't you worry, De'Vannon. Your goal is only the quota, you can't help everyone. Just keep checking the next name off the list and doing what you can."

I did wish I could help everyone, but Mallory was right. I had to learn to accept my own limitations which was not something I was accustomed to doing.

* * *

That night, I got all dolled up and was headed out from my apartment to Brianna's birthday celebration when my heart stopped.

Where's my Corvette? It wasn't where I'd parked it. That's when I noticed the envelope at my feet, right outside my door. "Notice of Repossession" it read on the front. *Well, shit!*

I still had my Cavalier, but losing my Corvette hit me like a gut punch. More than missing my car, I missed the feeling of driving up to any location with confidence and style. I loved feeling like I was the coolest person everywhere I went. It sucked to have that feeling taken away from me. At least I didn't have to make the payments anymore, which was a huge relief.

* * *

A few weeks later, as I walked from the parking lot to the office, I began to think of a new strategy to meet my quota of getting twenty people hired per month. *Hotels and restaurants hire the most laborers, and there have been a lot of immigrant workers coming in lately. They are incredibly humble and hardworking people, and just want a chance to be successful like all of us do. Maybe I can connect the two directly?*

When I got to my desk, my supervisor, Wyatt, greeted me warmly. He didn't mention the fact that it had been more than a week since I'd landed someone a job. I'd already hit my quota for the month, but I still worried he'd see me as underperforming. Thankfully, he acted graciously toward me.

"Hey, Wyatt?" I asked.

"Yes?"

"Where are the immigrants coming to us from?" Wyatt looked at me puzzled. "Not what country, I mean, how are they staying here in the U.S. without work?"

"Oh," Wyatt said, suddenly understanding. "A nonprofit organization we partner with called Catholic Charities sponsors them when they come here and directs them to us for work."

"I see." I started connecting the dots in my head. "So, what if I could connect hotels and restaurants looking to hire workers directly to Catholic Charities and get a dozen jobs filled all at once, before the listings are even posted? Would those count toward my quota?"

Wyatt thought about this. "I don't see why not."

"Great!" This was going well. "I would love to work something out with those businesses, but to do so I'll have to leave my desk. Is that okay?"

"Sure." Wyatt shrugged.

Hallelujah!!! That conversation could not have gone better.

By early afternoon I had three bulk employment orders. When I returned to the TWC offices, I made a call to Catholic Charities and found people to fill the jobs. By the time I clocked out I had twenty-seven job offers lined up from a single day of work. I easily surpassed my quota for the month.

That night I hit the clubs extra hard.

* * *

I hammered the words into my keyboard: *"I don't know why everybody I meet wants to do meth... What the fuck!?"*

I had been attending the clubs every weekend and hooking up with guys from Craigslist, which was fun. But I noticed that the majority of them wanted to do meth with me, which I had no interest in. I was tired of that drug soiling my sex life. I hadn't even been on a second date with anybody because once they saw that I didn't do drugs (or "party," as they called it), they didn't seem to want to see me again. What was it with gay guys and crystal meth?

"Why would I ever want to do meth? I don't need a drug to make me happy, and I don't understand why every guy I meet has to make those fucking chemicals a dealbreaker! I mean, what if I get drug tested at work? I don't want to lose my job! This isn't fucking normal!"

Without thinking, I hit 'post' on my Facebook page, and slammed my laptop shut.

* * *

"Mr. Hubert, I'm calling about your outstanding debts."

Wham!

The debt collectors were calling relentlessly, always threatening me with the "next step." Not only that, but they had called my brother, Mother, and even Brianna, too. I needed to do something, so I got online and started researching.

I came across a website for Sofia McIntosh, Bankruptcy Attorney, which stated that if I could provide the appropriate paperwork and $1,800, I could declare bankruptcy and eliminate my debt. It would destroy my credit for a decade, but I would no longer owe anybody money. Paying the requested amount in order to make over $50,000 in debt disappear sounded like a fair deal. I just needed to find $1,800.

Well, how have you always gotten money? My credit wasn't completely ruined yet, so I went and got myself a $2,500 loan, then drove over to Sofia McIntosh's office.

Sofia was a quiet woman with thick rimmed glasses and bright red lipstick. She was very orderly and appreciated that all my paperwork was together. The military had trained me well when it came to organization. Sofia went patiently through my bank statements and identified all the people I owed money to.

I didn't say much as she scheduled my court date for an arbitrator to approve my bankruptcy, and promised to send out cease-and-desist notices to all my debt collectors immediately. I took a big breath. I felt lighter, as if a physical weight had been lifted off my shoulders.

When I got home, I put my Building 429 CD in and was about to hit play when the phone rang. My jaw clenched. *What now? Why can't they just leave me the fuck alone!* I picked up the phone ready to scream at the debt collector, and then relaxed at the sound of Brianna's voice. I didn't relax for long, though, because she was *pissed*.

"De'Vannon! Why am I getting calls from fucking bill collectors after your ass? Don't you have a job? What the fuck is going on?"

"I do have a job, but–"

"No, you listen to me, De'Vannon! My company is having a job fair at our Downtown location in six weeks. Now your ass better be there, you hear? We've got entry level work and a lot of potential for growth. So don't you fucking skip out on me! Are you hearing me?"

"Yes, ma'am," I said numbly. I heard the click of her hanging up on the other end of the line and placed my phone back in its holster. I had heard Brianna yell and throw fits before, but I hadn't heard her take control in an angry fit like that.

I knew I had to go to this job fair. Brianna was right. Opportunity for growth was something I lacked at my current job with TWC. While I liked everyone there, my $17/hr. wage would see little increase over the years, and there weren't many positions to promote to. I needed work that could turn into something better down the road, and the power company where Brianna worked in marketing would provide a chance to move up.

* * *

The job fair Brianna sent me to was at CenterPoint Energy in Downtown Houston.

"Hi. I'm wondering which table I should talk to," I said, stepping up to the information desk at the job fair. "I'm a former Air Force mechanic and recruiter."

"Can I preview your resume?" the woman asked with a smile.

I passed it across the table and she scanned her finger over it quickly. "The boys at Table Four will see you," she said, handing it back.

"Thank you."

I navigated to Table Four, handed them my resume, and waited.

After a minute, one of the men addressed me. "You'll need to pass a test, but it's pretty easy. Just follow the instructions. After that we'll teach you everything you need to know on the job, but to make sure it's a good fit I'll set some realistic expectations."

"Sure," I said. "Go ahead."

"This job is at the Call Center, meaning long hours, high volume, and low pay. It's $13 per hour, but it gets your foot in the door, so you can transfer to something better later on."

"That makes sense," I nodded.

"Very well," he said, "Fill out the forms in this packet and we'll get you scheduled for your test."

I glanced through the papers he handed me and signed them all on the spot.

When I arrived at the Texas Workforce Commission that afternoon, I delivered my two weeks' notice. It was a solemn goodbye. I was going to miss Mallory and Wyatt.

* * *

The boys from Table Four had been right: the test for the Call Center was easy. Training, on the other hand, was three weeks of hell.

If I didn't make it through training, I wasn't going to get the job. It was as simple as that. And the people training me were super serious about the intensity of their course. Each day they critiqued my competency in communicating with customers, typing to keep up with their requests, arranging payments, adjusting bills, reporting gas leaks, and keeping my tone calm and agreeable. It was grueling.

It was like boot camp all over again.

By the time I took the final tests, I knew how to read gas bills in three different states, type eighty-five words per minute, and operate a switchboard.

The company had a deal with the Hyatt Hotel that allowed CenterPoint employees to park in the hotel parking garage and use the skywalk to cross over to our building. As I made my way through the skywalk on my first day of work after training, a man caught up with me. I recognized him from the first week of training. He'd been two weeks ahead of me, but he was hard to miss. Sam was an immigrant from Somalia who had done very well for himself and was by far the hottest and hardest working person I had met at CenterPoint Energy.

"Hey Sam!"

"De'Vannon! How are you feeling? Are you ready for this?"

"Is it really as intense as everyone says? I mean, seriously?"

"Oh, yeah!" Sam said with an odd, twisted smile. "Think about it. People only call when they can't pay their bill and are desperate to stop us from cutting off their gas."

"So… We're like debt collectors?" I asked.

"Kind of, but even better! I mean, think about it. Debt collectors can make threats and shit, but do you know how much it costs to sue someone for outstanding payments? I mean, unless you've amassed a shit load of debt, they're not actually going to sue you. We, on the other hand, can cut the gas off with the flip of a switch. See, we don't make threats. We just communicate the facts."

I thought about the debt collectors who had chased me for months.

"People will say and do some crazy shit," Sam continued. "Man. I'm telling you, one chick I heard was fucking the meter man so her gas wouldn't get cut off."

We stepped into the elevator to go up.

"Are you liking this work?" I asked Sam.

"Look, I mean, it's alright. It's no permanent gig, but it's not too hard once you know how everything works. You just kind of do what you're told and get on with it. Don't say anything stupid, because managers are listening, but our direct supervisor never leaves his office, so the boss situation could be worse."

The elevator door opened to the 30th floor and my heart sank. The noise of dozens of workers on calls from a maze of cubicles hit me like a wall. The light coming in from the floor-to-ceiling windows was nice, but no sooner had I started to take in the view did a manager bark at me to "Get to work!" It turns out hell has a view.

I clocked in, sat down at my cubicle, and put my weeks of practice to work.

I answered my first call and nearly ripped my headset off before adjusting the volume down. *"Waaaaaaaaaaah!"* A baby was wailing on the other end of the line. Then a woman screamed, *"Please don't turn off my gas!"*

"What's your name and address?" I asked, following protocol.

Thankfully she answered me, but the crying baby got worse. I pulled up her information and, sure enough, she had three months of outstanding payments. My stomach felt sick for her.

In the center of the floor was a glass office with a sign that read: "Managers." Above the sign was a red meter indicating the number of callers on hold. "72." I felt beads of sweat form above my brow. Adrenaline shot through my veins as I realized this call was going to take a while. I explained to the woman with the crying baby that we could accept a payment plan.

"How can I afford a payment plan if I can't afford to pay at all! Please don't cut off my gas!"

The red meter at the center of the floor continued to climb. I tried not to pay attention to it, but the flicker of the rising digits demanded my attention. "75."

"How soon would you be able to make any payment at all?" I asked.

"I don't know?" the woman whimpered.

"Could you pay $20 by the end of this week?"

I heard a sniffle. *"I don't know. Let me look."* The baby continued to squeal.

"78."

Just then I heard a voice over my shoulder. "Let's hurry it up here, De'Vannon. And button your shirt all the way up. What's the point of wearing buttons if you're not going to use them?"

As the manager walked away from my station, I thought, *What the fuck! Sam said the supervisor doesn't bother you.*

"What are you laughing at! Get back to work!" I heard the manager shout a few cubicles away.

"81."

I resisted the urge to pressure the lady with the crying baby to hurry the hell up.

"88."

I bit my tongue. *If this lady doesn't hurry up, I'm going to lose my job on the first fucking day!*

"99."

I heard another sniffle on the other end of the line. "Um, I think it's possible. I might be able to get $20 by the end of the week."

"That's good to hear, miss. Let me get you set up on that plan right away." My voice was shaking, but she didn't seem to notice.

When I finally ended the call and moved to the next one, the cue was up to 111 people. I wanted to scream, but I said, "CenterPoint Energy, thank you for calling. How may I help you?"

Walking back to the parking garage at the end of the day, I wanted to punch Sam in the face. "You lying son-of-a-bitch! I thought you said our supervisor never left his office!"

"Easy, man. I said our *direct* supervisor never leaves his office. That doesn't mean we don't get other bosses micromanaging us."

"We can't laugh! We can't smile! I can't even undo the top buttons of my shirt to stop myself from suffocating and show off my chest a little! We can't even take a piss without clocking out! How are you okay with this job?"

"Look, it's really not that hard. Our job is primarily customer satisfaction. If someone's not gonna pay, and I ask the super what to do, he always ends up giving the person an extension. So after about five minutes, if they're not gonna pay, that's what I do. Calm down, man, you'll be fine."

I wasn't fine. I was stressed. I needed relief. I wanted a drink so bad, but I wasn't in the mood to go clubbing because I had work the next morning. Instead, when I got home, I dug out the brochure with the picture of the Lakewood youth pastor on it and jerked off to his gloriously chiseled body.

*   *   *

I was officially accepted into the tenor section of the Lakewood Adult Choir just in time to stand with the group on Easter Sunday. This was exciting because Easter Sunday always boasted the largest crowd of the year. On the Tuesday before weekend worship we had our last Easter rehearsal, and I was given the uniform I'd been fitted for. The girls wore ocean blue dresses with frills on the sleeves that wavered in the wake of their movements. The guys wore dark blue suits and ties. When I received my choir suit, it instantly became the nicest piece of clothing I owned, next to my Air Force dress blues.

"Be sure to get this to the dry cleaners tomorrow so you can pick it up on Friday!" Gabriel, the choir director, emphasized to us. *Yes, sir*, I thought.

*   *   *

On Easter Sunday I woke up bright and early. I had to be at church ninety minutes before the first service to settle in with the choir, do final prep-work, and pray.

I sang along to the CD playlist on the car ride over. I wasn't worried about forgetting the lyrics, and I was definitely getting into the groove. The sky was clear, and the sun was bright as I accelerated up the ramp to merge onto the 59 Freeway.

The first thing I saw when I rounded the corner at the end of the ramp was the look of horror on a woman's face before she ducked behind the smoldering wreck of her vehicle. I yanked my steering wheel to the left and slammed on the brakes. I felt my tires lose traction with the pavement, and swung my steering wheel back to the right to try and regain control. My car swerved out of the way of the woman's car, but there was another car crunched up against the left shoulder of the ramp.

I closed my eyes and braced for impact. The jolt of my front tires regaining traction and throwing my car back on course was sudden. I opened my eyes as my body slammed against the door and my car shot the gap between the two wrecked cars and rocketed up toward the highway.

I gasped. I hadn't heard a scratch. Somehow, I had made it through unscathed. I screamed.

"WOOOO! NOT TODAY, SATAAAAN!"

Then I caught my breath and tried to calm down. I had worshipping to do.

Backstage at Lakewood was quiet but buzzing with energy. The band was doing sound checks on stage, and I mingled with my new choir friends and whispered excitedly. The ladies looked gorgeous in their blue dresses, and the men looked handsome in their suits.

When the soundcheck was over, we gathered for prayer. I could sense the electricity in the air as the subtle vibrations of people filling the sanctuary oscillated through the walls. Gabriel spoke up as the choir gathered in a big huddle.

"Friends, let's seek God in Spirit this morning as we prepare to minister through song and praise. Let's remember that God speaks through our music."

Gabriel's words resonated with me. I looked forward to hearing his words before every Sunday service, and then God answering his prayer as we ministered to the congregation. I felt honored to be a part of that.

As we lined up in preparation for our entrance, butterflies finally invaded my stomach. Blue light bled into the choir corridor from the sanctuary, and thousands of happy murmurs rippled through us from the crowd. We were told it was a packed house, and while I believed it, I couldn't imagine it. The normal eighty percent capacity felt like a lot of people. I couldn't imagine what the church would sound, look, and feel like with every seat filled.

Finally, the moment came for me to find out. We filed out into the choir section above the stage in an orderly fashion. On either side of us, water fountains put on an entrancing aquatic show which ran over large rocks and foliage. Standing next to those displays in our blue dress outfits, we looked like a living work of art. I heard and watched the opening music video play on one of the two large screens that flanked us, then the platform lifted the band up to the stage.

The sanctuary, especially from this view, was breathtaking.

Beyond the blinding blue lights was the sea of souls that I was so accustomed to swimming in. Adrenaline shot through my veins. I had once ridden the waves, but now I would be the wind behind them.

The synthesizer swelled and I watched the choir pacesetter in front snap her hands above her head to the rhythm of the beat. Then she gave the signal.

Her arm swayed subtly to the right, and when it swayed back to the left the whole choir swayed in sync. The frills on the girls' dresses moved back and forth, and it was stunning, even from my viewpoint in the choir.

We entered into our first song, "We Win." The words projected from my mouth before I realized I was singing. I was definitely in the groove.

By the 11am service my butterflies were gone, and I was no longer nervous about the cameras that were constantly trained on us. There are no words that can fully capture just how magnificent this experience was.

* * *

Gabriel was impressed with me in the choir. He appreciated my charismatic energy and that I had every song memorized backward and forward. Gabriel wasn't the only person to take notice of me. One day after service, Molly approached me and asked if I would step up as a worship leader for KidsLife during the Wednesday worship services. Of course I accepted this offer.

As I did, a sense of calm fell over me. *I'm doing it*, I thought. I felt like I was laying down reliable roots. I could see myself staying in Houston for the foreseeable future, getting on staff at Lakewood, and finding a long-term boyfriend. There was no military to relocate me, and while I hated the Call Center it was still a stable job.

That night I began going through some of the guys I'd slept with over the past month. If I was staying in Houston long-term, I didn't have to be sleeping around like I'd never see anyone again. One guy immediately came to mind.

"*Yo, De'Vannon! What's up, man?*" I loved how overtly masculine Sebastian sounded.

"Hey, Sebastian," I said, trying to be cute. "How've you been?"

"I'm good, man! I was actually thinking about you earlier today. I was worried I wouldn't hear from you again."

"Oh? What made you think that?" I asked.

"I don't know. I guess I was just worried I went too hard on your cute little ass last time."

I laughed. "Honey, please. My ass can handle whatever you got and more."

"How about you come on over show me?"

"I'm on my way."

Ten minutes later Sebastian was dropping his pants, but he stopped to give me a look. I knew he was waiting to see if I would make him put on a condom like last time, but I didn't. I let him enter me raw.

I loved the feeling of Sebastian inside me without protection. I felt so much closer to him. He forced my ankles behind my head as he took full advantage my asshole. Then I wrapped my legs around his waist and held onto his neck, gazing deeply into his hazel eyes to reassure him that it was okay for him to finish. When he came, the warm semen bursting inside me was surreal. I asked if I could stay the night, and he said that was fine as long as I didn't mind him watching *The Golden Girls*. I tried to imagine super masculine Sebastian watching something so girly, but I couldn't picture it. Sure enough, at 2am, we were cuddled in bed watching Betty White command the screen as Rose Nylund.

* * *

The subject line of the email read: "ALL HANDS ON DECK."

I had lived through my fair share of hurricanes, but Hurricane Ike was a different motherfucker. The wind ruined neighborhoods, crushing houses under its pressure and toppling trees and powerlines. Now CenterPoint had to fix all that shit, and I was going to have to answer to the thousands of people calling in to ask when their power would be restored.

While the wind had subsided, it was still pouring rain as I drove into the Call Center. After parking at the Hyatt and walking over to CenterPoint, I stepped into pure chaos.

"De'Vannon!" one of the managers yelled as I entered. "We've got five hundred people on hold wanting to talk about their electricity! I know you're on the gas team, but it's really the same fucking shit! Now sit your ass down and get to work!"

I did as I was told. I thought I caught a whiff of alcohol in the air. All of the managers on the floor had coffee mugs, and I was willing to bet they had whiskey in there. I answered the first call.

"Thank you for calling–"

"I see your workers fixing up power lines on every fucking street other than my block! Who the hell is assigning those motherfuckers? I pay my bill on time every month and y'all are treating me like shit! Now I expect some goddamned service in the next hour, or else!"

I took a deep breath and calmed my nerves. "I'm sorry, sir, but that's not something I can help with. We will get to your street when we get to it."

"Excuse me? Now listen to me you son-of-a–"

I hung up and answered the next call.

"Can you explain to me why when I look out my window, I see your workers sitting around doing nothing while I'm in here without power?"

"Because they're human, ma'am, and they need to rest at some point."

"Now I just cannot accept that kind of answer, mister–"

I hung up and answered the next call.

"Hey, I'm smelling smoke in my building, but I can't tell where it's coming from. I'm worried there might be an electric fire or something."

I smiled. Now, here was someone who knew their shit. Either that or he was telling the truth. "What's your address, sir? I'll put in an emergency order right away."

Then I answered the next call.

"I've been without power all fucking day! How long until you guys fix it!"

"We're working as fast as we can, sir."

At 7pm, one of the managers put an envelope on my desk. It had a room number and a Hyatt hotel key card in it.

"Go home and grab your shit, then come right back to the Hyatt. Get some rest and be back here at 7am sharp," the manager said.

"What about my car?" I asked.

"We'll get everybody's parking validated when we're able to get out of here, but expect to spend the next few days in this room at the Hyatt. Sorry."

*   *   *

When I got to the Call Center the next morning there were red and blue lights flashing all around the building. The managers didn't bother to stop me as I went to the window to see what was going on outside.

At the ground level, rows of police cars, policemen in riot gear, and metal blockades surrounded the building. I turned to the nearest manager, and before I could ask, he explained, "Someone called in a bomb threat. Said that if we don't fix his power in the next two hours he's gonna blow the place to shit."

My eyes widened in shock, but the manager just shrugged, took a sip from his mug, and walked away. "Get back to work," he called numbly over his shoulder.

The second day was worse. The calls were illogical. People complained and vented and made ludicrous threats. Of course, I couldn't do anything to help people unless they reported a fire or a gas leak. Then I could fast-track a crew to their location. Whenever I got someone who sounded calm, I tried to bait them by asking, "Do you smell gas, or do you see smoke coming from any of the downed power lines?" Unfortunately, no one was wise enough to take the bait. They always lost their cool and snapped, *"No, I just need you to fix my fucking power!"*

By the end of the day, all the men in the office had ugly five-o-clock shadows.

On day three, the women didn't even bother putting on makeup. We all shared identical bags under our eyes, and hair that pointed in every direction. We were drowning in negativity.

"I-I-If you d-don't f-fix my p-p-p-power ... r-r-right n-now ... I s-swear I'm gonna ... k-k-k-kill myself!"

I stared at my screen. *How the fuck do I respond to that?* I wondered. We weren't trained to deal with suicide threats. I looked around the office, but everyone else was busy responding to their own bullshit.

"Do y-y-you hear m-me?" the man on the other end of the line asked.

I hung up. *Better to say nothing,* I thought, and then answered the next call. *And if someone does ask, I'll just blame a bad connection.*

At the end of day four, my manager passed me an envelope with a parking pass in it. "Go home," he said. "Still, be back here at 7am.

Tomorrow's another 12-hour day. But go home in the meantime."

I wasted no time getting the fuck out of there and heading to my apartment. But first I stopped at a Spec's liquor store and bought myself a damn near gallon-sized bottle of Jack Daniels. I was so stressed.

When I got back to my apartment building, I was surprised to see the power on. Every other building in the surrounding neighborhood was dark, but somehow mine looked just fine. I hadn't reported any false fires or gas leaks for myself, and normally hospitals and businesses were fixed before residential spaces.

Then I noticed the business complex across the street from my apartment, which also had power. *We must be hooked up to the same line as those businesses.* A pang of survivor's guilt twisted in my stomach.

I took five shots of Jack Daniels and passed out.

*   *   *

"You lazy motherfuckers! I ain't had no power for two goddamned fucking weeks! Who the fuck is sucking y'all's dicks that I gotta wait so damn long to get the power I motherfucking pay for turned back on! Fix my fucking electricity, NOW!!!"

"Fuck you," I said, and hung up the phone.

I saw a manager's eyes dart in my direction in shock as he overheard my closing comment, but he didn't say anything. None of the managers said anything, so "fuck you" became my normal close for irate customers after that.

Sam overheard me and suggested I stop. He couldn't believe I wasn't fired on the spot.

That night, I called Brianna.

"Listen, do you know of any job openings elsewhere in the company? I can't keep doing this shit at the Call Center. It's so fucking stressful!"

I took a big sip from my glass of Jack and waited for her response.

"Lemme look. One second." She sounded tired.

I sipped from my glass impatiently while she typed on the other end of the line.

"You know you can do this research yourself, right?"

"I know, but I figure your word can get me outta here sooner."

"Lazy motherfucker. I don't suppose you want a job working in the sewers?"

"I'll take any fucking thing that gets me outta the Call Center."

"Hey, how about this! There's a job opening for Substation work. That would be more in line with your background in mechanics in the Air Force, right?"

"That sounds fine fuckin' dandy! Send me the link."

I opened my email inbox and saw the link she sent me. I also saw an email from my direct supervisor's supervisor, Laurence. *"See me in my office tomorrow."*

I downed the rest of my Jack, followed the link Brianna had sent me, and applied for the Substation job. I ignored the email from Laurence. *If he's gonna fire me, he's gonna have to show his face to the whole fucking office and axe me in person.*

I never went to his office. The next morning, he sent the same email, and I ignored it. Instead, I opened the email from CenterPoint HR. I had an interview lined up for transfer to the Substation department.

Hallelujah!!!

*   *   *

I had to take an exam to qualify for work at the Substation, and it was fucking hard. It didn't help that I didn't study. There was shit to calculate, and a couple handfuls of words I had to guess the meaning of. After finishing the test, I called my best friend in the adult choir, Janine.

"Girl, I need a drink!"

One hour later we were drinking tequila at a nice Spanish restaurant. I felt like shit, but Janine was lifting my spirits.

"When did you first know you had such a grand sense of style?" she asked.

I was wearing a half-buttoned maroon shirt, Seven jeans, and my California cowboy boots. To top it all off, I was crowned with a curved Dos Equis cowboy hat that I had gotten as part of a promo from some shot girls at a nightclub a while back. "As soon as I could walk, I could strut," I said.

"How was it in California? Is it as cool and glamorous as the magazines make it seem?"

"It's even better! I love California! It's my favorite place in the whole world! If I had a sense of style before Cali, I perfected it in Cali. Why do you ask? Are you thinking of going there?"

"A girl can dream."

"Damn straight," I said, and took a celebratory drink from my pink glass. "So, what's your dream?"

Janine blushed. "Well," she started, getting ready to confess her secret, "I want to be a photographer."

"Okaaaay!" I approved. "What kind? Portrait? Landscape? Fashion?"

Her eyes lit up. "Fashion!"

"Well, you know who just happens to be a semi-professional model?" I asked teasingly, waving my free hand to frame my face.

Janine gasped. "No way! Really?"

"Well don't act so surprised. Yes, I've been in a commercial or two, and done my fair share of photoshoots."

No sooner had the words left my mouth did Janine grab my forearm and look me in the eyes. "Can I take your photo?"

The request caught me by surprise, and I had to catch myself from spilling my drink. I held onto her gaze teasingly.

"Please?" she begged. "My camera is in the car.".

I downed the rest of my drink. "What are we waiting for?" Janine grinned.

Back at my place I poured drinks and began digging through my wardrobe. I kept the cowboy hat on.

"Hey there! Show that hat off!" Janine yelled. I posed. "What else have you got?"

I went back to my wardrobe and found a shirt from my favorite store in Houston, Duo, with a rip in the torso. As I was changing into it, I was stopped by the flash of the camera. I looked over at Janine and she was smirking, holding up the photo of me with my shirt off on the screen of her camera. "You wanna see it?" she asked.

It was my turn to smirk. "You wanna see this?" I retorted, and tore the sleeves off the Duo shirt. I put just the sleeves over my forearms and flexed my bare chest. Janine snapped away on her camera.

"Very nice," she said. "Now what else have you got to drink?"

* * *

The next morning my head was pounding. Janine hadn't stayed the night, and that wasn't a surprise. We had fun, but we both knew sex wasn't going to happen. I checked my liquor cabinet.

I had six liters of six different types of liquor, and we had made a significant dent in the vodka. "I'm gonna have to get more of that," I muttered, and went to the fridge to pour myself a tall glass of water.

Then I checked my email to find several messages from Janine. She had shared the photos with me, and I began to browse.

The photos were fantastic. At some point I had ended up in just my cowboy hat and underwear. I loved the images and was proud of them. *I have to share these!*

I pulled up my MySpace page, uploaded the photos, and clicked 'share.' Then I made the one of me showing off my cowboy hat in my underwear my new profile picture.

Then I returned to my email inbox. There was a new message from CenterPoint Energy. I had passed the exam. My transfer to the Substation department was approved.

I smiled and jumped up to celebrate, but my head throbbed, and I doubled over in pain. *Damn. Celebration's gonna have to wait.*

* * *

There were several Substations throughout Houston, and none of them were at the CenterPoint Energy Tower where the Call Center was located. So, my new job would take me all around the city, which I loved.

I purchased steel toe boots and wore them with tough jeans, as instructed. I was issued a CenterPoint Energy T-shirt and hardhat upon arrival. Then I filled out a bucketload of paperwork. This was a union job after all, which I was excited about. It meant stable, consistent hours, and fair benefits. Also, my pay jumped from $13 per hour at the Call Center to $22 per hour at the Substation basically overnight. On top of that, the Substation provided the possibility for advancement with pay raises up to $35 per hour. There was also overtime as well as double-time pay granted for extended workdays! I had a lot to look forward to.

My outlook got even better when I met the group of guys at my location: Sid, Jerome, Bob, Lucas, Emilio, Hanz, Cooper, Sal, and Josh. They were nine ripped, masculine maintenance dudes who weren't afraid to cuss and say perverted things all fucking day. It was wonderful.

In one transfer I had gone from white collar to blue collar, and I absolutely loved it. It was more like the military. And like the military, there was a lot of responsibility.

"Alright, looky here," Sid explained to me on the first day as he chewed tobacco. "We got the blueprints and schematics of this buildin' where repairs are being done. We gotta control the power output to that buildin' durin' repair time, but be sure to cross reference the coordinates to the grid, a'ight? The last thing we need is your fat fuckin' finger pressin' the wrong button an' killin' the power to a fuckin' hospital, y'knawhatimean?"

I understood. *Don't kill the power to any fucking hospitals. Got it. Now what are the odds any of these nine guys are gay?*

CHAPTER 11: DEHUMANIZED

Several leaders at Lakewood decided to rally volunteers to join up with an organization called Cruise with a Cause which had made plans for a mission trip to The Bahamas. I had never been on a cruise before, so my interest was piqued immediately.

I didn't have anyone to split a cabin with, so I paid the entire $1,900 fare myself. Soon it was off to Miami and on to a cruise ship!

The ship was huge and unlike anything I had ever seen. There were a couple thousand people on board, and I was placed on a team with people I had never met before. Other than nightly prayer sessions, the teams were free to do whatever we wanted throughout the cruise. Most people elected to spend time at the restaurants, pool, sundeck, and game room. Me and one other sinner kicked it at the bar and casino. I had no interest in socializing with the rest of the church crowd, and neither did this dude. We'd nod respectfully to each other, but other than that we just enjoyed our time.

Every night I stayed in and ordered room service. That was all I could do since none of the nightclubs were open due to the cruise ship having modified its operations to accommodate the religious patrons. My favorite meal was steak sandwiches, cheesecake, and either a screwdriver or a greyhound to drink.

I got the sense the other passengers were judging us from a distance, but I didn't care.

It was a relief when we finally arrived in Freeport, Bahamas. The team

I had been assigned to consisted of a preacher, worship leader, and prayer leader. Each team was assigned one school where we would put on a backyard event with music and minister to the kids. I was the worship leader on my team. I had a collection of worship CDs, and I was ready to party.

The school we went to looked like it could have fallen apart if I flicked a toothpick at it. I was startled when hundreds of kids came out of the brittle buildings and gathered in the courtyard. A woman I assumed was the principal approached us.

"Thank you for coming! Whatever you need, just let us know."

We asked for something to play the CDs on, and they brought out a janky little box with a speaker and a slot for CDs. I put a disc in, and we started to sing. To my amazement, the kids knew the lyrics to every song. I was happy to be less of a worship leader and more of a participant as we offered up our reverence to God. It was an honor to share in their joy.

I wanted to thank the school as much as they thanked our little team. We prayed for whomever wanted prayer, and they gave us a cart of sodas to take with us as we left. I was in awe. *How can these people live in so much poverty and have so much gratitude?*

A new anger arose within me. *How can millions live in comfort in the U.S. and be so ungrateful?* Other than the glistening beaches of the Bahamas, everything around me was poverty. And yet, all the people I met greeted me with gratitude, positive energy, and respect. They thrived more in their poverty than many Americans seemed to thrive with all our comforts.

I drank a lot that night.

* * *

The beaches were so fucking hot. I wanted to go for a swim in the ocean, but as soon as my toes touched the water I retracted them. It was freezing! How could the water be so fucking cold when the air was so hot? I didn't know what to do, so I went back to the cruise ship.

There was a signup sheet for an excursion to an all-inclusive resort on one of the islands. If they got enough names, they would rent a boat and take us over for an entire day. I immediately put my name down, right underneath the name of my fellow sinner from the bar and casino.

That afternoon there was a big concert. Some well known Christian artists were set to sing, including Mary Mary! I could hardly wait.

A tiny stage had been set up in a park, and hundreds of kids and adults from the surrounding neighborhoods were gathering for worship. We roamed the crowd, greeting people and praying for anyone who wanted prayer. And when the music started, we danced. It was a wild afternoon, and Mary Mary was far better live than I ever could have imagined.

I was sad when our time in the Bahamas ended, but I was even more sad when I found out no one else signed up for the excursion to the island resort.

What the fuck! Why are Christians so fucking lame?

I tried not to get too down, though, because there was one more event that I was looking forward to. I arrived at the small room where all the tables had been cleared, and less than a hundred people were gathered, waiting in front of a small stage. It was bound to be an intimate show.

An MC dressed in a Hawaiian shirt and khaki shorts came onstage. "Hey everyone, thanks for joining us tonight. I hope you've been enjoying the cruise so far. And if you haven't, please exit the ship on the starboard side so as to not block the view of the happier guests."

Some people chuckled politely at the joke, but I just tapped my foot impatiently, waiting for the music. The MC continued, "Either way, hopefully tonight can be a little bright spot. We've got a wonderful band from Fayetteville, North Carolina, and they're going to sing some uplifting songs for us tonight. Please give a warm welcome to Building 429!"

I clutched my face and gasped as Jason Roy and Building 429 took the stage. *Is this for real? My favorite band, live, in person, in this room.* Even though I knew they would be the ones on stage I still couldn't believe it.

Then the guitar riff I was so familiar with from their song "Not Gonna Let You Down," started. I shook my head. This was unreal. *Fuck it, I'm dancing.*

The people in the crowd around me felt the vibes too, and soon the whole room was dancing and singing along.

The end of that song bled right into a kickass worship set, and then they sang "End of Me," and then "Overcome"... I sang along to every line, and never stopped dancing.

Just when it seemed like the concert was coming to a close, they played my two favorite songs: "Glory Defined" and "No One Else Knows." My heart was on fire.

After what I was sure was going to be their last song, Jason Roy called out to the room, "I need some volunteers to come up on stage for this next song!"

Say no more. I jumped on stage with five other people. Out of nowhere the speaker system blasted a song that I instantly recognized, "Gonna Make You Sweat (Everybody Dance Now)" by C+C Music Factory! "Dance with me!" Jason commanded, and we boogied with Building 429. I pulled out all the 90's moves: I danced the Running Man, the Cabbage Patch, the Roger Rabbit, and I did it all in flip-flops! *Hell, a girl's gotta throw down when she gets called on stage.*

As the song died down, Jason Roy suddenly approached me and passed me his microphone before running off stage. I stood there, stunned. The microphone was as light as cardboard and padded with foam. *What kind of fancy ass mic is this?* Then a guitar riff I'd never heard before started and the rest of the band launched into a new song.

I stood frozen on stage. *What am I supposed to do?* I listened to the song for a verse and a chorus, and caught on. The lyrics weren't that difficult, but they were singing two octaves higher than anything I was used to.

Come on, man, when are you ever gonna get a chance like this again? If you can sing with the Lakewood tenors, you can sing with Building 429.

Adrenaline was coursing through my veins. I took a breath, and joined in with the rest of the band on the chorus.

I hit every single fucking note. At the end of the song, Jason Roy came back out onstage and invited me to join the band in a bow. I gave him his microphone back.

"Thanks, man," he said. "Hey, why don't you come backstage with me."

Say. No. More.

* * *

"Dude, you almost took my job!" Jason joked, and I laughed. "That was pretty impressive."

"Thanks," I replied. "I mean, I've been listening to your guys' music for almost two years now, and you guys are *my favorite band.*"

"Awe, thanks man. Hey, I never caught your name earlier. What is it?"

"My name's De'Vannon, and don't worry, I already know who you are," I teased. "But hey, can I ask you a question about one of your songs?"

"Sure thing, De'Vannon."

"So, my favorite song of yours is 'No One Else Knows.' It's a song that I just keep feeling like God is using to speak to me. I can't help but wonder, though, what is the real meaning behind the song? What's it about?"

Jason shuffled uncomfortably, but then nodded. He looked at me and answered, "So, there was a time when a very close friend of mine went through a really confusing time. It was even more challenging because this person didn't tell anyone else except me about what was going on. As we would talk about what was happening my friend kept saying, 'no one else knows, no one else knows, no one else knows.' Those words stuck in my head and reverberated down to my soul and thus this song was written. I wrote that song as a reminder that whenever we go through quiet battles in life we are not alone. God knows and He cares for us no matter what."

I stared at Jason in awe. "Wow, thank you for sharing that."

"Sure thing, man."

I nodded. "Yeah, well I'm just so thankful for your music. You know, I'm a worship leader at Lakewood Church in Houston, and God never ceases to amaze me with the ways we can minister to people through music."

At the mention of Lakewood Church, I could see Jason tense up. He stared stiffly at his knees. *Shit, he seems like he's ready to end the conversation right now! Does he hate Lakewood or something? Was I too arrogant in saying I was a worship leader?*

I cleared my throat and asked more generally, "I mean, what have been some of your experiences with ministering to people through music?"

Thankfully Jason entertained the question, but it still took some time for the tension to ease. I made sure not to mention Lakewood again.

It was almost two hours before we decided to part ways. I thanked Jason graciously for allowing me to sing with the band and spend time with him backstage. When I re-entered the dining room where the stage was still set up, a wall of people rushed toward me with pens, Sharpies, menus, brochures, tickets, and all sorts of shit for me to autograph.

"I'm not part of the band! You guys know that, right?"

They didn't give a fuck. They just continued to beg me for my autograph. So, I obliged.

Back in my room, I ordered room service and collapsed on the bed.

I needed to share the joy with someone, but I didn't want to socialize with anyone on the cruise. I decided to text Molly.

"Hey! You won't believe this! There was a Building 429 concert on the cruise, and I got to sing onstage with them! Then I got to hang out with Jason backstage! Am I dreaming? Tell me I'm not dreaming."

I sent the message and sighed contentedly. I waited for a response. And waited.

My room service order arrived, and I ate the meal heartily.

When I checked my phone there was still no response, so I sent another message.

"Frieeeend! Are you there?"

I never heard back from her.

* * *

My MySpace page started recording an abnormally high number of views.

Who the fuck is looking at my MySpace page? Modeling agents? In my dreams.

I started to think about the underwear pictures Janine had taken. They weren't necessarily nudes, but they were rather revealing. I switched the photos to private. I loved them, but hiding them from the public seemed to make sense—at least until I could figure out why my page views were spiking all of a sudden.

I thought of the guys at work, but that didn't make sense. I never got the impression they gave a shit about social media. If they did, I would have pointed them to my MySpace profile back when I first met them. I was crossing my fingers at least one of my coworkers was gay.

* * *

"Brianna! Hey, girl! Whatchu doing?"

"I'm knitting you a new jockstrap! What the fuck do you think I'm doing? I'm drinking a beer and watching the Rockets play! Whatchu want?"

"I want to ask your opinion on something."

"Okay, hold up, lemme mute this shit. What's going on?"

"So, you know how I've been working my ass off at church and how I'm hoping to get on staff at some point?"

"Yup!"

"Well, I got an email from Molly yesterday asking me to come in for a meeting before tonight's service."

"You think they're gonna hire you?"

"Well, I don't know–"

"What's going on? You sound like you're about to tell me someone died or some shit!"

"I just– I gave Molly a call to ask her if I was in trouble–"

"And what did she say?"

"She said, 'Oh, no. We just need to have a friendly chat.' What does that mean?"

"I don't fucking know. Sounds like your meeting's either gonna be really bad or really good. Either way, 'friendly chat' sounds like some fucking Christianese bullshit to me. I'll tell you what. Whatever it is, let's plan on grabbing drinks at that sushi place on Eldridge Parkway afterwards and you can tell me all about the good or bad or ugly meeting. Sound good?"

"Cool. I'll give you a heads up when I'm on my way."

* * *

I arrived at Lakewood Church one hour before the Saturday night service as I was accustomed to doing. I was wearing my bright red KidsLife volunteer jersey so the children could easily recognize me. When I walked up to the second floor, Molly and Gabriel were already there to greet me. I had not expected Gabriel to be in attendance. This didn't feel right.

They led me to an elevator. Inside, Molly scanned her badge over a black pad on the wall and a green light turned on. She then hit the button for the highest floor, which I knew was for employees only.

The top floor was immaculate. All the surfaces were made of beautifully varnished wood. The doors to every room were glass, and the furniture inside each office looked brightly polished. *Dear God, I hope I get access to this floor! Joel and Victoria's offices have got to be up here!*

Molly and Gabriel brought me to a 15-foot long conference table which was out in the open, just to the right of the elevator. They invited me to sit at one end. Then they walked all the way down to the other end. With the sunlight on their backs and a dozen chairs between us, they looked like fucking mobsters.

"So, De'Vannon," Molly started, "we on staff have been talking about hiring you as a full-time employee for a while now."

WOOHOO!

"The amount of time you've been volunteering is no secret. And we were going to hire you, but–" she paused. "Before we could bring you on staff, HR had to look you up. This included checking all of your social media pages."

I felt my jaw tense and my chest tighten. Molly took a deep breath.

"De'Vannon, we saw the pictures on your MySpace page! We know what you've been up to! And in Montrose no less!"

'What I've been up to?' Molly's words echoed in my mind. But she kept talking.

"How could you be doing *that* with *them*?" She spoke as if there was mud in her mouth. "You can't be hanging out in Montrose. You can't hang out *there* with *those people*."

The condescension in her use of pronouns was harrowing, as if she thought the people in Montrose were less than human. I felt my head burn hot with anger. Molly pressed on.

"We're relieving you of your volunteer supervisor and teaching duties in KidsLife effective immediately. There's a certain standard we expect from our volunteers, and we can't have you around the kids anymore. You're not the kind of person we feel we can trust around our children. I mean, one of them could have gone onto MySpace and seen that you were hanging out in Montrose, and… I don't even want to think about that."

Her words cut deep. Being told I wasn't wanted around the kids I had loved and served for so long hurt worse than being fired. Molly wasn't just stripping my volunteer positions away, but my humanity, too. I hadn't conformed, and therefore I couldn't be trusted.

Tears pressed underneath my eyes, but I held them back. As much as it hurt, I would not show weakness to these people. I would not give them the satisfaction of knowing they could affect me in this way.

Gabriel spoke next. He didn't say much, but he spoke curtly, and his brows furrowed in self-righteous anger as if *he* were the victim. "This also means you can no longer be a part of the adult choir." He may have had the name of an Angel, but he had the heart of a devil.

With Gabriel's rebuke out of the way, Molly swiftly picked up her lecture where she'd left off. "And you certainly can no longer lead worship in KidsLife! Look, we've completely removed people from the church for similar reasons before. We don't want to do that to you. In order for you to work your way back into the church's graces, we've prepared a selection of books we'd like you to read on how to deal with your *feelings*. In the meantime, you may continue to serve but only as an usher on Sundays."

The back of my neck and head hurt from the tension. I was *pissed. Books to become un-gay? So, basically conversion therapy? They want me to brainwash myself!*

I thought of the professor at the seminary who talked about controlling people in church. *This is what he was talking about! This is what they are trying to do to me!*

There was nothing I could think to say to them, and they weren't interested in hearing my perspective anyway. This decision was final before I ever arrived. As far as I was concerned, I had two options: I could beat the living shit out of them and go to jail, or I could leave.

I decided to get up and walk the fuck out. *After all these years of volunteering at Lakewood Church, this is how it ends.* These two jackasses had fully expected me to take the conversion therapy package they were offering. The last thing I saw as I exited the conference room was the shared look of confusion on Molly's and Gabriel's faces.

*   *   *

"What the fuck? You're telling me they were shocked when you left? Like they actually expected you to agree to fucking *conversion therapy*? That's some Nazi-level bullshit! Those motherfuckers!" Brianna echoed my thoughts exactly between bites of sushi. My nerves were far too rattled for me to even think about eating, so I drank instead.

"They thought they could control me because I was a volunteer," I said. "Like, I'm expected to fit a certain mold to help them reinforce the image they try to project to the public. They used my service as a means to try and control who I hang out with and where. It didn't matter that I wasn't paid. It didn't matter that the ways I was serving were coming from a place of genuine love. And nobody ever told me to watch my MySpace profile because the kids might look me up. There was no communication about that in any of the shit load of trainings and screenings I had to go through!"

I took a big sip from my whiskey and coke. I'd been venting to Brianna for several minutes, but I hadn't said what I really wanted to say. Finally, the words slipped out.

"None of what I did for them mattered."

I reached for my drink again, but before I could bring it to my lips the tears finally fell from my face. I put down my drink and cried.

"I didn't even get to say goodbye to my kids!" I wailed, no longer caring about the other people at the restaurant. I was still wearing my KidsLife volunteer jersey, and I lifted it shamelessly to my face as I cried into it. *How could they say I was bad for my kids? My love was not perverted and I'm not a pedophile just because I'm not straight. And yet they fired me without letting me say goodbye. My relationship with Lakewood seemed like it had been nothing more than transactional this whole time.* I cried for a long time.

Eventually, Brianna gently broke the silence.

"Listen," she said, "I've been wondering for a long time how churches that preach all week long about Jesus can be so incapable of showing grace and mercy. I don't have a good answer for that. It doesn't make sense to me. But I *do* know that you loved those kids. In spite of all their lying, stealing, and cussing, you loved them. The only reason they even stay remotely interested in Jesus is because there's some weirdo named De'Vannon, rocking some kickass Cali cowboy boots, who isn't gonna use the name of Jesus to judge them. You just show love, De'Vannon. Like Jesus, you just show people love. And Lord have mercy on the poor soul who's gonna have to explain to those kids why their superstar, Mr. D isn't there tonight to love on them. And Lord have mercy on Lakewood, because without you there's only gonna be less Jesus in that bitch tomorrow than there was today!"

I blew my nose on a restaurant napkin and laughed.

"And as for you," Brianna continued, "you'll be just fine. Because Jesus ain't giving up on you. Jesus is never giving up on you. And neither am I.

And you don't need to change or do anything to make me think otherwise."

I could feel more tears coming, so I stood up and walked around the small square table to where Brianna was sitting. She stood up, and we hugged.

"Brianna?"

"Yes, De'Vannon?"

"Thank you for being like Jesus to me."

"Of course," she said. "That's what we're here for. If the church won't be like Jesus then somebody has to." She took a step back, wiped a tear from my face, and sat back down. I sat too, finished my drink, and ordered several more.

When I got back to my apartment after drinks with Brianna, I realized I was still wearing my KidsLife volunteer jersey. I thought about lighting it on fire, but I decided to throw it in the trash instead. I went to my closet to see what other Lakewood attire I had so I could add it to the rubble. The deep blue of my adult choir suit popped out at me, and I pulled it down from its coat hanger. But as I held the fabric in my hands, I remembered all the worship services, album recordings, and fun times I had with my fellow choir members who I would never see again. I couldn't let go of those memories, though they now seemed to be tainted, and I couldn't let go of this incredible suit. Gently, I hung it back up in its place.

Then I got myself dolled up. I was going to a place where I knew truly everyone was accepted: Fancy's in Montrose. *Time to hit it, bitch!!!*

PART IV
(2010-2012)

CHAPTER 12: A FUCKING WRECK

One night I woke up in my car. My head was spinning. I'd only had two drinks at Fancy's, but after working a 12-hour shift at the Substation my energy levels were completely depleted.

As I began to rouse from my sleep, I noticed my car was slanted and the road in front of me looked oddly pale. That's when I realized it wasn't a road at all, but a sidewalk. My passenger side wheels were riding up on the elevated pavement, and the car was still moving! I lifted my foot off the gas just as a streetlight pole appeared seemingly out of nowhere.

My front right headlight went out with a *CRUNCH!!!* My airbag punched me in the face. And then my whole world started spinning. I was dazed and confused, but I looked up just in time to see the streetlight pole I had hit fall in my rearview mirror, slowly, like a tree. My car shook violently again as my car hit a short pillar made of cement, spun around, and came to a screeching halt in the middle of Eldridge Parkway.

Everything was dark. My other headlight had gone out, along with all the lights on my dashboard. Still, I could recognize the shapes of the buildings in my neighborhood, and I knew exactly where I was. If I could just get my car to start, my apartment was right around the corner, and I could sort everything out from there.

I tried the ignition, but it just clicked, lifeless. I noticed that my wrist was cut up from the airbag, but it didn't look too bad. Finally, I tried my driver's side door. Thankfully it opened.

I stepped out of my car just as several motorists pulled over to offer assistance.

"Are you okay?" one woman asked as she cautiously approached what was left of my vehicle.

"I'm fine!" I yelled back.

One man started to approach me. "Hey, are you okay there?"

I started to panic. "Hey, I'm fine! Just go away and leave me alone! I live like, right there!" I pointed in the direction of my apartment.

More people started to gather, but they kept their distance. Then the cop car came. I could see the lights of the patrol car before I heard it, and my heart sank. The crowd dispersed as the police pulled up, and five men stepped out.

How the hell are five police officers fitting in that one patrol car? I wondered. *They're either going to go fuck a bitch, or fuck up a donut shop…*

"Hey there," the one who'd been driving said. "Uh, have you been drinking?"

"No, sir," I lied.

The officer nodded. He looked relaxed. They all did. "Look," he said, "you don't have to lie to me. I'm not one of those asshole cops, okay?"

Two of the officers had started checking out the damage to my car. I saw one of them cringe at the sight of my passenger side. "Damn, buddy! The entire front axel's been ripped out!"

"That's okay," I said. "My apartment is, like, right there." I pointed again. The two remaining cops stood casually by the first cop's side. They looked like they didn't want to be here anymore than I did. "Okay," I said to the first cop, "I had one or two drinks earlier, but I've been working 12-hour shifts at my job and I'm really just tired. I'm certainly sober now! Just tired though."

The officers all exchanged quick glances. A couple of them shrugged. "Okay," the first officer said. "If you say so. We'll call a tow truck for your car. Once he picks it up, we suggest you get some rest, alright?"

I nodded. The five officers piled back into the vehicle and drove away.

I couldn't believe I wasn't getting arrested! *Not that they could've fit me in their car anyway.*

The next day I bought a brand new 2010 white Ford Mustang with a football-brown leather interior. The dealer said I'd be the only one in Houston with a Mustang like this.

The next week I moved right across the street from Fancy's Bar. I had to stop drinking and driving, and since I wasn't going to stop drinking... well... the move only made sense.

* * *

I normally didn't get hangovers, but one Sunday morning I woke up feeling miserable. My head felt like there was a hole in it. And so did my soul.

I immediately began to guzzle water and ibuprofen, begging the pain to go away, but the more awake I became, the worse the sick feeling in my stomach felt. *I wish I could go to church today but I can't. I won't be welcomed at any church. Dammit, how long is every Sunday gonna make me think of the bastards at Lakewood Church?*

I couldn't eat, but I had too much nervous energy to sit still in my apartment, so I showered off, made myself look fabulous, and (even though I felt like a goblin) walked outside.

Fancy's was open early. *Why did I not know Fancy's opened early on Sundays? Oh duh, because I used to always be at church on Sundays and only just fucking moved here.*

"Hey! Back for more, De'Vannon?" It was Grayson, the bartender I held responsible for my hangover.

"What the hell did you put in my drink last night, Grayson?"

"Hey, just what you ordered. And then a little more." He winked.

I couldn't help myself. Grayson had jade green eyes, he was tall, yellow skinned, and he had curly black hair. And he had a girlfriend named Ava. Still, he was every gay guy's fucking dream, and he couldn't stop me from dreaming.

"Grayson, I don't know why the fuck you guys are open this early on a Sunday, but–"

"Sunday Funday, De'Vannon!"

"What?"

"Sunday Funday! One dollar drinks all day long! As soon as everybody's sobered up from last night, it's gonna be fucking *LIT!!!*"

I stared dumbstruck at Grayson. *How did I not know Sunday Funday was a thing?* "Well, in that case," I said, reaching for my wallet. I slapped my credit card down on the bar. "Open me up." As he reached for my card, I then slapped a $20 bill next to it. "And this is for you if you spend the whole day with your shirt off."

Grayson smirked. He pocketed the $20. "This gets you an hour," he said. Then he took his shirt off.

He had beautiful green, black, and red tattoos all over his abs and chiseled back. The green matched his eyes. The red matched the color of the drink he served me. And the black matched the color of my memory of the rest of the day.

* * *

Sebastian and I continued to hookup but our relationship never evolved beyond incredibly intense sex, which I wasn't particularly upset about. But I still held on to the dream of finding my dream guy and so my search continued.

"Wanna get high?"

I had been on a date with Rory before and slept with him. He was kind and I trusted him, but he wasn't the first kind and trustworthy guy to offer me drugs. He *was* the first one to offer me drugs after my fall from grace at Lakewood. No one was depending on me to show up to volunteer at church and my Substation job was part of a union, so they didn't do random drug tests. I had no reason to say no to this perfect distraction from the anguish and rage that was seething inside of me.

"What do you have in mind?" I asked him.

Rory looked excitedly at me, and then reached into his backpack by the side of his bed. He had all sorts of toys in his fuck bag that I had respectfully declined, but the red tabs he pulled out of the side pockets piqued my curiosity.

"What's that?" I asked.

"Ecstasy!" Rory said excitedly. "Have you done it before?" he questioned eagerly.

"No," I answered honestly. "The only drug I've ever tried is weed. I smoked it a couple of times, but I didn't even inhale."

Suddenly, his eyes got sharp and intent as he seemed to delight in my innocence. "Oh, it's like nothing you've ever experienced! But you gotta drink a lot of water. Lots of water, and no alcohol, okay?"

I nodded and he passed me the tab. I was ready to learn what all the hype was about. Rory went to his kitchen and brought back two tall glasses of water. We downed them along with the tabs.

I waited for the sensation to hit me while Rory went to refill the glasses. Then we downed more water. I felt nothing except a little bloated.

"Okay," Rory said, "ready to hit the club?"

I shrugged. If the drug didn't affect me, I could still have fun dancing.

Rory drove us to Fancy's. The whole drive I waited for the feeling to hit. *Maybe it's like alcohol, and it just needs time to get into my system.* But by the time we got to Fancy's I still felt the same.

"De'Vannon! Who's your friend?" Grayson asked. Someone had already paid him to take off his shirt. I introduced Rory. "Hey, a friend of De'Vannon's is a friend of mine!" Grayson said, and reached for three shot glasses.

"Oh, we're actually just drinking water tonight," Rory said.

Grayson looked at me for confirmation, and I nodded.

"Alright, if you say so!" Grayson conceded and got us two glasses of ice water.

I was starting to feel more embarrassed than high, but I didn't say anything. I just drank more water, tipped Grayson, and waited.

"Rory, I'm not feeling anything."

Rory looked at me, and when he did, I saw that his eyes were black and fully dilated. "Let's dance," he said.

I hit the dance floor like I normally would, making it clear that I was the Queen in the club. Then I felt a chill pass through my body, like my skin had frills that danced in my wake. The lights in the room multiplied, and suddenly the dark club was heavenly. And the music...

The music was more real than it had ever been before. While previously I had danced *with* the music, now I was dancing *in* the music, hearing sound like I had never heard it before. I could feel the bass vibrate through every cell in my body, like a never-ending orgasm.

No song could be too long. I didn't want the music to end. Eventually I did have to go to the bathroom, though. Standing at the urinal, I couldn't see straight. When I stood in front of the mirror, I saw that my eyes looked just like Rory's had. And my shirt was drenched in sweat. I felt phenomenal.

Back on the dance floor I carried on. I would have danced until the sun came up but at 4am the music stopped, and I was ushered out politely along with the other party people.

Rory spent the night at my place. As soon as he got inside, he collapsed on my couch and passed out. I managed to make it to my bedroom.

Sleep came quickly, but before it did, I had one last lucid thought. *Lakewood ain't got shit on this party.*

* * *

"Damn, De'Vannon! Seven boxes of pizza? How many people do you invite to these things?" Adam peeked inside each of the boxes, confirming there was in fact a variety. It was the first time I'd seen him since we were enlisted in the Air Force together. I was excited to have him visit Houston from Virginia. Better yet, I was thrilled to have him over for a kiki at my apartment in Montrose.

I'd started hosting house parties with friends I'd met at Fancy's and other bars around the area. I'd order pizza because I didn't want to cook, and we'd drink, pregame, and then walk across the street to dance the night away. Having Adam over was a huge bonus.

When people started coming over, I gleefully introduced them to Adam. "Hey! This is my friend, Adam, from when I was in the Air Force. And no, he's not available, he has a wife and kids, but don't worry, he can dance like a motherfucker!" But it turned out that Adam wasn't the only new face at my event.

"Hey everybody!" Márquez announced when he arrived. "This is my boyfriend, Jaxon! He's from Lafayette and just moved to Houston!"

Jaxon was a goofy blonde nerd who looked like he was still in college. I don't think he ever blinked, and that was fine with me because his blue eyes were captivating. I caught Márquez by the arm. "Now he is what I call a snack," I muttered mischievously.

"Don't I know it, honey," Márquez said, playing along.

The first box of cheese pizza was destroyed within the first ten minutes. I made my way to the kitchen to fetch the second box of cheese, and Jaxon was munching on a messy slice of veggie. He waved awkwardly as I entered, and I couldn't help but smile. He was so weird, and I was in such good spirits. I grabbed the box of cheese as Jaxon put down his pizza slice and began fumbling in his pockets.

I was about to leave with the box when he said, "Hey, want some?"

I turned with a smirk on my face, thinking he meant dick, but then I saw the bag of white powder.

"What's that?" I asked.

"You've never done coke before?"

"Nope"

Jaxon chuckled as he pulled out a pair of keys, dipped one into the bag, lifted the little mound of white dust to his nose, and snorted. Then he passed the bag and keys to me.

I hesitated only for a second before saying, "Fuck it! Whatever!" I mirrored Jaxon's actions as best I could.

As soon as I inhaled, the back of my eyes burned. I could feel the powder dissolve and drip down the back of my throat. It touched my tongue, and my tongue went numb. My whole face was turning numb. But my vision was sharp. I felt like I could see and experience everything. And Jaxon, smiling giddily across from me, looked more gorgeous than ever. I smiled back. *What other treats could life have to offer that I've been missing out on this whole time?*

* * *

Grindr had become my favorite dating app, and even with Adam in town I spent time browsing for guys to hook up with. If Adam was out visiting with another friend who happened to live in Houston, or just on a call with his family, I couldn't stand being left alone.

I found one cute guy in the neighborhood with the username, *MilesLong*, but before leaving for his place I snorted some coke. It turned out that buying coke at Fancy's was easy. After just five minutes of asking around the night before, I was introduced to Nikki, a lesbian girl dealing coke *and* ecstasy!

I loved being able to walk to my hookups. I was located right in the middle of the party in Montrose. A ten minute walk in any direction could end in almost any fantasy I dreamed of. *MilesLong* was only five minutes away.

"Come in! The door's unlocked!"

Inside, all the windows were blacked-out. The guy who greeted me around the corner was pasty white. Whiter than his picture on Grindr had looked. He looked like a vampire, and just like the vampires in pop culture, he was hot.

"Hey, I'm Miles," he said. "Can I get you anything? Or do you wanna just get down to it?"

I suddenly wanted something to drink, but I knew that I couldn't get drunk when I was high on cocaine. "Do you have any weed?" I asked.

"Sure, man," Miles said. He went to a drawer and pulled out a joint and a lighter. There were other baggies in the drawer, too.

"Where do you get all that shit?" I asked.

"I have a handful of dealers," he said. "The only guy who's consistent, though, is my meth dealer."

I nodded, taking a drag from the joint. I felt my body begin to relax a bit.

"Do you want some?" Miles asked.

"What?"

"Do you want some meth? It's pretty good, you know, from the guy I get it from."

I stared at him, contemplating, letting the concoction of substances that I had already put into my body take effect.

Miles started picking at his fingers. "Or, you know, we could fuck first–"

"No," I replied. "I'll try your meth."

Miles smiled nervously before hurrying back to his drawer. He took out a small packet of pink crystals, and then opened a small cabinet door underneath the drawer. All alone on the shelf was a glass bong, already filled with water. He brought the supplies over to me.

We sat down on his couch, and he loaded a tiny bit of the crystals into the bong. Then he brought his lighter to it and breathed in the other end. I watched as the water bubbled and smoke flowed through the glass spouts of the device. Miles closed his eyes, sat back, and exhaled a thick white cloud of smoke. He passed the bong and lighter to me, and I replicated his actions.

The meth didn't hit me at first. I exhaled and passed the bong back to Miles. He promptly took another hit and passed it back to me. I wasn't feeling anything, so I took another hit as well.

"Hey," Miles said, "I know your profile said you prefer to take it, but would you mind topping me instead?"

"Sure," I agreed. It was the least I could do for him since he let me try his drugs.

The high hit me out of nowhere.

I had just finished topping Miles when my skin started to tingle. I stood to get a glass of water and had to catch myself in the doorframe. I couldn't see straight. I couldn't walk straight. But the tingle grew and warmed my skin.

I pressed up against the doorframe and breathed slowly. Sensually. I wanted friction.

"Feels good, doesn't it," I heard Miles say behind me.

I could feel my heart beating in my chest, rising against the steadiness of my breath. I forced my legs to walk again as I stumbled back to the bed and fucked Miles a second time.

* * *

A drug hangover is worse than a normal hangover. No amount of water and ibuprofen can solve that shit. And the morning after meeting Miles, I felt like a fucking zombie.

My phone buzzed. It was Adam. "Shit," I muttered to myself, remembering that I had promised him a ride to the airport. I answered.

"Heyyyy. Adam." My voice was hoarse from the smoke.

"Hey De'Vannon, I'm almost done with breakfast at Katz's. I'll walk back in a few. Just wanted to call and make sure you were up."

"Yeah. Listen. Man. I'm sorry, but I feel like absolute fucking shit this morning. Like, I have the worst hangover of my life. I don't need to be behind the wheel of a car."

"*Seriously, bro?*"

"I know I promised you a ride, but look, you got kids. And a wife. You don't wanna die. Lemme just buy you a taxi back to the airport instead."

"*If it's really that bad, then sure.*"

"It's that bad."

By the time Adam got back to my apartment, he had gotten over the fact that I wasn't driving him to the airport. I said goodbye, squinting at the bright yellow cab as he got in and left.

Then I hurried back inside. It was so fucking bright out!

I felt a tingle around my groin and I started breathing heavily. I was horny again. I got on Grindr and found some 19-year-old kid just looking for a fuck to come over. And when he did, he fucked me sober.

CHAPTER 13: TINA

Crystal meth was an all encompassing drug, and I started using it hard. I redid my apartment to look like Miles'. I blacked-out all the windows and installed black lights. I even bought several packs of glow sticks since a party could break out at any moment. The only reason I ever went out during the daytime was to go to work. Otherwise, I only went out at night.

The streets of Montrose are home to a lot of streetwalkers, and I was curious about their stories. One person in particular passed by my apartment frequently, but I tended to miss him.

One day I finally saw him. Her. She was wearing a maroon short-cut blouse and a short black skirt showing off her skinny dark legs. Her black hair was still short, but it was getting long enough to fall over her eyes. And she had a small, black purse.

"Hey there!" I said, walking up to her as I strolled through Montrose.

"Hey, sweetie!" she said, and flicked her hair back. "I've seen you around a lot. What's your name?"

"I'm De'Vannon."

"Ooh. I like the sound of that!"

"Thanks." She was really, genuinely nice. "I've seen you around, too. What's your name?"

"I'm Carmen," she said, wiping her lips.

"If you don't mind me asking, Carmen, I'd love to hear your story.

How'd you end up walking the streets of Montrose?"

"Wow," she said, looking away for a moment before looking back at me. "No one's ever asked me that before. I mean, I guess it's really simple. As soon as my dumbass Christian parents found out I was trans, they kicked me out, so…" She shrugged.

I was shocked by how matter-of-factly she had answered me. "What the fuck. Really?"

"Oh, please," Carmen said, rolling her eyes, "that hardly makes me special. There's dozens of kids walking these streets with the same fucking story, whether they're bi, gay, trans, or whatever."

Still, I was in shock. *How the fuck could Christians, of all people, be responsible for creating homelessness? Shouldn't they be the ones trying to end homelessness? But how can I be so surprised when that's exactly what happened to me at Lakewood? When I had been kicked out, it felt like I was being evicted, and now I was spiritually homeless.* Of all the people I had worked with during those years, no one had even called to see what had happened to me. The only person who had kept in touch with me was Brianna, who I still saw from time to time.

The anger in me welled, but I could see that Carmen wasn't interested in talking more about it. "Well, I'm still sorry," I said to her. "And I'm sorry that that's normal–"

"Why? Are you a Christian?"

"I'm not so sure anymore. I haven't dared to step foot in a church since something bad happened to me at the last one I attended." Carmen winced. "Listen," I said, "my place is just a block up that way. Can I offer you a place to spend the night?"

Carmen thought about it. "Listen, honey, that's very kind of you, but understand, you can't buy me with just a sleepover."

It took a moment for what she was saying to sink in. "Oh. I'm sorry, no, that's not what I meant."

Carmen fumbled about in her purse and pulled out a popsicle stick with a bump of cocaine on it. She snorted it and rubbed her nose. Through watery eyes she said, "You know, you're really kind, but this shit ain't free. I gotta work for it."

I didn't know my heart could break for her more, but it did. "Carmen, if it's coke you want, I've got coke at my place. On me, don't worry about it."

Tears continued to fall from her face. I began to realize that she wasn't crying from the cocaine. "Free coke?" She tried to smile, wanting to believe it. "That doesn't make sense. Come on, what do you really want for it?"

I wanted to insist that I didn't want anything in return, but she didn't seem like she would accept that answer. "I'll tell you what. You be my eyes and ears on the streets, and you can spend the night at my place whenever you want."

Carmen wiped her eyes, and then wiped her hands on her skirt. She stuck her right hand out in my direction. "Deal." I shook, and we walked back to my place.

Soon I had a new variety of friends sleeping over at my place most nights of the week. Some of the guys from the streets staying over were lean, ripped, tattooed, and so sexy that it seemed unfair. They also had a dangerous air about them, which I was drawn to against my better judgement. I eventually learned that they were known as "Trade," which meant they were sexually negotiable and would do anything for drugs. Absolutely anything. It fucking turned me on.

I begin to realize that the power I could wield over drug users was a high in and of itself. This new power was intoxicating and on par with my bourgeoning affection for crystal meth.

* * *

"Yo, you should meet my dealer," Miles said after taking a hit of meth from his bong.

We stopped having sex after our first meetup, but we kept in touch to get high together. I had already taken a few hits and was waiting for the high to hit. Except I couldn't wait. I squirmed and fidgeted on Miles's couch. My skin itched for the warmth of the drug. The boredom was torture.

"Sure, that sounds good," I said. As long as it meant not sitting still, I was ready to do anything.

"Yeah? Cool! Lemme find a fucking piece of paper and I'll write down his number for you."

"You mean we're not going to see him right now?"

"Nah, man! You can't just roll up on Casey like that! He's, like, super fucking organized and shit. You gotta call him. Besides, you can never tell if he's staying at his place or a hotel half the time. Just give him a call and say something like, 'Tweaker Miles gave me your number.' I'm sure he'll be cool about it."

Miles finished scribbling on a pad of paper, ripped off the top sheet, and handed it to me. The paper scratched my hands and I wanted to tear it. With shaky fingers, I managed to fold it up and put it in my pocket.

"Fuck! I'm so fucking bored!" I yelled.

"Want some weed?" Miles asked.

How could I refuse?

* * *

The nervous energy was intolerable. If I wasn't high on meth, I needed a distraction from the fact that I wasn't high on meth. I needed to *do* something.

I thought about all the weekly work I had done for Lakewood's KidsLife and adult choir. I did some quick math and added up a 10-hour hole in my week. *10-hours a week for over two years! That's over a thousand hours of dedication and passion I gave to them, and after seeing a few photos online they banish me? So much for fucking grace and mercy!*

Suddenly I was angry *and* bored. I paced and fumed in my apartment. There was no trade for me to manipulate at the moment, and no Carmen to kick it with. The emptiness of the space around me, and within me, collapsed on me all at once. I was lonely, angry, *and* bored. "FUUUUCK!"

I need to do something. I want to do something. What can I do? What can I do? ... What do I want to do?

I felt my body crave more meth. More drugs. More alcohol. More sex. But in a moment of clarity, I knew...

I want to do something to help people. I want to do something good again. Professionally this time. I really fucking want to make a difference.

But how?

All of my knowledge seemed to lead to dead ends. I was skilled enough to not die on the job at the Substation, but navigating the political world of the higher corporate ladder at CenterPoint didn't fit my personality. At best I would be stuck with field work. A good hourly rate, but nothing more than dangerous field work. I needed something else. I needed a new skill. But what?

Then it hit me: *I want to run my own business.*

I thought about Evangelist Nelson back in Baton Rouge and the way she ran her own clothing store and several other businesses aside from leading two churches. I wanted to be like that. But what kind of business would I run?

I don't know why, but at that moment I thought of my grandmother. *What would you be proud of me doing?*

Massage Therapy.

The thought came to me seemingly out of nowhere, and it felt right. Something inexplicable in my heart warmed at the thought of healing people through physical touch. In less than an hour I had looked up the two massage therapy schools in Houston and applied to both. And then I waited.

And waited.

The feeling of excitement quickly faded, and I was bored again. Angry, lonely, and bored.

I rubbed my shoulders, trying to calm the itch in my skin. Then I rubbed my legs. Then I felt it, the folded piece of paper still in my pocket.

I was out of distractions. Without even thinking, I pulled it out, unfolded it, picked up my phone, and called.

A deep, raspy voice answered in perfect English. *"Hello? Who is this?"*

"Hi, my name is De'Vannon. I'm a friend of Tweaker Miles. Is this Casey?"

"Ah, yes. And how may I help you, De'Vannon?"

"I'm wondering if we can meet up?"

"Why of course. Is this your cell phone?"

"Yes."

"Very good. I will text you the address to my place in the Heights. You can meet me there tonight at 10pm. And don't be shy, drive all the way up the driveway and come in through the back."

* * *

Based on the look of the houses, I judged the Heights to be a fairly conservative neighborhood. The houses were quite Victorian, and everything was so quiet. The streets were sparsely lit, but I still managed to spot the address on Casey's front door.

I followed Casey's instructions and drove to the end of the driveway. I knocked on the door. I had showered myself off and was wearing a white pinstripe shirt tucked into my Seven jeans, but my skin still itched. It took a great effort to stand still as a middle-aged man with evenly combed salt and pepper hair and searching blue eyes opened the door. From somewhere behind him, farther into the house, I could hear the faint sound of someone moaning. *In pain or in pleasure?*

"And you must be De'Vannon."

I nodded and smiled nervously. "Yes," I said, trying to hide my discomfort.

Casey looked past me for a moment. "That's quite a car," he said, noticing my white Mustang. "All one color." He returned his gaze to me. "And you're looking quite sharp as well! Come in!" He stood aside and gestured to me with a single wave of his hand to enter his house.

The kitchen had an art deco design with a rectangular, marble top island and tall, white cabinets. Four tall square chairs lined one side of the island neatly. Casey pulled the nearest one out for me and sat in the next adjacent one. The backs of the chairs were very low, and it was impossible for me to sit comfortably in them, and the echo of the moaning only put me more on edge.

Casey moved in swift, decisive movements. I thought of the formal protocol for addressing the generals in the Air Force and figured this was a business casual version of that. I felt a bead of cold sweat drip down from my armpit.

"So, De'Vannon, what does a neatly dressed man like yourself, driving an eye-magnet of a car, do for a living?"

"I work in the Substation department at CenterPoint Energy," I said matter-of-factly.

"The Substation" Casey echoed. The moaning got louder. It sounded like a man—I was sure it was a man—moaning just around the corner of the kitchen. Just one man. *He's either in a lot of pain or watching one hell of a porno.* "And do you like it there?" Casey asked.

"I like the money," I answered, managing a smile. I was relieved when Casey reciprocated.

"Yes, don't we all. And it would seem you know enough Benjamins to keep yourself comfortable."

"Well, the job is stressful as hell."

"Oh?"

"I mean, everyday lives are at risk on the job–"

"One moment." Casey cut me off with the wave of a finger and turned in the direction of the moaning. "WOULD YOU SHUT THE FUCK UP?" he belted. Immediately, the moaning stopped, and Casey turned back to me. "Lives are at risk?"

I forced myself to continue. "Like, for example, if one of us accidentally touches something that's hot, that's 345,000 volts of electricity we have to reckon with. We'd fry like a turkey."

"Stressful indeed." He sat as still as a statue, piercing me with his blue eyes, but he managed to maintain a comforting smile the whole time. To hide my discomfort, I kept talking.

"What I really want to do is massage therapy."

"Massage therapy?"

"Yes, I decided that that's what I really want to do, and as long as the military's willing to pay for my tuition, I don't see why not to just go for it."

"You served in the military?"

"Yes, in the Air Force. Six years."

"Why did you leave?"

I realized I might be telling this man too much information. *He is a drug dealer after all! With a man who sounds like he's in a lot of pain just right around the corner!* "I just got tired of the political bullshit," I answered as vaguely as possible.

"I see," Casey said, and paused. "Will you excuse me one moment? I will be right back."

He got down off his highchair and I gulped as he stepped around the corner. I couldn't see around the square corners beyond the kitchen, but I could hear by Casey's footsteps that he hadn't walked far. *Did I say something wrong?* I wondered.

"Oh, hush," Casey's voice echoed from around the corner. "You'll be fine."

Moments later Casey returned with a long narrow pipe with a bowl at the end of it and a small bag of blue crystals. He sat back down at his seat and loaded the bowl. "I'm very proud of my product," he said as he sealed the bag with the remaining blue crystals. "You know, I could tell from the moment I saw you that you were a man of fine tastes. And it's clear from your story that you don't settle for anything less than what you want, which is quite admirable."

He passed me the pipe and a lighter. I took a hit. The smoke was clean and smooth. Whatever he was selling Miles, it wasn't this.

"Wow," I said, exhaling a white cloud. I stared in awe at the pipe in my hand, wondering if it would be rude to take another hit. Casey saw my longing gaze.

"Well go ahead, have another."

I did, and it was better than the first. I could already feel the warmth emanating from my lungs, saturating my body, and comforting my skin in its sensual embrace.

"How much?" I asked.

"Two hundred bucks a gram," Casey said unflinchingly.

I pulled out my wallet and presented four Benjamins. Casey took the money and folded it into his pocket. He then walked out of the kitchen and returned moments later with two bags of the same blue crystals. After passing them to me he sat down again and stared right at me. I felt frozen in place by his look.

"How would you like some extra work?" he asked. Before I could think about an answer he pressed on. "Nothing too complicated. Just run some errands as needed."

I looked at the blue meth in my hands, and then back at Casey.

"I can pay you in cash, meth, or a split of each."

My eyebrows raised.

"I'll take the split," I said.

"Wonderful. You can await my call."

* * *

I heard from one of the massage schools before I heard from Casey. As expected, my G.I. Bill from having served in the military would pay for my entire tuition. I could begin participating in classes three nights per week effective immediately. I was also told that I would have to complete fifty hours of massages outside of class at the clinic within a year in order to be licensed to do massage. It all seemed fair and sensible to me, so two nights later after work I drove to my first class.

The class was small. Only six other people attended. One of them was Landon.

Landon had a long, dirty blonde hippie hairdo that immediately caught my attention. He was *cute*. I gazed flirtatiously at him, making my attraction obvious. When he didn't return my stare, I followed his gaze to a girl, who was looking curiously at me. As soon as I turned to her, she looked away.

"Welcome, De'Vannon, my name's Mel." The instructor was tall. He practically had to bow to shake my hand, but his greeting was warm. "The other students are Lindsay, Ethan, Megan, Chris, Landon, and his girlfriend, Chloe."

Chloe was the girl who had been giving me the curious look. Now both she and Landon avoided eye contact with me. *They're so cute,* I thought. *This is going to be so much fun.*

Massage classes entailed taking turns practicing massages on one another while Mel guided us through the techniques.

"Ok, De'Vannon," Mel was saying, "massages are different for males and females. Have a preference?"

"Give me a man," I said with a smirk.

"Great! Landon, you're up."

Landon went into a changing room and came out with a towel around his waist. When he turned around to lie down on the bench, his back muscles were more precisely defined than I ever could have imagined. *How do I do this without getting hard? ... Oh, fuck 'em if they care.*

"Now," Mel instructed, "we're going to start at the base of the neck, then work on the shoulders, and go down from there."

This is a fucking three course meal!

"Now, once you find a knot, don't be afraid to really dig in. Anyone can give themselves a shoulder rub. Your job is to put your whole soul into loosening those fibers up."

I bent over, arched my back, and pressed in. Landon groaned. I couldn't help but look at Chloe. She had a purple fingernail hanging on her lip, and her eyes were glued to the proximity of my hip to Landon's as I massaged his neck.

She's fucking digging this! Oh, this class is going to be so much fun.

*   *   *

One week after my first meeting with Casey, he called.

"I have a job for you. How soon can you be at my place?"

It was just after 10pm on a Thursday, but I wasn't sleeping. I wasn't even sleepy. I was only getting about two or three hours of sleep every night, and that was only because my body forced me to rest. As long as I could help it, I stayed awake.

"I'm coming over right away," I said. "No more than twenty minutes."

Fifteen minutes later I was back in Casey's kitchen. Two other men sat with Casey at the kitchen island, smoking from a rather large glass pipe. They looked at me unassumingly.

"This is Twack, and Kiwi," Casey said, indicating each with an open palm. "And this," he said, passing me a sealed, white envelope, "is your job. Now get out your phone, I'm going to give you the address."

I took the envelope and did as I was told. Casey gave me an address in Downtown Houston and the number for the guy I was supposed to meet in case there were any complications.

"Now, the man you'll be meeting has been told to wait for you outside. All you have to do is drive up, hand him the envelope, and return. He's already paid, so don't worry about handling any money. Any questions?"

"No."

"Good. Off you go, then!"

There was absolutely no traffic, which made sense for 10:30pm on a work night. It took me ten minutes to drive to the address, and when I turned the corner there was a guy in a hoodie standing right in front of the address I was told to go to. I rolled down my window as I pulled up. I passed the envelope to this hooded stranger, and drove off in less than a second. Ten minutes later I was back at Casey's.

When I entered the backdoor to the kitchen my heart nearly burst out of my chest. A man I hadn't seen before was completely naked, blindfolded, and hogtied on his knees. Twack was violently fucking the guy's face, and Kiwi was jerking off to the scene.

"Any complications?" Casey asked, rounding the kitchen island to greet me.

"No," I managed to say without stuttering.

"Good," he said with a delighted grin. He handed me another white envelope, unsealed. "This is for you."

I peered inside. $100 and five little bags of blue crystals shined up at me from the little fold in my hands. *All of this for twenty minutes of driving in my Mustang!* I looked up at Casey, my face shining with delight.

Casey grinned back at me, and over the sound of heavy moaning behind him he declared, "From now on, I'm going to call you Token!"

CHAPTER 14: THE CRUCIBLE

"My husband's cheating on me," the woman said between groans. "What should I do?"

It was a surprise to me when I first learned that massage therapists were bound by the same confidentiality laws as clinical therapists, but every client seemed to be aware of this as they shared their most intimate struggles. To them, a massage therapist was as good as any therapist. It had been made clear during my lessons, though, that I was not allowed to give any advice.

"I can't say that I miss him in bed most nights," the woman went on. "He snores like a foghorn. But the smell of other women on him when he returns home... oh..."

She trailed off as I began to work on her lower back.

"What should I do?" she asked again, sounding on the verge of tears.

Stab him in the heart while he sleeps, I thought. "I don't know. I'm sorry. That sounds really hard," I said instead.

She was quiet for a while longer. Then, as I worked on her right calf, she said, "I'm afraid he's going to leave me. How can I make him love me again?"

Hire a hitman to take out the bitch he's fucking, I thought. "I don't know. I'm sorry. That sounds horrible," I said instead.

The woman didn't say anything for the rest of the massage. I was sad I couldn't help her. I wanted to help her. It touched me that she felt safe enough to be so vulnerable with me, but I knew what my boundaries were, and I didn't want to cross them. It had been several months since I started massage school, but I still had thirty more hours of free massages to give. Then I could graduate, take the national exam to become a licensed massage therapist, and open my own practice.

* * *

I lived for the endless night. On meth, I could go three or four days without sleeping. And unless work at the Substation demanded it, I avoided the sunlight at all costs. Plus working four ten-hour shifts afforded me the luxury of three-day weekends so I could party even longer. And now, freed by the darkness above, I drove, surfing the midnight airwaves in my beautiful white Mustang, seduced by the night.

My cell phone buzzed. "Hello?" I answered, turning down the volume on the radio.

"Token!" It was Casey. "*I placed an order at Katz's. Pick it up for me.*"

"You got it," I said.

"*Oh,*" Casey went on, "*and there'll be a boy out front named Lorenzo. Pick him up, too.*"

"Ok, sure thing, Casey."

My heart began to race in anticipation. Casey's errands always promised more meth.

Lorenzo was a tall, lanky guy and I recognized him from Casey's kitchen on the night of my first drug drop. He didn't make eye contact or say anything as he got in the passenger seat, and that was fine with me. I liked the quiet of the night, and it was a short drive from Katz's to Casey's; too short for a conversation.

I walked him into Casey's kitchen where he joyfully greeted the two of us. "Lorenzo! Token! Yes, come in!" He did not pull out any of the highchairs at the kitchen island. There was already one man sitting there wearing plain khakis and a neatly tucked sky-blue button-down shirt. He was hunched over a clear cocktail with two green olives skewered and drowned, and he did not look up from his drink when we entered.

I was about to move to get a better look of the man when Casey spoke again. "Token, this is Baker. I need you to give him an escort. He has the address. Just a quick errand. I expect the two of you will be back before Lorenzo and I have finished our fun. I'll leave your payments in the drawer. Ta-ta now!"

The man named Baker downed the rest of his drink and stood up. I finally got the look of him I'd wanted. He was not a big man, but his face was stiff and square, cleanly shaven, and his black hair was shaped in a rigid crew-cut above his high forehead. Nothing about him was intimidating, but his dark, blank, blue-eyed stare suggested that I not try to converse with him on the errand. *This man belongs on Wall Street*, I thought to myself.

I opened the door for Baker and we stepped out. As the door closed, I could hear Casey address Lorenzo, "Now, my dear, can I get you a drink?"

Once in the car, Baker passed me a small piece of paper. It had the address of a place a short drive north of the Heights. Casey was right. It would be a quick errand. *But what is Baker doing that Casey couldn't ask me to do?*

Fifteen minutes later we pulled up in front of a single-story house in a quiet neighborhood with other single-story houses.

"Turn the engine off," Baker said. I was surprised to hear how soft his voice was; almost like a sigh. I did as I was told.

Baker reached into his pockets and pulled out a pair of black gloves and put them on. Without saying anything, he exited the car, and walked up to the house, but not to the front door.

As far as I could tell, all the lights in the house were off. It was already 2am and fair to assume that everyone on this block was asleep. Instead of knocking on the front door or ringing the doorbell, Baker began going from window to window, checking them to see if they would open. Eventually he rounded the side of the house and disappeared from my view.

I waited in my car. All was silent, except for my thoughts. *What is this guy doing?* The question kept echoing in my mind, louder and louder as the minutes ticked by. I felt like I knew the answer, but I didn't want to think about it in case it was true. Instead, I just let the question continue to ask itself on repeat, *What the fuck is Baker doing?*

Only eight minutes had gone by when Baker returned. I didn't look at him when he entered, and he didn't say anything. I just started the car and drove back to Casey's.

*   *   *

"Do you take the drugs, cash, or split?" Baker asked. He sounded tired.

We were back in Casey's kitchen, and as promised our payments were in the drawer on the kitchen island. Two white envelopes, one with "Token" and one with "Baker" written on the front.

"I take the split," I said.

"Same." He tucked the envelope into his pocket. He was no longer wearing the black gloves. I couldn't remember if he was wearing them when he returned to my car after doing his job. I imagined the gloves were crumpled in his pocket with his payment.

Baker straightened his shirt, although it did not need much straightening. He looked ready to leave when he asked, "Do you hot rail?"

"Excuse me?" I asked, caught off guard. "Hot rail?"

"Yeah. It's kind of like smoking, but a lot more intense. The high is insane."

My eyebrows shot up in earnest at Baker's last few words. "How insane?"

"Like, a snorting type of high, times one hundred thousand."

"Bullshit."

"No bullshit. If you're interested, I can show you." He pulled out his phone.

I wanted nothing more to do with Baker, but I latched onto the thought of such an extreme high. My skin tingled at the thought.

"What's your number?" Baker asked. "I'll text you my address, and you text me on your next free night."

"What's wrong with tonight?" I asked. The tingle had turned into a crawl. I couldn't wait. If there was a high as intense as this, I wanted it now.

Baker smiled. "Alright. I guess tonight's as good as any."

I followed Baker closely in my Mustang. His car was a boring, dark blue Toyota Camry. *How could a guy with such a boring sense of style have the secret to the highest high?*

His house had a garage. He parked his Camry in the garage, and I pulled up behind him in the driveway. I could see Baker getting out of his car and waiting so I hurried to join him.

The night got darker as the garage door closed behind me, and then

Baker turned on a bright fluorescent light. I could see all sorts of drills, hammers, rakes, saws, and tools of every kind organized neatly on cork boards spanning the entire length of both sides of the garage. There was a small work table on the side opposite the door, and Baker pulled out a small drawer underneath the table.

"Aw, shit," he muttered. Turning to look at me he said, "I left the pipe inside. I'll be right back. Would you mind crushing two of the crystals from the drawer? And make sure they're crushed as fine as ash. It needs to be the lightest powder possible for this to work."

I nodded and again did as I was told, taking a credit card from my wallet, and getting to work on two of the brittle crystals. Baker was only gone a moment, and when he returned, he looked over my shoulder to see my progress.

"Yeah, even more," he said. "Even finer."

This better be fucking worth it, I thought to myself. My skin was starting to itch, and my hands were starting to shiver in anticipation of the rush.

"Ok, that should be good," Baker said. "Line one up for me."

Using my credit card, I cut a line for Baker. Moments later I heard a *whoosh*! I turned to see Baker holding the tip of a long, glass pipe to the flame of a torch lighter. *What the fuck?*

The pipe sat in the flame for what couldn't have been more than twenty seconds before Baker shut the torch lighter off. The tip of the glass was glowing bright red.

"Ok, stand back," Baker said, and I immediately scooted back from the work table.

Baker bent over one of the lines and snorted it through the glowing hot pipe. His eyes immediately shot wide open, and a thick white cloud of smoke plumed from Baker's mouth and engulfed his entire head.

"Ok, your turn," Baker said, gently setting down the pipe, still red hot, on the work table. His voice sounded even softer than before, and his face was completely relaxed. He leaned back against his car, letting his eyes gaze off into some fantastical wonderland in the top corner of his garage.

I tried to keep my hands steady as I picked up the still glowing pipe. Slowly, I positioned my head over the remaining line of meth, and brought the pipe to my nose. The air was warm before the glass hit my nose, and then I inhaled sharply.

My nose burned, and my face immediately went completely numb. Then, I exhaled the thickest cloud of white smoke I had ever seen in my life. My head buzzed with the rush of energy.

I watched the smoke dance toward the corner of the ceiling where Baker was looking. *I want to dance like that. I want to dance so fucking bad.*

"Wow. I'm gonna go now," I said to Baker. "Thanks. This is insane."

It was insane. My head felt detached from my body, and I could feel my blood throbbing through me at a million miles an hour. It took all of my focus and energy to drive safely back to my place. I then sprinted across the street and danced the rest of the night away at Fancy's.

* * *

"Hey, do you guys want to go in on an 8-ball of coke?"

I was at Fancy's with my friends Thiago and Miles, and I had spotted Nikki, my badass lesbian coke dealer across the room. I intended to make a purchase from her no matter what, but I had an idea.

"Man, I haven't done coke in years," Thiago said. I knew his drug of choice was crystal meth, but I was holding out hope.

"Well, what the fuck are you sitting back waiting for?" Miles teased him. "Let's do it!"

"Nah. I'm good," Thiago said.

"Suit yourself, Miles replied. "What do you need, De'Vannon? $100?"

"Yes, sir!" I said excitedly. I had hoped Thiago would go for it, but a split with Miles would still be just fine.

I collected the $100 from Miles and strutted my way across the dance floor to where Nikki was sitting at the bar. She was drinking a pink drink that I knew had tequila in it as she flirted with two other girls. I interrupted.

"Is my wholesale rate still good?" I asked.

"Should it not be?" Nikki replied.

I passed $160 discreetly under the bar. She glanced down for a second to verify the amount, pocketed it, and then handed me back four baggies of white powder: A quarter ounce of coke divided into four teeners of coke. *Two 8-balls and only $60 out of my pocket! Score!*

"Thank you, darling!" I waved as gracefully as I could before strutting to the other end of the bar where I had seen Grayson mixing a drink. He was pouring a long row of shots when I walked up. He looked as yummy as ever as he winked at me. I smiled deviously.

I noticed a cocktail napkin and pulled it close to me. I then leaned over the bar and asked, "What do you like, Grayson? What's your poison of choice?"

He looked at me slyly as he put the bottle of liquor back in the well by his crotch. *What a fucking tease! Looking this delicious, working at a gay bar, and being fucking straight?*

"Who's asking?" Grayson replied.

"Oh, just someone who wants to know the price of a night of free drinks," I said.

Grayson put his hands on the bar and looked down, considering. Then he looked up with a glimmer of light in his beautiful jade green eyes. "I'll tell you what. If you give me enough coke to wake me up tomorrow, I'll give you enough juice to knock you out tonight!"

I was already sliding one of the teeners underneath the cocktail napkin which Grayson made disappear immediately.

"I know you know where I'm sitting," I said, looking over my shoulder as I turned to strut away.

I returned to my friends with butterflies of excitement in my stomach. *My plan is actually fucking working!* "Here we are," I said, presenting two of the baggies on the table in front of my friends. "And here we have one 8-ball! One teener for you and one for me!" I said proudly. They didn't need to know about the remaining baggie still in my pocket.

Miles swiped one of the two baggies.

"I'm gonna get myself another drink," Thiago said as Miles and I headed off to the bathroom to snort up.

By the time we came back Thiago had what I guessed was a rum and coke, a server had delivered me a scarlet red cocktail in a chilled martini glass. It smelled like watermelon. It burned like jet fuel. *Damn! Grayson mixes a strong fucking drink!*

I was served ten more of those drinks before the bar closed at 4am, each one just as strong. Miles was giving me curious looks after the third one. I just shrugged.

When the house lights turned on to signal the bar was closing, I could barely stand up straight. I stumbled my way to the bathroom. Gathering my composure in a stall, I pulled out my extra bag of coke and bumped half of it with my apartment keys.

Grayson had definitely served me enough alcohol to knock me out, but my plan had worked, and I had more than enough coke to keep me up and going for at least another day.

I hurried home, eager to escape to the safety of my blackout shades before the sun rose. Back in the safety of my apartment, I prolonged the night with only one thought circling in my head: *How much more dope can I get?*

* * *

"Hi, Casey. How are you?"

"Just fine, Token! What can I do for you? Is there someone with a drug problem I can help?"

"I'm wondering if we could meet."

"Of course! I'm currently staying at the Hyatt next to the CenterPoint Energy Tower. Room 722. Just come on up!"

I knew that Casey did most of his selling out of hotels, but I did not expect myself to be revisiting the Hyatt next to the CenterPoint building I used to work in. I didn't exactly have fond memories of there from Hurricane Ike, but I wanted to make a purchase off of Casey. I wanted to see how well my plan could work with meth.

Moments after knocking on the door of Room 722, Casey opened it and greeted me as if we were meeting in his kitchen. "Token! So good to see you. Come in!"

He was wearing one of the hotel's white bathrobes and looked as if he had just come out of the shower. Among the scents of lemon and lavender bath soap, though, I caught a whiff of the spicy smell of whiskey. Sure enough, there was a glass of the brown liquid on the desk, right next to the bed where a naked Lorenzo was blindfolded, gagged, and hogtied. Next to Lorenzo's head was a laptop opened to a spreadsheet. Casey walked over to it.

I expected him to slam the laptop shut. I could see names, numbers, and dollar signs, and wondered if I should have seen it at all. But instead of concealing this incriminating information, Casey just ruffled Lorenzo's scraggly black hair and sat down on the bed with his ass against the naked man's face. He placed the laptop casually on his lap and motioned with a firm, open palm for me to sit next to him. I sat down a foot away from Lorenzo's dick, and as I did, I could see it get hard.

"This here is my entire business," Casey said, drawing my attention back to the laptop. "Every paying customer, where they live, where their mothers live, how much they've purchased, and how much they owe me." He scrolled down. The list went on for hundreds of rows. "I've got to be fucking organized if I want to keep it all straight in the head. Organized and honest." With a flare of showmanship, Casey waved a finger and looked me in the eye. "I *never* fuck with the product. If I knew someone was cutting the shit they were selling me, I'd cut their face just as badly."

I nodded, taking in what he was saying, but itching for the meth.

"This is an honest fucking business," Casey went on, shaking his finger with every word. "It's a shame this service requires so much discretion, but whatever. The rules are the rules." He took a sip of his whiskey and stared at his laptop. "I don't like moving from hotel room to hotel room, but I suppose the work more than pays for the expense." Behind us Lorenzo moaned. "Excuse me, *expenses*," Casey corrected.

"Why do you have to change hotels?" I asked. I was afraid that if I didn't say anything, Casey would have blabbed on forever. But I didn't want to sound like I didn't care.

"Why do I have to change hotels? Ha!" Casey took another sip of his whiskey and turned to glare at me with devilish blue eyes. "Because that's the fucking loophole the morons who make the law don't care to fix up!" He leaned forward putting his hands on his knees, pressing his words into me. "If they want to make a case against me that can stand up in court, they have to make two controlled buys from me at the same location within a small window of time. But if I keep moving, then sure they might arrest me, but they won't be able to make anything fucking stick."

I gulped. *Why is Casey telling me this? Is he suspicious of me? Does he think I'm a cop?* The thought concerned me, but my mouth was dry, and I wanted meth so badly. I started to grind my teeth uncontrollably.

Finally, Casey asked, "Now what is it that I can do for you, Token? Here to make a purchase?"

I nodded. I kept my mouth shut, afraid that if I spoke, my voice would quiver.

"How much?" Casey asked.

I thought about asking for a wholesale deal so I could run the same scheme with my friends that I did with the cocaine, but there was something vile in the look Casey was giving me that made me think twice. I kept my dry mouth shut, pulled out my wallet, and presented Casey with $400. Casey snatched the money out of my hands.

Standing up from his chair, he walked over to the minibar and opened it. There was a safe in there, but to my surprise he didn't open the safe. Instead, he pulled out an ice chest and a scoop. When he pulled the black lid off the ice chest, I saw that it was filled to the brim with beautiful pink crystals. I nearly gasped.

Casey placed the crystals on a scale that I hadn't noticed, sitting in plain sight on top of the minibar, and measured out the meth that I had paid for. These were the most beautiful shards I had ever seen.

Walking back to where I sat on the bed, he held out the bag of meth with a stiff arm. "Anything else?" he asked, motioning with his eyes toward Lorenzo.

I shook my head and took the bag from him. "No. Thank you."

"Very well. I'll see you out." Casey walked me to the door. "Good evening, Token."

The door closed. I tried to catch my breath. My body had been so tense inside his hotel room, and now my nervous energy was crawling to the surface.

Casey is fucking insane!

Just then I heard a loud *SLAP* and a whimper from the other side of the door. A violent shiver ran down my spine. *Fuck this, I need to get fucking high.* I hurried back to my car so I could drive home and smoke the shit.

My heart was still pounding when I turned on the ignition. As my Mustang roared to life in the parking garage, a realization hit me. *Casey just showed me a spreadsheet with his entire business on it. He showed me an ice chest filled to the brim with crystal meth. And he straight-up confessed to why he jumps from hotel to hotel.*

Casey isn't suspicious of me. Casey trusts me! He was just trying to intimidate me.

I was impressed.

* * *

My apartment was packed full of tweakers, and I loved it. Almost as much as I loved my outfit.

I had gotten in the rhythm of changing outfits twice per day: one outfit for while the sun was up, and one for while the sun was down. When I did brave the sunlight, I had gotten accustomed to rocking sunglasses so I wouldn't burn up like a vampire yielding under the strength of the suns unforgiving rays. On this night I was wearing a neon pink tank top, flashy yellow short shorts, brand new orange Skechers, and two wrists-full of glow-in-the-dark bracelets. I was looking and feeling *hot!*

My phone buzzed in my pocket: *"This is Baker. Sorry to bring this up, but I need you to pay me back for the T we railed. $200."*

What the fuck? I thought. *He never said I'd have to pay him for that shit! Why the fuck is he bringing this up now?*

My front door burst open and Thiago came running in. "We need to check on Daniel!"

The room went quiet.

"Who the fuck is Daniel?" I asked.

Thiago seemed caught off guard, surprised his urgency wasn't met with equal intensity. "Uh, he's my friend. And I'm worried about him! He hasn't answered any of my texts or calls in two days!"

"Ok, I'm sure he'll get back to you eventually," I said, trying to sound reasonable.

"No, no, you don't understand," Thiago stammered.

"What?" I was getting frustrated. I didn't want to have to deal with whatever Thiago's problem was. "Is there a reason he might *not* be okay?"

Thiago fidgeted with his fingers and rubbed his shin with his sneaker. He was growing increasingly uncomfortable. "Come on, man. My car is in the shop, otherwise I wouldn't be asking. I just need to check on him so I know he's okay. Can someone please just give me a fucking ride?"

I sighed. Thiago wasn't going to let this go. "Alright, who's coming?"

* * *

Me, Thiago, and two other tweakers filled my Mustang as we drove to the southern outskirts of Houston. I was beginning to get frustrated with how far of a drive it was when Thiago directed us onto the street Daniel would supposedly be on.

We pulled up in front of a two-story house with a rusty chain link fence and chipped white paint. The air was cool as we got out of the car and approached the front door. Something about the house and the air reminded me of the old dream I had where I was standing in the doorway of a rundown house, staring at faces made of black static. *What the fuck am I walking into?*

The door was unlocked and Thiago wasted no time opening it and rushing in. I could hear heavy bass music reverberating from inside. Trying to look confident, I followed Thiago in.

Like my apartment, everything was blacked-out. Suddenly a nude man walked around the corner, quickly followed by another smaller guy, dicks swinging. "Sup," they said as they passed us and walked up the stairs. Rounding the corner of the entry way I saw blue light from a projector glowing from what I assumed was the living room. As I approached, more laser lights shone out from around the corner, and the rumbling bass music got louder.

A gay porn playlist played on silent as it was being projected onto a blank, white wall. Tweakers smoked and shot up all over the living room floor. Laser lights of every color streaked across their naked bodies, as if the lights had painted the room into existence and were still hard at work. I turned to look in amazement at the two tweaker friends who had accompanied us. Their eyes were also wide with wonder.

Behind them was a small TV on a counter that I hadn't noticed when I walked in. This TV was playing a different type of gay porn: 100 man gangbangs. *This house is glorious,* I thought to myself. *I have to get my place decked out like this.*

Behind my friends I saw two figures walking down the stairs. I recognized one as Thiago. The other was a smaller man with jet black hair that gleamed in the blue light of the porn room. He had his arm stretched out over Thiago, who supported his weight as they finished their descent from upstairs and rounded the corner to us.

"Hey guys, I found him!" Thiago said. "Everyone, this is Daniel."

Daniel looked dead tired, but he lifted his free hand in a polite wave.

I returned the gesture. "Hey, nice to meet you. Is everything okay?"

"Yeah," Daniel said. "I was just sleeping. Hadn't slept for a week. I just passed out cold."

"Yeah, don't I know the feeling," I said. "Is this your place? I absolutely love it!"

"Yea it is. Thanks, man," Daniel seemed to brighten up. "Yeah, the hardest part was the laser lights. Oh, and setting up the projector. But fucking worth it."

"Oh, of course! Totally fucking worth it!"

"Well, hey, enjoy the place. And if you need any T, just let me know."

My eyebrows shot up. "You deal?" I asked. *If I can't get my plan to work with Casey, maybe I can work up a relationship with Daniel.*

"Sure, man. Just give me your address, and I'll arrange a drop."

Suddenly, I was very glad Thiago had dragged me to meet Daniel.

As soon as I got back to my apartment I began renovations to make my place look like Daniel's, with one improvement: I got a TV that was dedicated to playing straight porn.

* * *

"Where are you?"

It was Casey calling me. It was half past three in the morning, but I was driving around Montrose and the surrounding neighborhoods in my beloved Mustang. The night lights of the city relaxed me more than sleep ever could, and the car made me feel in control. It was also normal for Casey to call me at all hours of the night, so already being on the road came with the perk of not feeling stolen away from some other task.

"I'm just driving around," I told Casey on the phone.

"Come to the Crowne Plaza on 59 South."

I did as I was told. As soon as my car pulled onto the block Casey called again and started giving me instructions, hard and fast.

"Alright Token, you have to go up to the fourth floor. You can't take an elevator. You must take the stairs. Next to Room 413 there is an ice machine. On top of the machine is a bag containing half an ounce of meth. Leave seven hundred fifty dollars in its place and leave. And remember, you must take the stairs. You cannot take an elevator."

He hung up the phone before I could say anything. I had barely managed to find a parking spot in the time he was talking, but already my heart was racing. *Half an ounce of meth? People go to prison for years for being caught with that much meth on them! And what's it doing just lying around on top of an ice machine in a hotel hallway?*

This wasn't normal. Casey had sounded much more intense than usual on the phone. As I got out of my car and walked to the hotel entrance, my eyes darted around on high alert. I wasn't sure what I was looking for, but in a matter of seconds I saw it: An unmarked white van with blacked-out windows parked casually across the street from the hotel. The feeling of being watched nagged in the forefront of my mind.

This is fucked up! Am I being set up? What is the fucking deal? Is Casey fucking with me? Is there something he's not telling me? What the hell am I doing?

I tried to push all thoughts out of my mind, focus on the task, and act normal. I entered the hotel.

The lobby was empty except for a single night clerk at the front desk who regarded me with a kind smile when I entered. I kept my feet moving, trying to act like I knew what I was doing as I scanned the lobby for a door to the stairs. The elevators were in clear sight, so I headed toward those while I kept trying to identify the entrance to the stairs. I prayed to God the clerk wouldn't say anything, and he didn't.

The stairs were just past the elevators, and I opened the door as quietly as I could manage. Four flights of stairs felt like an eternity. I was nearly sweating by the time I got to the landing on the fourth floor and entered a hallway with antique lamp lighting on white walls and an oddly patterned red and gray carpet. I saw a little sign on the wall across from the stairway that pointed me in the direction of Rooms 410-419. I rounded the first corner and saw the black ice machine before I saw a door with a room number.

There was nothing discreet about the situation. The bag was nearly hanging off the top of the ice machine, begging to be picked up. I grabbed it. Half an ounce of meth. *Fourteen fucking grams of meth!* And it was all in crystalline form. At first glance the crystals just looked white, but as I moved to stuff them in my pocket, I saw a shift in color. I looked more closely. There was a bubbly, iridescent rainbow sheen to the crystals that I had never seen in meth before. I wanted to examine them more closely, but I was still holding a felony in my hands in the middle of a hotel hallway, and unless Casey somehow knew of a blind spot, this was almost certainly on a security camera.

I pulled out my wallet, left $750 in cash on the top of the ice machine, and hurried back to the stairs. When I exited the hotel, the cool night air shocked me. I didn't realize that I had started sweating. Wiping my brow in disgust, my phone rang. It was Casey.

"Token! Did you get it? Did you leave the money?" He sounded furious.

"Yes! I did everything you told me to!" I was aggravated by this job, and his sharp tone was pissing me off.

"And you left nine hundred fifty bucks on the ice machine?"

"Nine hundred what? You said seven hundred fifty bucks!"

There was a pause. When Casey spoke again his voice was no longer harsh, but almost whimsical. *"Oh, silly me. I should have charged you more. Go back up and leave another two hundred on the ice machine."* I was about to object when he added, *"Now!"*

As if I'd been kicked in the ass, I whirled around and marched back into the hotel. I dared not make eye contact with the night clerk. It was getting close to five in the morning, and I could only imagine what the man working the graveyard shift thought I was up to. *I hope he doesn't call security, or the police.*

I ran up the stairs. If the night clerk did feel like investigating, I wanted to be done with the job and out of the building before he had the chance to do anything about me. As soon as I landed on the fourth floor, I pulled out my wallet and readied another $200. And as soon as the top of the ice machine was in reach, I slapped the extra money down on top. It reverberated with a sharp CLUNK.

My heart jumped in a panic, and I ran back down the hallway for the door to the stairs. I nearly tumbled down the stairs several times as I ran down, no longer caring how I looked. I wanted to get the hell out of the hotel. If there were any security cameras that had caught what I had done, I was fucked.

I could see in my periphery that the night clerk was still at his post when I passed through the lobby for the fourth time. I kept my hands stuffed in my pockets, paranoid he might have x-ray vision and see through my pants to the bag of meth crystals. The drugs may as well have been sending out a beacon for my arrest. I half expected an army of patrol officers to spring on me at the door to the hotel.

The sweat was dripping profusely from my face and bleeding through my shirt as I exited the hotel again. I walked as briskly as I could for my car, knowing that Casey would call me again, but hoping I could be in my car getting as far away from this place as possible before he did.

Casey didn't call until I had merged back onto the 59 South and the sun was bringing about the morning crack of dawn. My hands shook as I answered. I just tried to drive straight.

"Congratulations! You passed my little test! From now on my new rates are going to be sixty bucks per gram, and you can by all means buy in bulk. Pleasure doing business with you, Token."

Casey hung up. I wanted to scream, but I was exhausted. *I can buy meth in bulk! And what a deal!* I couldn't believe how much access I now had to this drug. I wanted to celebrate, but I didn't have the energy to organize a party. Instead, I drove straight over to my friend Ridley's place.

I knew Ridley would be awake because he worked in the service industry and his shifts normally wouldn't end until 4 or 5am anyway. Also, he was a fellow tweaker. Sure enough, he opened his door when I knocked.

"Token! Come on in, man!" I entered his beautifully blacked-out abode. "What's going on?" he asked.

"Man, I just had the most fucked up night of my life," I said, and proceeded to tell him about all the crazy shit Casey had put me through. When I showed Ridley the meth, though, his eyes lit up.

"Holy shit! Look at that!" Ridley reached for the bag and took out a crystal to examine. "I've never seen meth that looks like this. It's so bubbly. It has that wetness to it like that good dope does though."

I nodded, sharing his awe and wonder, but also a little disappointed he couldn't explain the meth color to me. Meth comes in all kinds of different colors and each color has its typical uses. If it's brown or green, it's great for shooting up. If it's pink or blue, it's good for smoking. White and yellow can be easily snorted. But a tweaker is gonna use whatever color he can get his hands on and get it into his system in whatever way he can. I had no idea what to do with these beautiful clear, bubbly, iridescent, multicolor crystals. And with that thought in mind, I passed out from pure exhaustion.

* * *

When I awoke, all my meth was still in the bag untouched. That was lucky. Most tweakers I knew would have taken the bag and run. I still didn't know what to do with this type of meth, so I figured I'd sell it and then buy some of a color I knew what to do with.

"Who do you think would buy rainbow meth?" I asked Ridley.

"I don't know about any one person," Ridley responded, "but I know of some meth orgies that would probably be game for a bag like that."

Five minutes later I was out the door with an address. I was surprised to see that it was night again. I had apparently slept all day.

The address brought me back to Montrose. I was familiar with the block, and surprised that there were meth orgies in my neighborhood that I did not know about. I knocked on the door.

"Who is it?" someone cooed from inside.

"Hi, I'm Token. I'm a friend of Ridley's."

"Ridley!" the voice responded excitedly. I couldn't tell if it was a man's or a woman's voice. "Is he here?"

"No," I said. "I was just looking for a party and he said I could try here."

I heard some shuffling of feet and the door opened to a very tall, very skinny man with soft skin and short mousy hair. And no clothes. He looked more curiously at me than I did at him.

Behind him, other naked men walked about, caressing each other, dicks swinging. And I saw some meth pipes and a shit load of syringes.

I reached in my pocket and pulled out the bag of rainbow dope. The tall man's eyes widened. He stood aside and motioned for me to come inside. As soon as the door closed, he said to the room, "Check this out everybody. Check out what Ridley's friend Token brought!"

I puffed my chest out proudly and held out the bag of rainbow crystals for all to see, and a room full of naked tweakers looked up at me like I was the fucking Buddha. "Whoa!" one small guy gasped. "Where did you get that? I haven't seen that shit in years!" He stood and walked up to the bag, reaching for it, but restraining himself from taking it out of my hands. I could smell fresh sweat on him. "This is the crème de la crème! We can bang this shit! Let me grab a point!" I assumed by *bang* he meant shooting up and by *point* he meant needle.

The tall man put his hand on my shoulder. "How much?" he asked.

I looked around the room. There were at least ten people present. "If each of you chips in a hundred bucks, that should cover it," I said.

Instantly, the room was a scurry of skinny naked tweakers, hustling to their jackets and purses strewn about the room. A minute later I was handed $1,500 and I relinquished the meth. They all looked at me admiringly, and I soaked in the attention. They still had no clue who I was, and they adored me. I loved the mystique.

"Will you be joining us?" the smaller guy asked, hopefully.

"No, darling," I said, "I'm afraid I have other affairs to attend to." That was a lie, but I wanted the mysteriousness of my presence to linger. I wanted to come back and make more drops in the future. If I joined the orgy, the mystique would have vanished. And I didn't want to lose the power I had over these people.

With a flirty wave of my hand, I turned and left.

This made me feel like I was an official drug dealer, and I loved it! I had found a new calling and I knew I could be good at it.

CHAPTER 15: LET'S MAKE A DEAL

"What can I get you in return for free drinks all night?"

It was a Friday night, and I had spent every night of the week bar hopping through Montrose to set up similar deals with other DJs and bartenders like the one I had with Grayson at Fancy's Bar. Only one bartender had ratted me out to their manager, which pissed me off because now I was banned from that club, but one strike still felt like good odds compared to the other deals I was making.

I was now at a gay club called F Bar, and I was getting to know each of the three bartenders on duty. I loved the vibe of this club. The black walls blended in with the dark shadows of the dimly lit room, making the space feel much larger than it actually was. Beautiful chandeliers hung from the ceiling, and laser lights shined over the dance floor from the stage where a DJ was playing Top 40's hits.

"One joint equals one drink," Sally, the bartender, said as she wiped off the counter. "And the shit better be good!"

I grinned. My shit was always good. I tested all of my products personally to make sure, and if I was ever sold something I didn't like, I stopped buying from that supplier. I could tell it was making a difference.

There was no shortage of dealers in Montrose, but once I connected with a new client, they always came back to me for more. And it wasn't even that hard! I showed up on time, I weighed the product in person when I could, and I never cheated my buyers in any way. My work as a recruiter had trained me well.

I picked out a few joints from my pocket and placed them on the bar. Sally's bar towel was out in an instant to wipe them out of sight.

"What does the DJ drink?" I asked.

"He likes his bourbon."

"Alright. Two bourbons then! And I'll come back for my third drink later!"

Sally poured bourbon on the rocks into two crystal clear glass tumblers, and I waltzed them over to the stage.

The DJ's eyes lit up at the sight of the brown liquor. I passed it up to him. As he reached down to grab it, he lifted his headphones to hear my request. He knew the shit wasn't free.

I then gave him the same message I had given every DJ at every bar earlier in the week: "My name's Token! Every time you see me walk in this club I want you to play 'Get Outta My Way' by Kylie Minogue! Starting now!"

The DJ gave me a thumbs up, put his headphones back on, took a long sip of his drink, and switched the track up. On the projector behind him, the highlighted silhouettes of Kylie and her gorgeous male backup dancers lying on a radiant floor took over the screen. I threw back the bourbon, letting the warm feeling take over my insides, and then I took over the dance floor.

I knew the swipe moves from the music video perfectly, and the lovely people of F Bar got well the fuck outta my way!

When I returned to Sally after a few more songs, she tried to be nonchalant, but I could see a twinkle of admiration in her eyes. "What'll the third drink be, Token?"

She remembered my name!

"What does the security guy at the front door like?" I asked.

Sally smirked. Then she reached for a top shelf bottle of an unmarked amber colored liquor. She poured some into another tumbler glass, neat. "You're lucky your dope smells legit," she said as she passed the drink to me.

I smiled. She smiled back.

The guy working security was named Isaac, and he liked rum.

*   *   *

It was the day after Amy Winehouse died, and I was throwing a party in her honor. No one could sing like she could. I wanted to celebrate her life. I got me a white tank top and wrote *FUCK REHAB* on it in big letters using a black Sharpie. This ended up being a total conversation piece throughout the evening.

Per usual, all drugs and alcohol were provided by me for free. I took one (or two or three) tabs of X before everyone showed up, and pre-cut lines of coke on silver serving trays. There were little black specks of dirt (that I later found out was heroin) in the white powder, but I didn't care, and nor would anyone else. I rolled several joints, set out some molly, bought several liters of alcohol, laid out a few gallons of GHB, and even managed to get my hands on some shrooms.

And then there was the T. Pink, blue, yellow, and green crystals serving as the centerpiece to my public display and personal high… I snorted much of it first just to secure my fix because I knew it would be popular.

We were playing Amy Winehouse's hit song "Rehab" for the third time in a row and having a ball, when suddenly I thought the music was slowing down. Then everyone slowed down. All of my friends were dancing and singing in slow motion. It was like I was partying in the fucking Matrix!

I turned to my nearest friend, Maggie. "IIIIs iiiit juuuust meeee oooor iiiis eeeeveryyyythiiiing mmmoooovvviiing sloooweeeer?"

"Nooooo bbiiittccchh IIIIt's juuuust yoooouuuu!"

I couldn't believe it. I had slowed down Father Fucking Time!

After we laid Amy to rest, I hung my commemorative tank top up on a wall in my apartment so she would never be forgotten.

*   *   *

"The streets are talking about you," Carmen said as she burned the coating off a Brillo scrub with a Bic lighter.

"Yeah? What are they saying?" I asked.

"There's word of some other dealers getting mad about some new Black, gay dealer stealing their business."

I shrugged as she pulled out a pipe and a coat hanger and started plumbing the Brillo into the pipe. "If they wanna complain, they can complain," I said. "Besides, it's not what I'm doing, it's what they're not doing! I show up when I say I will, I don't cut my dope, I don't cheat people on the measurements, and hell! My shit is good!"

"I'm just telling you what I hear," Carmen said. She dropped some crack rocks onto the pipe, held up her lighter, and began to smoke.

I felt my phone vibrate and checked the message. It was Baker: *"Hey, did you get my last message? I need you to pay me back."*

I was about to type a response for him to come on over when Carmen said, "What the hell is going on?"

Red, white, and blue lights were flashing through the cracks of my blackout shades, and Carmen was going over to peak outside.

"What's going on?"

"Damn, there's like twelve cop cars in the parking lot at Fancy's! And an ambulance!"

"Hey, could you run over there and find out what's going on? Make sure everybody's okay over there?"

"Sure," Carmen agreed, and left my apartment. I instantly regretted not going myself when I realized I was left alone.

I looked at the remaining specks of white powder on my kitchen table from where Carmen had cut her a line of coke. I thought about sweeping it back into my personal coke bag, but then decided against it. I liked Carmen, and she was doing me a favor by scouting the scene at Fancy's for me so I didn't have to show my face to a bunch of cops.

I pulled out more coke and dumped it on the table for Carmen to find when she returned. Under the UV glow lights of my blacked-out apartment, the powder glowed as white as the sun.

I then rolled myself a joint and lit it up, waiting for Carmen to return. When she did, her eyes were wide.

"Someone got stabbed in the parking lot in front of everybody, but no one's saying anything! He's dead!!!"

* * *

Sometimes the streets talk, and sometimes mouths stay shut.

The stabbing was in the paper the next morning, and the morning after that. There had apparently been more than two dozen witnesses outside the club, waiting to get in, but not one person could identify the killer. There wasn't even a description.

Carmen had gathered from some people that the kid ran up to the bouncers and begged to be let inside the club. He was talking about someone trying to kill him, but the bouncers didn't want anything to do with him. If only the kid had known that just across the street was a string of dark alleyways where he could have hidden out all night had he just kept running.

Instead, a guy in a hoodie caught up with him. The kid only made it as far as the parking lot before a knife found its way into his guts. He bled out on the pavement.

A few days later, I saw a pile of flowers in the parking lot where he died, placed there by Fancy's I assumed but couldn't be sure. The club hadn't been nice enough to allow someone passage who was clearly in trouble. Why would they grow a heart after the fact and spring for a bouquet?

A few days later, the flowers were gone. But I could still see the black stain on the pavement where the kid's life had spilled out.

* * *

"Hey, thinking of you. Want to come over?" It was a text from Hayden, a guy I had met on the Adam4Adam dating app. We had only hooked up once, but it was an experience I was down to indulge in again, so I agreed.

"Be there soon!" I replied.

Ten minutes later, I pulled into a parking spot in the lot in front of Hayden's apartment. That was a mistake. Before I had even turned off the ignition, a dark car pulled up behind me boxing me in.

The driver's door opened, and out stepped a man in fresh khakis, a blue pinstripe button-down shirt, a square head with neatly cut hair, and black gloves. It was Baker.

I jumped in my seat as he slammed his gloved fists against my window.

"Listen you motherfucker!" he yelled. "Don't you dare think you can take my fucking dope and not pay me back for it! You know what I can fucking do to you, so stop ignoring my texts! Pay me back my fucking money!"

"Okay, okay!" I said, pulling out my wallet. My heart sank. I didn't have any cash on me. "I don't have it right now, but I'll pay you back tomorrow!"

Baker slammed my window again, and again I jumped. For a second, I thought he was going to smash it in and strangle me. "You fucking better!" he yelled. Then he marched back to his car and drove away.

I tried to catch my breath. I felt helpless. *He could have killed me if he wanted to,* I thought. *And he probably would have gotten away with it.* I felt my eyes well up with tears. I didn't want this kind of drama in my life. Slowly, I caught my breath and calmed down.

My phone started to ring. It was Hayden.

"Hello?"

"Hey, I can see you from my window. Are you gonna come up?"

"No, no, no, no, no. You do not get to sell me out like that and still expect to get a piece of this ass. Fuck you! Fuck you! Fuck you! I don't ever want to hear from you again!"

I hung up. I felt better. Cursing Hayden out returned a sense of control to me, and that was enough to get me to wipe my eyes, back my car out, and drive back to my place.

The next day I paid Baker back the money I owed him.

* * *

"Hello, thank you for calling Drugs 'R' Us located on the corner of Happy and Horny. How may I help you?"

"Hey, Token. It's Thiago. Are you around?"

"Of course! You know me!"

"Can I come up?"

When Thiago entered my apartment, he looked defeated. His eyes were puffy as if he had been crying, and his head was slouched. As soon as he entered my apartment, he slumped down onto my couch.

"What's going on, Thiago?"

"Daniel's dead."

"Oh. Shit." I remembered Daniel, the soft-spoken meth dealer with the pimped-out place that inspired a renovation of my own apartment. I had only met him that one time, but I'd developed an affinity for him, and I knew from Carmen's reports that he was the most respected meth dealer in Houston. "What happened?" I asked.

Thiago sniffled, holding back what I could tell were more tears. "AIDS, man. He's had HIV for a while, but I thought he was taking his medication. Turns out he gave up and stopped taking his meds a couple months ago."

I felt my stomach twist into a knot. I recalled the ugly pictures from the videos in grade school of people's bodies shriveled up and discolored as they suffered the effects of HIV and AIDS. I couldn't imagine Daniel coming to that sort of end. I didn't want to think about it.

"I'm so sorry, Thiago. Is there anything I can do for you?"

Thiago shook his head. "No. Just having someone to talk to is good enough."

* * *

"Hey, I'm good, buddy. Thanks, though!"

"What the fuck? What do you mean *you're good*?"

I had motioned to pass Fancy's bartender, Grayson, his drugs for my free drinks, per our routine, but he had waved away the drugs.

"Don't worry," he said, as he loaded a cocktail shaker with vodka and lime juice, "I'll still get you your free drinks. I'm just taking a month off from drugs."

"Bullshit!" I was incredulous. "What's the fucking point of taking a month off of drugs if you're just going to go back to them when the time's up?"

"It's important, man. I don't want drugs to play too big a role in my life, and this month helps me prove to myself that I'm not addicted. It'll also reset my tolerance." He capped the cocktail mixer and began shaking it over his head, making a point to show the flex of his bicep.

"Oh, come on! Why this month? What difference does it make if you do this sober thing next month?"

"Sorry, buddy. You can't crack me. This is my month."

"Fuck that! I can get you to get high!"

Grayson just smiled, calling my bluff. I had no idea how I could convince him to get high. I was so used to selling to people who actually *wanted* on some level to take drugs, even if they were reluctant. But Grayson genuinely did not want to take my drugs.

Grayson poured the cocktail into a chilled martini glass and pushed the pale-green drink toward me. "Get drunk my friend! And have fun!"

I took the drink and scowled at him. I was not used to rejection as a drug dealer. I didn't like feeling like I had no power over Grayson.

Grayson returned my scowl with a courteous smile and sauntered on to the next person at the bar. I turned my head in the opposite direction. My gaze landed on golden blonde hair and two bright blue eyes looking hungrily at me. I met this wondrous gaze evenly.

Golden boy grinned, sticking his tongue out teasingly. "Wanna play Hide-the-Weenie?"

It was the nerdiest thing I had ever heard, and I was instantly infatuated. I laughed and asked, "If that's what I think it is, then yes."

"It's a board game," my golden boy responded.

"Oh my God! You're so fucking cute! I love it!" I walked up close to him so I didn't have to yell as loud. "I'll tell you what. You can bring your Hide-the-Weenie game over to my place *after* you fuck me in the bathroom."

Golden boy put a hand on my shoulder. It was as firm as I'd hoped it would be. "If you insist," he said.

* * *

"Have you ever taken time off from drugs?" I asked Thiago as I placed a blue meth crystal in the bowl of my pipe. I was staying over at his place because I needed a break from selling to all the tweakers swarming outside my apartment.

"Yeah," Thiago said. I looked at him in surprise. "I mean, I've taken a few days off here and there."

"But, like, have you ever taken an entire month off?"

"A month?" Thiago contemplated, "No I don't think so. I think the most I ever took off from drugs was a week. And even then, I was still drinking."

"Oh, drinking doesn't count," I said, turning my attention back to the pipe. I set my torch lighter underneath the pipe and let the blue flame go to work. I watched in awe as the shiny blue rock melted into a heavenly pool. The sheen of the liquid was appetizing. The moment I saw the vapor, I brought the pipe to my lips, took a deep pull, and exhaled. The rush was perfect.

"Why do you ask?" Thiago asked.

"Grayson told me he's taking a month off of drugs. Says he does this every year."

"Oh yeah, Grayson." Thiago's gaze instantly drifted into a fantasy, undoubtedly about the sexy Fancy's bartender.

"And after I talked to Grayson, I met this super sexy, nerdy guy with absolutely glistening hair and blue eyes. He said he wanted to play Hide-the-Weenie or some shit. I didn't care, he was fucking cute. We fucked in the bathroom and oh my God his dick is so pretty and juicy I just want him to fuck me upside down. But when he said he would come by my place the next day, he never showed up. I've been texting him for two days and haven't heard from him."

"What's his name?" Thiago asked.

"Julian."

"Oh."

"Yes, put the word out and let it be known that I want him to call me." I took another puff from my pipe. "Here," I said, handing the pipe to Thiago. He gladly received it and took a hit.

A couple hours later I drove back to my apartment. As soon as I pulled up in my Mustang, car doors opened and a swarm of tweakers amassed. I led them all up to my place and began doing business. *This is too many people,* I thought to myself. *I need to start selling out of hotels like Casey.*

My phone buzzed in my pocket. I pulled it out and my eyes widened. It was Julian. "Hello my golden boy," I answered.

"Hey there, Token. I heard you've been looking for me. Sorry I haven't responded to your texts. Do you want to play Hide-the-Weenie again?"

"Desperately," I replied. "Don't keep me waiting."

* * *

I adored Julian. His "board game" was everything I'd hoped it would be, but I also enjoyed spending time with him.

"Can I share a secret with you?" I asked him after sex.

Julian nodded.

"I have an underwear fetish."

"Nice!" Julian replied as his dick got hard again.

"I may turn my fetish into a business one day if I can learn to control myself and not wear all the shit."

"I'm sure you'll do well at whatever you set your mind to babe."

"Ah thank you honey! Say, would you like to go with me to the underwear store across the street!?" I asked.

"That sounds fun," Julian responded to my delight.

I had Julian try on everything. I already had my own version of every piece of merchandise the store owned, except for one brand new red leather jockstrap, which I immediately tried on. Julian cooed at the sight of me in it.

"Sweetie, you are the sexiest stick I have ever seen!"

I blushed. Meth had lost me a lot of weight, and I agreed I looked good. "Would you believe a guy I dated recently had the nerve to fat-shame me?"

"Was he fucking blind?"

"Only when I made him wear a blindfold," I joked.

"Kinky. And I thought I was the one with all the toys. I did see your Godzilla doll." Julian smiled teasingly.

"That doll is sacred," I said. "You can do whatever you want to this ass, but don't you ever fuck with Godzilla."

Julian put his hands up in mocking defense. "I promise, your ass will be the only thing I fuck with."

My phone started buzzing away in the changing room. I went to check it. Casey was blasting me text after text.

"Get out of the fucking mainstream!"
"Get rid of that fucking Mustang!"
"Start taking the fucking bus!"
"And stop going to that fucking underwear shop!"
"You're too easy to fucking locate! Lay fucking low!"
"And get over here fucking asap! I want to buy some fucking coke!"

I ignored Casey's advice. There was no fucking way I was getting rid of my Mustang. *He's so fucking intrusive. How does he even know that I'm at the underwear store?*

When Julian and I returned to my apartment, I invited Thiago and a couple of tweakers to join us in going to visit Casey for my drop-off and we packed into my beloved Mustang.

* * *

Hundreds of meth baggies were piled on top of the island in Casey's kitchen next to a larger open bag of pink meth crystals. Casey was nowhere in sight, though.

"Casey?" I called into the house, wondering why he would leave his shit unattended. I motioned to my posse to follow me as I walked cautiously around the corner.

There was a single step down into the living room and the floor turned to carpet, making our steps even quieter. I searched for a light switch and found one. When I clicked it on, warm light from a standing lamp shone brightly over Casey's sleeping face. He was passed out on a long, white couch by a window.

I hurried over to Casey and shook him awake.

"What the fuck?" he muttered groggily, waking up.

"Casey, what are you doing? All your shit is just sitting out in the open in kitchen. If anyone else had come over, they would have fucking robbed you!"

Casey scowled up at me, still emerging from his slumber. "Why didn't you?" he growled and then pulled himself up. "Fucking weak," he grumbled. "What, did you think you could bring Christian values into the criminal underworld? That shit doesn't work, Token. Now did you bring my coke?"

Casey walked slowly ahead of me back into the kitchen, ignoring the other guys I'd brought with me.

"Yes," I answered, trying to sound composed. His disapproval surprised me. I thought I'd win points with him for not stealing. I didn't think I'd look weak and naive.

I gave Casey his coke and he gave me my money and an address.

"A drop-off?" I asked.

"No, just an address. I want you to meet her, but don't bring any of your fucking friends with you. She enjoys her privacy. Do you understand?"

I nodded, eager to get back on Casey's good side.

"Good. Now fuck off." Casey poured his coke out on the island and pulled out a metal credit card that clanked on the marble as he cut himself a couple of lines.

Dragging the tweakers reluctantly away from the mound of meth, I promised to give them some of my own back at my apartment.

* * *

The address Casey gave me brought me to a small house in the Greater Eastwood area east of Downtown Houston in an entirely unassuming neighborhood.

The tall woman who answered the door gave me a quick scan before saying, "You must be Token. Come on in, baby."

I admired the way her dark curls bounced as she turned to lead me inside. She carried herself proudly and didn't wait for me. I had to walk quickly to keep up. She led me into a cramped, dimly lit kitchen with chipped wood cupboards and fake marble countertops.

"What can I get you, baby, anything to drink? Smoke? Snort? Shoot?"

"Smoke," I answered. "I love your hair, by the way."

"Why thank you, baby. I'm glad you like it. Now tell me, what's your favorite color?"

I thought about answering simply with 'blue,' but then I stopped myself. This woman seemed so tender and motherly, I wanted to be more open and honest. "Aquamarine," I said with a smile.

"*Aquamarine*," the woman echoed. "Well, I haven't heard that one before. Doesn't mean I don't have it, though," she said with a smile of her own. "Follow me."

She turned and opened a small door behind her and ducked underneath the frame. I followed her down a narrow hallway and around a tight corner. A light switch was flipped, and white fluorescent light illuminated a large room full of metal tables topped with all kinds of flasks and lab equipment. There were also several large cylindrical vats in neat, orderly rows. In one corner was a blue crib with a baby sleeping soundly in it.

The woman walked over to a wall of buckets and started cracking the lids on a few of them. Different shades of blue crystals filled each one. "Come here, baby, and tell me which one is *aquamarine*."

In a daze, I approached the wall of buckets. None of the blue crystals struck me as aquamarine, but I didn't want to tell this woman that and offend her. I looked up at the wall of buckets. "I once had a bag of meth crystals of an iridescent, rainbow color. I sold it to some tweakers who said it was the 'crème de la crème' of meth."

The woman smirked. "Yeah, I cooked that shit. You want that one instead?"

"Can I smoke it?"

"Oh, no. I wouldn't recommend it, baby. That glory is for shooting only. If you want the smoke-show of smoking-ice, lemme get you this. It's not *aquamarine*, but this'll make you so fucking horny that a goblin will look like Brad Pitt!"

She sealed the buckets containing blue ice and opened another bucket at the end of the wall. As she did, the baby in the crib stirred and whined. "Oh, Dougie! Mama's coming!" She left the open bucket and hurried over to the crib.

She picked up little Dougie swaddled in a white blanket and rocked him gently in her arms. She saw me looking affectionately. "Here, Dougie. Uncle Token's gonna hold you while I take care of him." She passed her baby to me. I felt Dougie's warmth against my heart, and instantly loved him. I rocked him gently as his mother collected some Ziploc bags and filled them with crystals. These crystals were so large that each of them could have doubled for the blue Hope Diamond.

"What's your name?" I asked in wonder.

"Aw, hell, did Casey not tell you? That fucker. My name's Scarlet, baby. Call me Scarlet."

Scarlet put three bags of Diamond quality ice down on a work table and retrieved baby Dougie from me.

"I gotta ask," she said, "how much did you sell that first bag of rainbow meth for?"

"I sold a half ounce for $1500," I answered.

"Ha!" Scarlet cackled. "Shit, brother, you could have sold that for two, if not three times as much! But you won't make that mistake again, now, will you?"

"No," I replied, smiling sheepishly. "I won't."

"Good. Now here, take down my number. Maybe sometime, when Dougie's staying with grandma, you can come back, and I'll show you how to cook *aquamarine* crystals."

* * *

I started selling out of hotels like Casey, and it worked like a charm. I transported my drugs in a safe in the trunk of my car, and put the safe in a suitcase before entering a hotel. And if tweakers didn't want to come up to my hotel room, I had no problem going for a walk to meet them at their car. Business was good.

One night in a hotel room, my phone rang... except it wasn't a tweaker. It was Evangelist Nelson. It was nearly midnight. *Why is she calling so late?*

"Hello?"

"De'Vannon?"

"Yes. Evangelist Nelson?"

"Yes, I'm sorry to call so late. But the Spirit is moving me to tell you, get ready to go through a rough time."

Evangelist Nelson had given me similar warnings in the past, after which I would usually ask how to circumvent the impending gloom. But this time her voice sounded solemn and resolute. The impact of her words stilled me, and I accepted her message as a matter of fact. I didn't try to fight the anticipation of a trial like I normally would have. Deep in Evangelist Nelson's words I understood that this trial was something I would have to do. And besides, she had said I would go "through" it. I wasn't going to die, but I would go *through* whatever was coming.

"Well, thank you for telling me Evangelist Nelson. And don't worry about the late hour."

"Yes..." I heard her sigh on the other end of the line. She sounded at a loss for words. *"Look, drink lots of carrot juice. And use protection, you hear?"*

"I hear you."

"Good. Alright. Good night, child."

"Good night."

I heard her hang up on her end of the line. I then dialed room service.

"Hello?"

"Hi, do you have carrot juice?"

"Yes sir. What's the room number?"

I ordered several glasses of carrot juice, but after drinking two glasses of the nasty-ass orange shit I stopped. I had no idea what I was about to go through, but I was going to have to do it without carrot juice.

* * *

I strutted up to Sally at F Bar, unmissable in a black and white shirt, a black vest, a fedora, True Religion jeans, and cowboy boots. I was dripping with sweat from my "Get Outta My Way" dance floor anthem. She was just finishing pouring a drink when I rested at the bar. I smiled and discretely passed her three joints. She did not smile back. Instead, she took two of the joints and returned the third one.

"Save this one for later, Token, you won't be needing a third drink. The new security guy doesn't drink."

"New guy?" I asked. I hadn't even noticed the new person at the front door who had still let me skip the line the same way Isaac always had. Somehow, he must have gotten the memo about me. "What happened to Isaac?"

Sally looked away. It looked like she was trying not to cry. "He died," she finally said.

"What? How?"

"He had AIDS," she said. She was trying hard to hold back the tears.

"Here," I said, "forget about my third drink. Just take the joint anyway."

She took the joint and nodded. "Thank you." Then she went to serve the next customer.

Damn, I thought to myself, *how many people around here are dying of fucking AIDS?*

I shook my head. I didn't want to think about the deadly disease. I wanted to dance! I downed my drink, delivered the other to the DJ, and was about to dive back on the dance floor when I saw her.

She stood underneath the crown of one of F Bar's chandeliers in an ocean-blue sequin dress with gold streaks going down the sides. She had Beyoncé bangs, decadent caramel skin, and her brown eyes were as cool as the chilled martini in her hand. Her other hand leaned elegantly against the bar as she watched the dance floor. She wore six-inch heels even though she was already tall. I had to know who she was, and so I returned to the bar.

"Hi! I saw you standing here looking like a queen and I thought, 'this woman either needs to be my new best friend, or my new arch-nemesis.'"

To my relief, she smiled. "What's your name, honey?"

"De'Vannon. And you are?"

"My name's Halle."

"Like Halle Berry?" I asked, excitedly.

"Mmm-hmm. Except more dangerous."

"Oh?" Halle tantalized me. I wanted to know everything about her. She took a long swig from her martini. The glass was nearly empty.

"Is that vodka?" I asked.

"Grey Goose."

I turned to catch Sally's eye, and saw that she was already watching me, waiting for my cue. Without a word, she immediately started making Halle another martini. Halle watched the whole exchange, and didn't bat an eye, almost as if she were expecting the service. *This woman knows her power*, I thought to myself in admiration.

"So, Halle, what are you looking for when you prowl the streets at night?"

She shrugged. "Mostly just a good time. But the nightlife is also where I find clients."

I raised my eyebrows. She didn't look like a drug dealer to me.

"I'm a lawyer," Halle said, answering my unspoken question. "One of the best you'll meet," she added unflinchingly. "My firm's been pushing me to become a partner for a while now."

"Wow. Why don't you?"

"I don't know. I guess I'm just waiting to see if there's something better out there. Besides, I like my job as it is right now. Why change that? I'm comfortable."

I nodded approvingly.

"Now tell me, *De'Vannon*, is that your real name?"

I blushed. "Why, of course it is!"

"Don't worry, you don't have to tell me your real name," Halle said, teasingly. "Just know that if you ever need my professional support, your real name's the first thing you'll have to give me. After my retainer, that is."

Sally delivered Halle's martini. Halle smiled, took a sip, and winked.

I was about to grab another drink for myself before asking Halle to join me on the dance floor when I felt a hand grab my arm. I turned to see Thiago, sweat dripping down his face, and in a total panic. "Token! It's Julian! He's at Fancy's with another guy!"

My stomach lurched. "That scandalous, motherfucking, son-of-a-bitch!" I screamed and then bolted out of F Bar with Thiago.

* * *

Diego, the bouncer at Fancy's, saw me drive up in my Mustang, and pushed the line of people aside for me to run into the club with Thiago. We ran up to the bar where Grayson had his shirt off.

"Where the fuck is he!?!" I yelled at Grayson. "Where's Julian?"

Grayson frowned. "The blonde kid? I think he went up to the balcony."

I stormed to the stairs and marched up to the balcony. I could feel eyes following me as I did.

When I emerged at the top of the stairs, I saw Julian straddling some other guy and making out with him.

"OH, HELL NO!"

Julian jumped up. "Token!"

"No!" I was already turning to go back down the stairs. I had seen what I needed to see.

"Wait!" Julian caught up to me and grabbed my arm. "I'm sorry!"

"Fuck you! No! Get the fuck off me!" I shook my arm free.

"I'm sorry, Token! Wait, let me explain!" Julian was starting to cry.

"Explain it to your ho over there! I don't need to hear shit from you! You don't get to humiliate me like this and then make up like it was nothing! Go fuck yourself!"

"Token, wait!"

I slammed the balcony door and ran downstairs. Thiago tried to keep up with me, but I lost him in the crowd of people in the club. I ran out the door and across the street.

"Token! I'm sorry!" Julian called, still on the balcony.

I ignored him, making my way up to my apartment.

I kept all the lights off as I cried alone in the dark.

CHAPTER 16: MORTALITY

"Are you a man who has sex with men? Yes or No."
I circled "No."

I had gotten used to lying on that question on blood-test paperwork. I have O- blood, so donating my precious resource felt like a justifiable reason to sin a little.

After having my blood drawn, I made my way back to the Hyatt where I had stationed my drug dealing operation for the weekend. It was odd being back at the same building I had been pent up in during Hurricane Ike, but I liked having a sense of familiarity about my surroundings.

My stash of drugs welcomed me back to my room, spread out on the bed and looking seductively delicious. I had already bagged the smoke detector and was reaching for my meth when I heard a key card slide into my door. The door unlocked.

The door opened two inches and then banged to a stop as the chain lock did its job.

"Mr. Moore!" a man called from the other side of the door, using the name on my fake ID. "Open the door please. This is the hotel manager."

I was already collecting my supplies and stashing them into my safe. "One second!" I called back.

"Mr. Moore, I'm afraid this cannot wait. Please open the door this instant!"

I sealed the safe and made my way to the door. When I undid the chain lock, two large men in gray hotel security uniforms entered, followed by another man in a navy-blue suit. He had a name badge that said, "Wesley."

"What's going on?" I asked angrily.

"One of our hotel maids served a welfare check to this room and reported seeing obscene amounts of narcotics."

"That's crazy," I insisted, feigning innocence. *Damn, why didn't the maid just steal the shit? Fucking weak ass bitch!*

"Don't play innocent with me, Mr. Moore!" Wesley suddenly became enraged. The hotel security men kept eyeing the safe. "Don't you dare suggest that one of my maids is a liar! And don't start thinking that you can bring narcotics into my hotel and get away with it!"

Wesley marched farther into the room, solidifying his presence. He saw the safe and looked at me. "Open that up."

I shook my head.

"Open that up right now!"

"No, I don't have to do that," I said, trying to remain calm. I could no longer pretend to be dumb. All I could do was stand my ground. They couldn't open my safe without a warrant, and it didn't look like they had one.

"Dammit!" Wesley yelled. He spied the covered smoke detector. "That right there is a $300 fine," he said, pointing to it. "And don't think you're going anywhere until you pay for it."

I knew he was trying to hold me until he could get actual police to arrive, but I called his bluff.

"I'm sorry, but I don't have $300 on me. I'll have to go to an ATM. I'll be right back."

"Hey! Where do you think you're going!"

I made a mad dash for the stairs. If the hotel security men chased me, they couldn't catch me.

At the ground level I ran out the hotel lobby and bolted around the corner. Five minutes later I ran into a sports bar, purchased a drink, sat down in a corner booth, and called Ridley.

"Hey, Token, what's going on?"

"Hey, sorry to bother you, but I'm in a bit of a pinch. Can you meet me?"

"Right now?"

"Yes! Right now!"

"Uh, okay."

I shared my location with him.

"I'm on my way."

When Ridley arrived, I ordered some drinks for us and explained the situation.

"So, lemme get this straight," Ridley said when I had finished. "You need me to go into the Hyatt, pay for your room and your fine, and ask them to collect your shit and bring it to the lobby?"

"That's right. And I promise to pay you in drugs, cash, or whatever. Here." I pulled out a stack of bills and handed him $1,000. "That should pay for everything at the hotel, and you can keep whatever is remaining."

Ridley took the money and held it in his hands. I could tell he liked the feel of so many Ben Franklins at once. "And once all your shit's in the lobby, you're just gonna go in and grab it?" he asked.

"Yep! If they've got the police involved, you'll be able to tell me, but there's no way they can keep cops waiting around for an undetermined amount of time. For all they know, I'm not coming back."

Ridley shrugged. "Okay. This seems fine."

"Thank you, darling."

One hour later, Ridley called to tell me everything had gone according to plan. Relieved, I ordered myself another drink, and waited. I wanted to outwait Wesley in case he was sticking around to try and catch me. My skin was itching for my meth, but I forced myself to wait.

It was 10pm when I called the Hyatt.

"Hi, is Wesley there?"

"No, I'm sorry, but Mr. Wesley left about an hour ago."

"Okay, good to know. Thank you! Bye."

I could taste my victory.

I walked back over to the Hyatt. Brand new staff greeted me in the lobby. I asked for my bags, and they brought them out from behind the counter. I made a speedy exit to my Mustang and speed the fuck off. Everything had gone according to plan.

* * *

"If you ever need someone taken care of, I'll do the deed for a $1,000 flat, no questions asked."

Cole wasn't a tall man, but his muscles were toned, and his skin was covered in smokey tattoos. Ridley had invited him over to my apartment, and tucked under his loose-fitting tank top I could see the hilt of a large knife. Cole was crazy. And I was embarrassed because I had also invited Halle over. It had only been a few weeks since I'd met her at F Bar, but I made a fast habit of inviting her over to my place as frequently as possible.

Halle drove up in a jet-black Mercedes-Benz and was dressed to kill in a black backless dress and matching six-inch heels. I had been sure to purchase a tall bottle of Grey Goose before she arrived, and she listened to Cole unflinchingly as she sipped from her ice-cold glass. "Why $1,000?" she asked, suddenly. "That seems like a small price to pay for taking a life."

Cole grinned, as if he'd expected that question. "If someone is willing to pay me the money, then the dead skin must've done something to deserve it."

Ridley crushed a meth crystal on my countertop. Halle seemed unfazed by the entire scene. In fact, she seemed to be enjoying herself. "And what kind of people are paying for these jobs?"

"Ah, come on!" Cole exclaimed. "I can't share that. That'd be bad for business! But I'll tell you what, some of the people I roll with would pay an even higher price for this T here. This is some good shit, Token! You should come to a party I'm attending tomorrow night! The people there would be all over this shit! It's at Hotel ZaZa in the Black Label Suite."

"Hotel ZaZa!" Halle spoke up. It was the most animated I'd seen her. *"Damn!"*

Based on Halle's reaction alone I knew I didn't want to miss this party. Cole was certifiably crazy, but I got the sense that he'd be worth the ticket to a party at Hotel ZaZa.

* * *

Every square inch of Hotel ZaZa was designed for royalty.

In the Black Label Suite a crystal chandelier hung over a marble countertop covered in champagne bottles resting on ice. Polished black leather cushions were on all the chairs except for two chairs so large they may as well have been thrones. Those chairs had zebra fur backings and arm rests, and alligator skin cushions.

Very few people in the room were sitting, though. Men were half dressed in their tuxes and women in bunny suits were walking around with their tits flying free. The wildest of these people were putting the bedrooms to *very* good use. Cole was quick to greet me when I entered, and he wasted no time introducing me to the other people in attendance.

"This is Mr. McMahon. He owns a manufacturing plant just outside of the city."

"This is Mr. Eldridge. He's a venture capitalist and owns about three multimillion-dollar companies."

"This is Mr. Powers. He's an assistant to the attorney general."

They all asked for my number, and I gave it gladly.

"This is Dr. Chaffley. He's a dentist."

"Nice to meet you, doctor."

"And *you*, Token. Do you sell molly?"

"I do! Is that your poison?"

"No, I prefer cocaine for myself, but I make molly. It's quite easy, and I'd be happy to supply it to you directly. You know, cut out any middlemen."

"That sounds fabulous!"

"Great! Let me get your number."

Then one girl approached me. She wasn't wearing a bunny suit, but she must have had triple-Z boobs under her skintight blue dress.

Cole introduced her. "Ah! Token, meet Nora!" I shook Nora's hand. "Nora owns three alcohol labels, and her husband owns the distillery. Now, if I remember correctly, Nora, your husband likes molly, but you like Tina."

Nora smiled and nodded. "That's right! Now if you'll excuse us, Cole, I'd like to talk about some private business with our dear Token, here."

Cole obliged, and Nora guided me to a table and poured us both a glass of champagne.

"Look," she said, "if Cole says your shit is good, I believe him. But I don't want any mainstream wholesale shit, no matter how good it is. What's your top shelf crystal, and how much does it go for?"

I thought about the rainbow meth and what Scarlet had told me about it, but Nora didn't look like someone who used needles. "How do you take it?" I asked.

"I prefer Ben Franklin to kiss it first," she said. I looked at her inquisitively, not getting the reference. "I snort it," she clarified.

I looked Nora squarely in the eye and said, "My blue Hope Diamond T goes for two hundred bucks a gram."

Nora smirked. "Now that's what I'm fucking talking about! Here, take down my address. I want you to come over tomorrow and show it to me."

By the end of the hour, I left the party with a dozen new high-profile clients, one guaranteed purchase, and two bottles of champagne. I fully intended to keep this party going.

* * *

Two blood red Ferraris slept peacefully in the semicircle driveway in front of Nora's four-story mansion on the border of Downtown and Midtown. I was glad I still had my white Mustang. I couldn't imagine parking a boring car—like Baker's Toyota—next to these upscale beauties.

The door was unlocked, just as Nora had told me it would be, and I entered into a brushed metal art deco wonderland. Gold and silver diamond designs covered the carpet and archways partitioned one room from the next.

"Token! Right on time! I love punctuality. Come in!"

White pom poms waved invitingly from the elbows of her silver satin blouse as she waved me into her kitchen. The white cabinets seemed to welcome the sunlight pouring in from floor to ceiling windows, which made me wonder how this house could be so brightly lit for someone who claimed to enjoy ice.

"Well, let me see! Let me see!" she begged excitedly, like a little school girl.

I presented an ounce of blue Hope Diamond crystals that rivaled the sheen of her black marble countertop.

"Oh my God!" Nora exclaimed. She picked up a crystal and held it to her eye. "This is fucking unbelievable!"

She placed the crystal back down on the counter and opened a drawer by her waist. She pulled out a Black Amex card. I watched as she impatiently crushed the crystal, returned the Amex card to the drawer, and pulled out a $100 bill in its place. Her hurried movements slowed down to a practiced, dainty approach as she bent over her triple-Z boobs and snorted the powder through the bill.

"Holy fucking shit," she said after soaking it in. "Holy shit!"

"I know, I know, it's the best," I said cockily.

"Okay, you can come over any fucking time you like. Seriously! My door will always be fucking open to you." She took a deep breath. "Holy shit this is fucking insane!"

She pulled out a wad of bills and handed it to me. I counted $600. *Easy money.*

"I need to tell my friends about this," Nora continued. "Seriously. They're all gonna want a piece of this shit. I'm giving them your number like right now!"

I grinned from ear to ear as Nora pulled out her phone and began typing away. When she finally stopped and put her phone down, she looked up at me and sighed in ecstasy. "Well, would you like a drink? Champagne?"

We drank and talked for hours. Nora turned out to be pleasant to be around. I loved observing her demeanor given the poshness of her lifestyle. And before we had even finished our bottle of bubbles, three of her friends had texted me to schedule drop-offs later in the week. I couldn't believe my luck. *With these rich-ass people as my clients, I could be making over $2,000 in weekly sales, easily!*

When the sun went down and I left to do my rounds among my familiar tweaker crowd, I only had one thought on my mind: *This is fucking awesome!!!*

* * *

Several weeks after I had donated blood, I got a letter informing me that my blood had been rejected due to the detection of Hepatitis B antibodies. I immediately made an appointment to go see my primary care doctor about it. The doctor informed me that I had "an extremely high viral load" for Hep B and referred me to a liver specialist. But after five minutes of talking to the specialist, something didn't feel right.

"The first step we want to take," Dr. Kang was saying, "are weekly shots, to try to get your viral load down which is now at about two million copies. I also want to order a biopsy to take a closer look at your liver to be sure there is no scarring. There aren't any other options. From all the research within the medical field this is as far as the treatment has come for your condition."

He had several forms in front of me and paged through them quickly, pointing to different spots that I assumed held decently valuable information as he talked. What I kept noticing, though, were the prices listed. The shots would total up to $300 per week, and the biopsy was going to cost $1,500.

Is this really fucking necessary? I wondered. *This guy probably just needs some extra dough for his dope.*

"Are there really *no* other options?" I asked.

"Well, we can do an ultrasound to see if we see anything, but that still won't be as conclusive as a biopsy."

I was hesitant. "Can I think about it?"

"Yes, of course. I cannot force any of this upon you. I can only tell you what I recommend. At the very least, I strongly recommend getting your blood drawn today so we can check for any other diseases you may have."

"Okay. The bloodwork is fine. Can you order the ultrasound first, and then give me time to think about the other options?"

Dr. Kang nodded. "Absolutely."

After the bloodwork and the ultrasound, I called Evangelist Nelson.

"I'm at the doctors."

"What's the matter, child?"

"It seems I have a liver disease."

"Have you been hurting?"

"Well, no. But the blood bank rejected my blood because they said they detected Hep B in it. Now I'm seeing a liver specialist, and he wants to give me all these expensive shots and chop up my liver for a biopsy!"

"De'Vannon, if you don't feel good about this, then don't do it."

"Will you pray for me?"

"Of course, child. I'm always praying for you."

"Thank you."

Knowing Evangelist Nelson was praying for me, I felt better.

I did not agree to the shots or the biopsy.

*   *   *

"You gotta sell that car, baby," Scarlet said.

"My Mustang?"

"Shit, what the fuck other car could I be talking about? Baby, you stand out too much. You can't be dealing at the level you're at and be playing like a high-roller, too."

"But my Mustang," I whimpered. "I love that car."

"I can see that, baby. But if you want to keep going down this path, you're gonna have to make some sacrifices. Have you ever heard of Frank Lucas?"

"No."

"Shit, he was one of the most prolific drug dealers, if not the most prolific drug dealer, in Harlem. He played the game masterfully and had the connections to stick around, but he got too flashy. Eventually his fucking brass caught up with him and he got busted. You remind me a lot of him, Token. And I'm worried you're bound to get fucking busted if you don't tone down your act."

After loading my fresh supply of meth into my safe, I got in my car to drive back to Montrose. I sat in the driver's seat without starting the ignition. I loved this car. I loved the feel, and I loved the attention. *How can I be a drug dealer and still have all the attention?*

I felt stuck. I couldn't argue with what Scarlet was saying. I knew she was right... but there was no way in hell I was letting go of my beloved Mustang. I turned the keys and closed my eyes, relishing in the sound of the engine firing up, and drove back to Montrose.

* * *

"So, I started dating a new guy," I told Carmen.

"Oh no way! Who is he?"

We were walking around Montrose and enjoying an evening out. She had been acting off, and was more reluctant to take my drugs, but I still liked her friendship. And I relied heavily on her voice on the streets.

"His name's Crimson, and he's beautiful. Tall, muscular, dark red hair, and he owns an auto repair shop."

"Are you in *love*," Carmen teased.

"Oh my God, no!" I objected. "I am infatuated, though."

"How did you meet him?"

"He's a friend of Nora's," I said.

"That rich girl you were telling me about?"

"That's right. I never imagined rich people would be such good clients, but I guess everybody wants their fucking drugs. They'll text me to just leave shit underneath their flowerpots, and they tip like twenty dollars per delivery. Sometimes they'll even leave the front door to their four or five story mansions unlocked and tell me to just leave the shit inside!"

"That's fucking insane," Carmen said. She sounded kind of distant, though.

"Are you okay?" I asked.

"Yeah. I'm fine. Tell me more about this Crimson. What's his place like?"

"Oh, he lives in a beautiful apartment on the top floor of this building with a fabulous view. It overlooks fucking everything."

"That sounds nice."

"Girl, it's glorious."

Carmen was rubbing her arms uncomfortably. "Hey, De'Vannon, do you have any drugs I could buy off you?" she asked.

I looked at her curiously. *She's been trying to avoid my drugs for weeks, and now she fucking wants to make a purchase? She's never had to buy drugs from me before. And what's she doing calling me by my real name?* Something didn't feel right.

"No," I lied. I had anything she could have asked for in my pockets, but I didn't want to do business with her until I figured out what was going on.

"Oh," Carmen said. She looked genuinely disappointed.

"Sorry," I replied. "I know. Unusual."

Carmen knelt down and pulled up one of her socks, both of which had fallen down to her ankles.

A police siren sounded, and I turned to see a patrol car pulling up beside us. With the window down, the officer in the passenger seat motioned for us to stop. "You boys doing alright?" he asked.

"Yeah, is something the matter, officer?" I responded.

There was a pause as the officer looked down at Carmen's socks and then the officer said, "Nope. Just doing a random check."

Without another word from the officers, the car pulled away.

I looked at Carmen, stunned. "What the fuck was that about?"

"I don't know," she said, but she wouldn't make eye contact with me.

* * *

The letter sat on my kitchen counter for a week, unopened. *"Your test results inside,"* the envelope read. It was from the lab that had done my ultrasound. The thought of opening it made my stomach lurch. I felt like inside I would discover the trial that Evangelist Nelson had forewarned I would go through, and I wasn't ready. Not yet. I wanted to get high first.

"What the fuck is this letter that's been sitting on your counter for a week?" Halle asked. I tried to ignore the question while I melted a meth crystal in my pipe, mesmerized by the blue rock's change in form. "Excuse me, you gonna answer? Or shall I just open it for you? The suspense might be killing me, but if there's something that's killing you, don't you want to know?"

I saw the vapor form in the pipe and took a puff. *I suppose it wouldn't hurt to have a friend open the letter for me.* I looked at Halle and shrugged. "Go ahead," I said. "You can open it."

In three clean tears, Halle ripped open the letter and looked at it.

"Oh no," she said.

I nearly puked. "What?" I asked, the pipe beginning to shake in my hand.

Halle put a hand to her face. "Oh my, I am so sorry."

"What? What the fuck, Halle! What does it say?"

"It says... You *are* the father! Hahaha!"

"What the fuck?"

"You're fine, fool! Stop torturing yourself by not opening your damn mail!" She slammed the letter down on the counter and I looked at it. "It simply confirms that there's no scarring on your liver." I took an eager, shaky puff from my pipe. My heart was beating uncontrollably.

I'll be fine, I told myself.

"Oh, I'm sorry. I suppose that was mean," Halle conceded. I just continued to stare at the letter. "Are you okay?" Halle asked.

"Something doesn't feel right?"

"What do you mean? It says you'll be fine."

"Doctor Kang, my liver specialist, kept making such a big deal about giving me all these tests, and Evangelist Nelson said I'd be going through a rough time, so it doesn't make sense that everything can just be fucking fine!"

"Evangelist who?" Halle asked. "Never mind. Look, if you're so worried that there might be a mistake or something, or if you feel sick, make sure they forward these results to this Doctor Kang so he can take a closer look. Maybe he or she can see something they overlooked."

I considered Halle's suggestion. "That's a good idea," I finally said.

"Well, what the hell. I'm good for more than just entertainment."

* * *

I had just come from an ATM to make a purchase from Casey since Scarlet was sick.

The man who sat in Casey's kitchen was small, bald, and angry. His name was Little D.

"Ah! Token, meet Little D. Not your biggest fan, I'm afraid, but perhaps this is good! You two can sort out your discrepancies. Also, do you have any coke? I'm not out yet but may as well re-up while you're here."

I pulled out my personal teener from my pocket and tossed it on the marble island. I had more blow in the safe in my car, but I didn't feel like disclosing that in front of this angry bald man named Little D. Casey counted out his payment and walked it over to me before collecting the teener.

"What seems to be the problem?" I asked.

Little D took a big, hefty breath, and then spoke gruffly, one word at a time. "Stop. Stealing. My. Fucking. Clients."

He wasn't blinking and his face was glowing red with rage. *This guy's a sociopath.*

"All of my clients came to me first," I said reactively. "I'm not stealing anybody's clients." Little D growled. "People want my shit!" I exclaimed. "I'm not going to turn down someone who's asking for *my* shit."

Little D clenched his fists. "Oh, you think you can get away with this? Bullshit! You motherfucker! Midtown and Downtown are *mine*!"

"Now, now, let's be reasonable," Casey said calmly. He seemed completely unaffected by Little D's rage. *Maybe this is just the way Little D is*, I thought to myself. "The last thing we're going to be is territorial. Are there any clients in particular that you feel robbed of?"

"All of them."

"Well, that sounds like a bit of an exaggeration if I do say so myself," Casey said in a snarky tone. "I'll tell you what, if it's business you need, Baker is coming in an hour and could use a driver."

"I'm not a fucking chauffeur," Little D snapped.

"Of course, you're not. You're a businessman, and you'll do what's best for your business the same way Token or I would." Casey gave me a sideways glare as if he meant to communicate something to me by that last statement as well.

Shit, does he still want me to sell my Mustang and take the bus? I scowled irritably back at Casey. *Fuck you.*

The room was silent for a tense minute. "Well, if that's all, I'll be going now," I said. I was going to buy dope from Casey, but the room didn't feel right for that.

I was happy to be free of Little D and safe in my car driving home. Two minutes after pulling away from Casey's, though, red and blue lights lit up my rearview mirror and a police siren wailed.

Fuck!

I took a mental stock of all of my dope. *It's all in the safe in the trunk, I'm sure of it.* I pulled over and shut the car off.

Two policemen got out and quickly flanked my car. I was blinded by two flashlights.

"License and registration," the officer by my driver's side door said.

I pulled my real ID from my wallet and handed it to the officer. "My registration is in the glovebox," I said.

"Okay. Open it slowly."

The officer on the other side pointed his light at my glove box in anticipation. I could see that his free hand was hovering dangerously above his gun's holster. As calmly as I could, I opened the glove box, retrieved my registration, and handed it to the officer.

He shone his light back and forth from the ID to the registration card several times. As he did, I could see that the Houston Police Department badge on his uniform said 'Captain.' "Sir, please exit the vehicle," the captain said.

What the fuck? I hesitated.

"NOW!"

I did as I was told. As soon as I was out of my car, the captain shouted, "Get on the ground!"

"What?" I asked. *I must have heard wrong.* The captain grabbed my shirt and pulled me forward, kicking out my feet as he did. My palms burned as my hands broke my fall, stopping me from face planting on the street.

"Keep your hands where I can see them!" the captain shouted. I then felt another sharp pain in my back as he knelt on top of me.

"Ah!" I wailed. "What the fuck!"

"Shut the fuck up!" The captain began patting me down. As he worked his way down my torso, the other cop walked around to my open door and started rummaging around inside. *Can they do this?* I didn't actually know what the rules were. All I knew was that all my dope was in the safe in my trunk.

The captain patting me down found a wad of bills in my pocket and pulled it out. "This is a lot of cash, Mr. Hubert. What are you doing with so much money?"

The words strained out of my mouth as I struggled to breathe under the weight on my back. "I just came from an ATM," I said, which happened to be the truth. "And I have a job."

"Uh-huh," the captain muttered, unconvinced. He slammed the money down on the street by my face and stood up, relieving me of the pressure on my back. "Find anything, Jack?" he asked the other cop.

"Not yet," Jack said from inside my car. Then I heard a *clunk*. My throat tensed. Jack had opened my trunk.

"What do we have here?" the cop asked. "Come here Mr. Hubert." I stood up and obeyed. Two bright flashlights spotlighted my safe in my trunk. "Open the safe, Mr. Hubert." I didn't move. One of the flashlights skipped back to my face, and I flinched. "Open the safe," the cop said again, more sternly.

"Umm," my voice shook, "do you have a warrant?"

"Do we need one?" the captain asked.

"I think so," I said. The cops were silent. *I think I'm right. I don't think there's anything they can do!* Emboldened, I asked them, "Hey, what did you pull me over for? Is there any reason I can't go now?"

The cops remained silent. They knew their suspicions were accurate, but there was nothing they could do. Finally, the captain broke the silence.

"Fine." His voice grumbled like Little D's. "You can go."

* * *

I ran down the middle of the street like a lunatic.

"DE'VANNON! WAIT!"

Carmen tried to keep up with me, but a crack addict like herself was no match for a meth fiend like me. And after the "random" stop by the police the last time I was with her I was convinced she was an informant. I was having nothing more do with this bitch.

"DE'VANNOOOON!"

I could hear her voice getting farther away. I'd almost shaken her, but the street was long.

"DEEEE'VAAAANNOOOON!"

I finally reached the end of the street and bolted around the block. Then it was a familiar maze of turns to make it back to my apartment where I locked the door and caught my breath.

What the fuck is going on?

Why can't the world just leave me the fuck alone and let me do my thing?

* * *

"You gotta cut that shit out. We can't be havin' none of that!!!"

I don't know how the fuck Scarlet found out about the incident with Carmen. Anyone could have been hiding in the shadows of that long street, I supposed, but that didn't matter now. I sat silently in Scarlet's kitchen as she blasted her motherly furor down on me.

"Someone shouting your real fucking name for all of fucking Montrose to hear? Un-fucking-believable! That shit ain't gonna fly, Token. Pull your fucking shit together!"

I hung my head in silence. I was ashamed.

Scarlet took a breath and sighed. "Look, baby. I like you, but if you don't learn how to stay low, the game's gonna get you? You hear?"

I nodded.

"Good. Oh, and stay away from Little D. I hear that piece of shit's got it out for you. Angry son-of-a-bitch."

"What, like he's trying to get me killed?" I asked.

"I'm just telling you what I hear, Token. But listen, don't be thinking you can have all this power and not be making enemies, too. The more powerful you become, the more your lifestyle needs to change so that you can survive long enough to solidify yourself here."

I nodded... and gulped. *I didn't sign up for this shit. Selling drugs and making money was fun, but since when did all this extra shit get thrown in, too?*

I wanted to get high before driving home, but Scarlet had to leave to go make drops to some other dealers she was supplying. So, with itchy skin and jitters, I went on my way.

I wasn't sure if the black car following me was real, or a paranoid hallucination, but by the time I got back to my apartment I had made up my mind. I was moving out of Montrose. *Maybe that will finally shake Carmen and the police. Maybe that will make them leave me alone.*

* * *

I spent the last two weeks of November finding an apartment in the Galleria Area and moving. I got a huge, mansion style apartment.

Maybe now I can invite Crimson over. My view almost rivals his. And I have two floors!

But that fantasy vanished as soon as I blacked-out all the windows. I didn't even furnish my new place beyond my disco lights, a glass coffee table, a wooden kitchen table, a couch, and a couple chairs. Even my mattress lacked a bed frame. It was simple. As long as I had my meth and my privacy, I was happy.

DECEMBER 31, 2011

When I saw the name on my caller ID a chill went down my spine. I tried not to think about why Dr. Kang, my liver specialist, was calling me again, for the fifth time in a row, on New Year's Eve. Plus, this was a Saturday but his office was only open Monday to Thursday.

I didn't want to hear from him tonight, I had other plans. In fact, I had the entire evening mapped out on top of my kitchen table in front of me. First, I was going to take two bright red King Cobra ecstasy pills. Then I had an 8-ball of cocaine to polish off in the bathroom when we got to the club. After that I would take a few hits of Tina from my skull pipe. The T I had was beautiful, with large blue iridescent crystals that were nice and thick. Finally, I had plenty of crack to finish out the night.

It was going to be a great New Year's, and the last thing I needed was bad news about a test result. The blood work results had been pending for over a month now and Dr. Kang didn't say anything during any of my calls to check up. *He doesn't get to crash my New Year's Eve party!* I pressed ignore and sent Dr. Kang's call to voicemail.

"You ready to go, D?" asked Halle, poking her head into my bedroom. She was looking fabulous in a black and silver sequin dress and brand new stilettos. "We're heading out, Player. Let's move." I grabbed my collection of goodies, popped the King Cobras into my mouth, and thirty minutes later we were strolling up to our favorite club, F Bar. We walked past the line of onlookers stretching around the block as the bouncer pulled back the velvet rope and waved us in.

Stepping into F Bar, I started to relax. The stress of the past few months melted off me. I could feel the music before I heard it. The beat thumped through my body as I stepped across the familiar black and white checkered floor and passed underneath a giant crystal chandelier bathed in disco lights. Those King Cobra pills were starting to kick in and I felt feisty. I caught my reflection in one of the full-length mirrors and noted that I looked damn good, too.

As soon as the DJ saw me, he waved and nodded. Then he immediately swapped the track to my favorite song, *Get Outta My Way* by Kylie Minogue. I made a mental note to get the DJ a drink later on. Then I let my body go free. Halle and I hit the dance floor like divas, and I reveled in merging myself with the throng of bodies all pulsing to the beat. I mouthed the lyrics along with Kylie and everyone else on the dance floor. It was good to hear my song.

The ecstasy was flowing through my system and soon even my skin was dancing. I started making eye contact with all the hot guys around me. Finally, one of them stuck his tongue out and winked. I grabbed him and pulled him into the bathroom. I drizzled a line of coke down the middle of his hard dick and snorted that shit for all it was worth. Then I inhaled his dick and sucked it until the surreal flavor palate of cum and coke danced across my tongue as he climaxed.

Then he took a bump and motioned for me to bend over. He stepped toward me, stroking his dick. I could see beads of sweat forming on his skin. The temperature in the stall suddenly felt ten degrees higher and I needed his heat to help me acclimate. Just then my phone buzzed in my pocket.

"I'm sorry, one second," I said as I awkwardly took out my phone. The stranger cuddled up temptingly close to me as I read the notification that I had "1 New Voice Message." It was from Dr. Kang. *It's bad. I know it's bad. Just let me have this one last moment of fun.*

"I'm sorry," I said again, motioning for the stall door, "I have to take this. It's an emergency." To my relief the stranger didn't protest as I made my way out of the bathroom.

The music from the club was so loud I had to walk a block away to find a quiet spot. Standing on the curb, I pulled up my voicemail. The night was calm and the winter air was crisp and clear as I navigated to Dr. Kang's message. *You can handle this*, I told myself. But I only half believed it.

I tapped the voicemail and let it play:

"Hi De'Vannon, this is Dr. Kang. I've finished analyzing your test results. You're HIV positive. Give me a call as soon as you hear this message, we need to make sure you're not out there spreading this disease around to anyone else. Also, how soon can you come into my office? This is urgent, please call me back at this number."

The air rushed from my lungs and my legs collapsed beneath me as I crashed to the curb. I felt like I'd been punched in the gut and I screamed as I fell but no sound came out.

Then, a few seconds later, came a wave of emotion.

Intense fear gripped me first. *I'm going to die*, I thought hysterically. Then I felt crushing shame. *I am disgusting, and less than human*, said the voice in my head. My hands balled into fists as my shame turned to rage. *How dare he leave this news on my voicemail!!! And on New Year's Eve!!!* I hated Dr. Kang. I realized his perception of me was that I needed to be warned so I wouldn't be out having sex with random guys. Then I felt an instant rush of guilt. I thought back to the bathroom stall just moments earlier. *I'm dirty and contagious. My life is a mess and now it's over.*

These thoughts rattled around in my head as I choked back tears. I'd learned to suppress my feelings with outstanding effectiveness while in the Air Force. But even I couldn't hold off this tidal wave of emotions. All the stress, trauma, and shame of the past few years was boiling over and spilling out. The church had rejected me, but my nightlife had allowed me to feel loved and respected again. Now my glorious lifestyle was crashing and burning all around me.

I felt hot mascara streaming down my cheeks. My chest heaved. For a moment I just let go and allowed myself to cry.

I cried so hard I couldn't breathe. I felt betrayed, naive, and alone. Between sobs I cursed myself for being so trusting and not taking better precautions with my health.

I couldn't go back to the club. I felt gross. *But this could also be my last New Year's Eve before my body goes to shit. I need to enjoy the time I've got left!*

I pulled my shit together, went back into F Bar, got a drink from Sally, downed it, found Halle on the dance floor, and danced harder than I had ever danced in my entire life. We dazzled brighter than the chandeliers and disco balls above our heads. We laughed, smiled, and then screamed when the clock hit midnight. Then we partied some more. And I savored every moment. *I need to remember this night.*

* * *

I cried a sea of tears as I sat alone in the darkness which was the void of my apartment. Every so often my phone buzzed but I ignored it. All I wanted to do was cry.

And then there was a knock at my door.

"Hello?" a familiar voice sounded from outside. "De'Vannon? It's Brianna. Are you in there?"

I stayed quiet. I wanted to see her, but I was too ashamed. *Look what I've become! She'll only think less of me.*

"De'Vannon, I don't know if you're in there… I sure as *fucking hell* don't know why you aren't answering my calls. But I'm worried about you. I haven't heard from you in a while. What the fuck's going on, man? Are you okay?"

I checked my phone. Not all the calls had been from Dr. Kang.

"De'Vannon, I feel like you're in there, can you please open up? I want to see you!"

I squeezed my eyes shut. I wanted to see her, too. But I couldn't bring myself to my feet.

I never saw Brianna again.

PART V
(2012)

CHAPTER 17: NOT LIKE THE PORNOS :(

It had been days since I had received my HIV diagnosis, but I lost track of how many. In the darkness of my apartment, I had no notion of when the sun was up or down. And I ignored everyone who came to my apartment looking to make a purchase. I needed my meth to last. I couldn't waste it on anybody else.

In my perpetual high, I didn't eat or sleep. I just drowned in my own tears.

I'm going to die. This is it. I'm going to die.

Fuck, I'm going to die! I'm too young to die!

I listened to Dr. Kang's voicemail on repeat. *Maybe I misheard something. Maybe this is a bad dream.* The words were always the same.

And so, with death now a certainty, I waited in a fog of meth smoke dazzled with neon yellow, green, purple, and blue disco lights.

The buzzing of my phone snapped me back to reality. *Oh no, not the fucking doctor.* When I checked to see who was calling, it was my boss from the Substation. I let the call go to voicemail, and then listened to the message: "Hey, De'Vannon. Missed you for a couple days now. What's going on?"

* * *

As soon as I arrived at the Substation, I headed straight for my boss' office.

"De'Vannon!" he said, startled, as I entered. "My God, look at the state of you. Are you okay?" Apparently, while everyone else had gained a few pounds over the holidays, I had lost several and looked like a skeleton.

"I'm sorry," I started to explain, but sensing the tears already beginning to form in my eyes, I pulled out my cell phone and navigated to Dr. Kang's voicemail. I couldn't find the words to say, so I just played the recording and handed my phone to my boss.

As soon as he heard the voicemail he closed the door to his office to give us privacy. By the time the short message finished, I was weeping uncontrollably. I could tell my boss was sympathetic but didn't know what to say or do. After a minute of watching me cry, he put a hand on my shoulder and tried to reassure me that everything was going to be okay.

I tried to work that day but I was way too emotional and so I went home early. I doubted I would ever be able to keep a clear enough head to do a job as dangerous as Substation work and I feared that I would get one of my co-workers killed. I never went back.

My massage school also left messages on my voicemail. *There's no way I could touch people now that I have HIV! Can I still be licensed?*

I never showed up to class again.

* * *

When I got back to my apartment I texted Halle to tell her about my diagnosis. Then I texted Scarlet because I had run out of meth.

I cursed the sun as I stepped out into a bright, clear noonday, and made the reluctant drive to Scarlet's place. She rolled her eyes at the sight of my Mustang, but thankfully didn't say anything. It was an easy pickup, and fifteen minutes later I was driving back to my cave of darkness and disco lights with an 8-ball of meth in my pocket. But then I saw red and blue lights glowing in my rearview mirror.

Fuck!

I pulled over across the street from an elementary school where the kids were out on their lunch break. I shuffled quickly in my seat to hide my fresh 8-ball in my underwear. *Why didn't I use my safe? I am definitely not thinking straight.*

"Get out of the fucking vehicle!"

I jumped in my seat, startled by the abrupt command. *Are you fucking kidding me? He hasn't even asked for my ID and registration!*

"Now!" the cop said, nearly yelling.

I unbuckled my seatbelt and exited my car.

"Hands on the hood of the car," the cop said.

I rolled my eyes and did as I was told. Immediately, the cop started patting me down roughly. His hands jabbed at my skinny torso searching for the dope I was certain he could not find. I began to have my doubts when he didn't hesitate to feel my ass. He practically jammed a finger up my crack, and I winced.

Then he worked his hands around my groin, and my heart sank. I felt the pressure of the 8-ball as the police officer's pat-down finally hit its mark. Suddenly, the cop's hands were unbuttoning my pants and pulling them down. Next, his hand was in my underwear reaching for the dope. *What the fuck? Is he allowed to do this?* Whatever the rules were, they didn't matter. The cop pulled out my 8-ball of meth with an, "Ah ha!"

Then he began reading me my rights.

The handcuffs were cold, and they bit my wrists as the cop yanked my thin arms behind my back and clasped them together. When he pulled me away from my Mustang to walk me to his patrol car, I saw a crowd of school kids lined up against the fence, watching me with quiet curiosity.

Crammed in the back of the patrol car, my legs were skinny enough to sit semi-comfortably. There were only a handful of inches between my knees and the partition between me and the front seats. As the car pulled away, I managed to twist my shriveled torso around so my handcuffed hands could reach into my pocket and retrieve my phone. I then crooked my neck and typed a quick message to Casey.

"Yo! I got arrested!"

* * *

"Hubert," one of the guards said in a monotone voice, unlocking the cell door. "Come with me." I gave the guard a confused look. "Now!" the guard insisted.

The guard steered me to a room with agonizingly bright lights and two chairs. I was thrusted down into one of them. The guard who brought me into the room then backed away to a corner while two other men entered, one wearing a gray suit and the other wearing a black one.

"De'Vannon Hubert, also known as Token," gray suit started, "the streets have a lot to say about you. You've got quite the reputation."

"I like to party," I said passively. "And where the fuck are all the hot ass guys with tattoos like they have in the pornos? This is not at all how I imagined jail would be." -

"Shut up and listen!" black suit snapped. "We know you're dealing all sorts of shit, and the system does not deal lightly with drug dealing fucks like you! If you want any hope of seeing the light of day without handcuffs, then you better listen up."

"We want to make a deal, De'Vannon," gray suit said, presenting a manila folder with a contract in it. "Be our eyes and ears on the street, and you don't have to go to prison. Help us get the bigger, badder, drug dealers supplying your business, and you can walk out of here today as a free man." He waved the contract in front of me, urging me to take it and look at it.

Even if these guys know I'm a drug dealer, what can they fucking prove? There's no way I'm betraying Casey, Scarlet, and my other connects. Plus everyone knows snitches don't live long on the street. I bet Halle could walk all over whatever bullshit they've scraped up. I'll take my chances, bitch.

I rolled my eyes and shrugged. "I'm good," I said.

"Come on," gray suit pressed. "What do you mean you're good? You're not good. But maybe for once you can–"

"Bitch, I said no! Now get that motherfucking paper out of my face!" I locked eyes with the man in the gray suit and made it clear that I wasn't going to take his deal.

The two men stood up and smoothed out their suits. "You'll regret this," black suit said before following his counterpart out of the room. Then the guard in the corner pulled me up and brought me back to the cell.

I laid on an uncomfortable bed in the City Jail cell and waited. I didn't eat, drink, or sleep, and I certainly didn't shit or piss. The cell had two beds, one toilet, and no partitions or curtains to create a sense of privacy. I was alone in the cell but I still felt exposed. *I'm not degrading myself,* I thought to myself. *At least, not yet. Not until I absolutely have to.*

"Hubert," came the monotone voice of the guard again. "You made bail. You're good to go."

I gave the guard a more confused look than the one I'd given him just hours earlier. "Someone bailed me out? Who?"

"Some guy named Afonso Santiago. Now let's go."

Who the fuck is Afonso Santiago?

* * *

"Token! Hey man!"

"Thiago? What the fuck?" Afonso Santiago was just tweaker Thiago, the same tweaker who had introduced me to Daniel. "Your real name is Afonso Santiago?

"Yeah, man!"

"Why the fuck are you bailing me out? How much was it?"

$500. I mean, who the fuck else am I gonna buy fucking dope from? Daniel's gone. I can't fucking lose you, too."

"What about Casey?"

"Nah, fuck that. I don't know Casey like that. I only saw him that one time when you took us to his house. And Casey never lived *in* the fucking heart of Montrose like you did. When you were in the middle of the fucking scene, everybody knew they could trust you. And lots of them still do!"

"Damn. I thought moving was a good way to get the cops off my fucking back. Now I got my ass thrown in jail and people might trust me less."

"I wouldn't worry about it, man. I'm sure it'll be alright."

I had no concept of time while I was in my cell and didn't realize I had been in jail all night until I walked out into the blazing sunlight. I had Thiago take me to the car pound where I paid to get my Mustang back, and then drove back to my place. As I drove I couldn't help but think, *Damn. Thiago has shit luck for only picking meth dealers dying of HIV.*

* * *

I stared out the window of my booth seat at the Grand Lux Café, waiting impatiently for Halle to arrive as I sipped the Sprite I had ordered. I only wished I wasn't out in the sun.

Finally, Halle's black Mercedes pulled up. Her six-inch black stiletto heel shot out of the driver's side door and planted itself firmly on top of the unworthy concrete. Halle's shades were blacker than her dress, and her strut murdered every square inch of ground between her car and the booth where I was seated inside. When the waitress came, Halle just said, "Water with lemon," and waved the server girl away.

My admiration turned to timidity the second Halle removed her shades to reveal the ire of her glare. "What the fuck have you gotten yourself into, De'Vannon?"

I explained everything that had happened with the arrest. I could see clearly that Halle wasn't going for any bullshit. She remained composed as she listened, but as I told her about the cop searching my pants, I could see her bite her tongue with relish, and her eyes lit up. *What is she thinking? Is there something here that she could use to help me?*

When I finished talking, Halle just looked at me.

"Well, what do you think?" I asked.

"Did you bring what I asked?"

I passed an envelope with $600 in cash across the table; her retainer, rated for friends and family. Halle opened the envelope and examined the contents. She smirked. She loved getting paid. As soon as the envelope was stuffed in her purse she looked at me and said, "While you clearly had an 8-ball of meth under your dick, it sounds like the cops searched and seized it illegally. I'll see what I can do. So long as you don't skip bail or do any other stupid shit, I should be able to get you a reduced sentence or possibly get the case dismissed."

I nodded, absorbing what Halle was saying. *I'm not gonna have to go to prison.* "Thank you," I said, appreciating that she was still willing to help me.

Halle shrugged. "Just doing my job."

"No seriously," I said, reaching across the table to hold her arm, "this means so much. Whatever you need, please, just tell me."

Halle patted my hand, and then stood up, collecting her stuff. "I like you, De'Vannon. You're a fun friend. I will try to get you a clean slate, but you gotta stop this shit."

I feigned stupid, even though I knew she was talking about the drugs. "What! Stop having fun? I thought that's why you liked me?"

"You can be fun without being a fucking dealer. Shit, you can be fun without even being fucking high. If you wanna pay me back as a friend, and not just as a professional service provider, then *stop this shit*. Hell, at the rate you're going, you'll end up dying like fucking Tony Montana with a face full of coke and a chest full of bullets. I don't want that for you, but it's up to you to knock this shit out."

Halle grabbed her purse and walked out. She didn't know that dying as fucked up and high as Tony Montana was exactly my goal. It sounded infinitely better than dying of AIDS.

* * *

I had just returned to the darkness of my apartment with a fresh supply of meth and was stripped down to my underwear, ready to get high, when Casey called.

"I'm out of coke—"

"I'm not calling about your fucking cocaine, Token. Now come downstairs, we need to talk in person."

"You're outside?" It was still only the afternoon, and the sun hadn't yet gone down.

"Yes, and I'm itching not to be. So hurry up!"

I put my clothes back on and went downstairs. Sure enough, Casey was waiting in the parking lot with the engine running.

"What's going on?" I asked after we pulled away. "I thought you just wanted to talk. Where are we going?"

"What did you tell the cops?"

My stomach jumped. There was menace in Casey's voice. *Does he think I snitched?*

"I told those bitches to fuck off! What do you think I told them?"

"How did you get out so soon then?"

"Thiago bailed me out. Fuck, Casey! I wouldn't snitch! They tried to get me to talk, but I didn't say shit!" We were on the highway and Casey was driving rather quickly.

"Thiago bailed you out?" Casey sounded doubtful, and he was raising his voice to match mine. "Who the fuck is Thiago?"

"I brought him to your house that one time when you had passed out," I offered. "Turns out Thiago's real name is fucking Afonso Santiago!"

Casey flipped the blinker on and eased his foot off the accelerator. We exited the highway, and Casey took a couple turns to get us headed back to my apartment. I calmed down. Casey took a breath and seemed to calm down, too.

"I'm sorry, Token," he said, wiping his brow. "I had to be sure. The police posted on the Texas VINE website that you had been released from their custody yesterday, after being detained for only two hours. They didn't say anything about you being bailed out. It made it look like you'd struck a deal."

I couldn't breathe. *Those dirty motherfuckers! They can do that? They can lie?* When I finally caught my breath I screamed, "WHAT THE FUCK?" I sank into my car seat. I wanted to get high so fucking bad. "What does this mean?" I finally asked.

"It means the whole underground thinks you're a snitch. I'll do what I can to ease the rumors, and buy you some time, but listen to me, Token. Snitches get stitches and end up in ditches. You've gotta skip town. Get the fuck out of Houston. Okay?"

I stared down at the dark floorboard under my feet. All I wanted to do was to get high. I didn't want to fucking move.

"Do you hear me, Token?"

"I don't want to leave."

Casey stuttered, taken aback by my objection. "Did you fucking hear what I just said? The criminal underworld thinks you're working with the cops! If you stay, you'll probably get fucking killed!"

"I don't care! I'm already fucking dying anyway! What does it matter if someone else kills me first?"

We pulled up to a stop light, and Casey looked at me. "What the fuck are you talking about? What do you mean you're dying?"

The tears came back and I quickly wiped them from my face. "I got HIV!" I cried.

Casey was silent for a moment. A car behind us honked, and Casey realized he had a green light and drove. "Well, fuck," he finally said. "I mean, isn't there medication for that? Like, this doesn't have to kill you–"

I waved at Casey to shut up. "All I want to do," I said, "is get fucked up and stay fucked up so that when I die, I die high."

Casey didn't say anything for the rest of the drive, and when he finally dropped me off I did exactly what I said I'd do. In the safety of my dark apartment, I got as fucked up as I possibly could.

But the tears never stopped falling.

* * *

"Your honor, shouldn't it be the 3.5 grams of methamphetamine that's illegal, and not the seizure of it?" The woman prosecuting me was sweating as she watched her case slip through her fingers.

Halle listened, poised and steadfast as my court session proceeded. Like a lioness waiting patiently for her prey, she stood with a deadly vigilance by my side, her six-inch stiletto heels threatening to stab the first idiot to get in her way. I felt safe. "And which of the elementary school children would you like to call as your first witness to tell us how my client's penis looks or how his behavior was ever inappropriate?" she jabbed. Her voice projected with the authority of a royal magistrate, weaving legal vernacular like a seamstress of poetry, and cutting down the prosecutor's arguments with surgical precision.

The prosecutor looked worried from across the courtroom. She scowled at me as if I were getting away with murder and not possession of a controlled substance below the belt. *"Fuck you!"* she mouthed at me.

In less than 20 minutes, Halle had done her job. My case was thrown out for illegal search and seizure.

Outside the court's chambers I hugged Halle with all my might.

"Alright, alright," she said. "Now listen. Remember what I said. You got a clean slate. Now cut this shit out."

MAY 2012

...BOOM!!!

My front door burst into the apartment, flying across my foyer. A shit ton of men swarmed in.

"Show yourself you dirty motherfucker!"

... Another loud *BANG* reverberated from the back of my living room. Another dozen men swarmed into my apartment. By now I could read the "S.W.A.T." signage on the backs of these men's uniforms.

CHAPTER 18: WHERE DO YOU LIVE?

Harris County Jail was cold and completely void of sunlight, but I breathed a sigh of relief as I settled onto the only bedding available, which was a two-inch floor cot. The suspense was finally over. The police raid had happened. My time had finally come.

My teeth clenched at the thought of drugs, and I shivered.

Merciful sleep came quickly, saving me from my body's desperate cravings.

* * *

"Yo."

I felt a nudge on my shoulder and opened my eyes. One of the other guys in the tank was trying to wake me up.

"What?" I asked, annoyed.

"You gonna eat your food?"

I looked at my untouched tray of food: rice with slices of gray meat, green beans, coleslaw, a bread roll, and an apple. My stomach turned at the sight of it. I tried to contain myself from convulsing. *Fuck, I need drugs.*

"You can have it," I said to the guy. His eyes lit up in surprise, and without asking twice he took my tray.

I curled up in a ball on the floor and went back to sleep. The others didn't bother waking me up again. I slept for the majority of the next five days.

* * *

Casey bailed me out.

The guards gave me a pair of shoes some other inmate had left behind. They barely fit but I was thankful.

It was midnight when he picked me up from County in a brand-new white Hummer SUV. Blue light from his dashboard highlighted the creases of pure rage on his face. I could see he was grinding his teeth, waiting to release the tension. "What the fuck," was the first thing out of his mouth when he saw me, his perfect English landing sharply on the consonants. "Did I not tell you to stay fucking low? Get in the fucking car."

I got in, but I wasn't ready to take shit from Casey yet. As soon as he started driving, I said, "You still owe me for my last order which I paid for in advance!" I was referring to the order of meth I had been waiting for when my apartment got raided.

"I knew you were gonna say that," Casey shot back. "You know how I knew you were gonna say that? Because you're fucking predictable! You put yourself out there for everyone to see! You were practically begging for this shit to go down! You want your fucking meth? It's in the fucking glovebox."

I opened the glovebox and sure enough, the meth was there.

"It wasn't all my fault," I argued. "Ridley fucking snitched."

"Bullshit!" His voice was on the verge of cracking. "Informants are part of the game, Token! That's no fucking excuse!"

I was silent. I didn't like Casey being mad at me, but he was one of the only people who could help me.

"That does explain why Ridley was seen driving around in your Mustang, though."

I looked at Casey in shock. *Ridley has my Mustang? What the fuck! Who else has been stealing my shit?*

"Take me to my place," I demanded.

"You shouldn't go back there," he shot back.

"Casey, I don't give a fuck what you think! I need to check on some shit at my apartment!"

Casey rolled his eyes, but he turned in the direction of my apartment. "I've got a lawyer I want you to use. He's good with narcotics cases."

"I didn't have any meth when they arrested me. Yo, the only dope in my place was Ridley's Adderall."

"Still, you'll want to use him. Trust me, he's good."

I wanted to call Halle, but I stayed quiet. Halle had gotten the previous case against me thrown out and I trusted her, but I felt like I owed Casey. If there was one thing I could do to ease Casey's anger, it was to speak to his fucking lawyer.

* * *

When Casey dropped me off at my apartment, I went in through the back. I didn't want to risk being seen walking in since the last time I was there I had been escorted out by a S.W.A.T. team.

The place was torn to shit. Other people had clearly been through since the cops completed their search. The front door was still smashed in and lying in the foyer.

I found my wallet and my passport. My cash had been swiped, but my real ID was still there, and so was a debit card (although it was probably out of funds). I hadn't paid rent in months.

There was broken glass in the kitchen, and most of my appliances were gone. Every single one of my knives had disappeared. The sink was dripping water. I shut it off before going to my bedroom as butterflies filled my empty stomach.

Socks and shirts were strewn about my room. Even my Lakewood Choir suit was missing. My heart sank. *They better not have stolen my underwear collection.* I opened the closet and walked in. Sure enough, most of my clothes were gone. All of my shoes had been stolen. I turned my attention to the shelf that held my prized collection of underwear. It had been wiped clean.

My chest tightened. "No, no, no, no, no! FUCK!" I yelled and ran out of the closet.

I can't live here. I can't even stay the night here. What the fuck am I supposed to do?

I found my backpack. Somehow that had survived the intrusions. I filled it with as much clothing as would fit, and then stuffed my new supply of meth on top. Somehow my phone had also survived, but its battery had not. *Damn!* I knew there was a communications store around the block, so after doing a final sweep of the apartment, I walked out for the final time.

* * *

The sign on the communications store said "Closed." *Of course, dumb shit. It's two in the fucking morning!*

I looked around the Galleria Area. I had no idea where to go, so I sat down in front of the store.

This can't be happening to me. My life can't end like this. I can't die a failure.

The tears came slowly at first, but the longer I sat outside in front of the store, the more defeated I felt. Eventually it was hard to breathe because I was crying so hard. My chest hurt from the agony of my despair. It was like I was drowning myself.

* * *

The store opened at 8am but the owners were hesitant to let me in. I insisted that I just needed to buy a phone charger and they opened the doors. They watched me closely, but I didn't play any tricks. *I can't believe I have to convince these people that I'm honest!*

I held my breath when they swiped my debit card. "DECLINED." The message popped back in red.

Before I could try swiping the card again, the owner pointed to the door. "Get out!" he said menacingly. I opened my mouth to argue, but he spoke again. "Now!" I tried to convey my desperation, but there was no sympathy in this man's eyes. I turned and left the store.

Then I headed to the first trap house I could think of.

* * *

Suggs' trap was the perfect hideout. I was ready to get fucked up. *I hope he doesn't think I'm a snitch like everyone else.*

When he opened the door and saw me, Suggs didn't say a word. He took a drag from what looked like a fresh joint, and waved me in. *Finally.* My hands shook with anticipation as I pulled out the bag of crystals from my backpack. Suggs looked at me inquisitively and asked, "have you ever shot up before?" "No" I replied matter-of-factly. "You look like you could use a stronger hit than smoking. You wanna try it?" Suggs asked. "Fuck it why not?" I said excitedly.

Suggs fetched me his supplies for shooting up. While I was waiting I swiped a phone charger, a pipe, and some crack rocks I saw lying around.

Suggs offered to help me but I insisted on doing this myself. I had been curious about the process of getting the syringe ready, mixing the crystals with water, and watching them dissolve into liquid as I had seen my customers do countless times before. My heart pounded inside my chest, ready to send liquid glory coursing through my veins.

I tried to keep the needle steady as I held it to the vein in the crux of my arm, but the adrenaline was too much.

"OW! FUCK! SHIT!"

Blood shot up from my arm.

"What the fuck, man!" Suggs yelled. "Clamp it! You're getting blood on my ceiling, yo!"

It took several minutes for me to get the bleeding under control. Dried blood crusted my arm. Only when Suggs was convinced I was cool did he offer to inject my other arm for me. Suggs leaned over my arm, placed the needle up to my vein, and delicately punctured my skin. I felt the pinch, and then the warmth. It was like lava filling my body. And then everything was fuzzy. My skin tingled and I breathed in sharply. The UV lights in Suggs's trap house bloomed into violet suns. And my stomach fluttered, like it was filled with butterflies having an orgy. I was completely engulfed in this new sensation as I became aware of everything all at once and yet I was unable to focus on anything, except one thing. *I need to fuck!*

There was one other guy in the room who was smoking a joint: Otto, and he looked like he knew how to swing his dick. He stared absentmindedly at me from across the room, unsure of what to make of me. I could have flirted, but I was impatient.

"Are you gonna fuck me or not?" I asked.

Startled, Otto jumped to his feet. I walked to Suggs' bedroom, making sure Otto was following. The door closed, and Otto started fumbling with his zipper. I watched as he dropped his pants and then looked up at me.

"You're a big boy," I said teasingly. "Undress me."

"Hey, fuck you!"

I didn't flinch. "I'm waiting."

Otto scowled. He was angry. *Good.* He spun me around, loosened my belt, and yanked my pants down. When he saw that I was not going to bend over on my own, he grabbed my shoulder and pushed me over the bed. *That's more like it.*

Otto fucked me angrily, his hard dick sending vigorous vibrations all throughout my body. The crystal made the earth move with each thrust, and I gasped as I ejaculated on Suggs' bed. Otto came shortly thereafter.

"Yo, let's get outta here, man," Otto said, zipping up his pants.

"Okay, where do you want to go?" I asked, ready for anything. I had nowhere to be.

"Let's grab a porno from a video store and go to my place."

It sounded hot, so I agreed. Otto had certainly earned another round of ass from me.

* * *

It was a 30-minute drive from Sugg's trap to the porno store near Otto's place. When we stepped out of his car, it was nighttime again. As I adjusted to the streetlights, though, I saw something that made me want to scream.

"Are those my orange Skechers!"

"I don't know what you're talking about, man," Otto said, blowing me off. He started walking quickly and I hurried to keep up.

"Where the fuck did you get those shoes?"

"I bought them, bro. Get off my fucking case, I've never taken shit from you."

"Right, and you just happen to be wearing a pair of Skechers that look exactly like the ones I had stolen from me, like, fucking yesterday!"

"Shoes can look the same, dude. Seriously, calm the fuck down. Stop acting like a little bitch."

Otto stormed into the porno store, hoping I would drop the conversation once we were inside. But I didn't.

"Who the *fuck* are you calling a little bitch?"

Otto tensed up, uneasy that I was willing to throw a fit inside the store.

"Excuse me," I pressed, "I want a fucking answer from you. And I want my fucking shoes back!"

Otto turned on me and faked a punch at my face, stopping his fist inches from my cheek. "Hey, I'm not looking for a pain in *my* ass, bitch! Get off my motherfucking case! Bitch, I will beat the living shit out of you! Fuck off!"

Otto walked out, slamming the door behind him, leaving me alone in the video store.

Behind me, I heard a snap. I turned to see a girl behind the counter waving her fingers. "He no good for you! You don't need him!"

I nodded, glad to have some kind of support, but I was still mad. *All my shit is just scattered across Houston, and people are wearing it right in front of my face!* I didn't want to go back outside. *Next thing I know I'll see Ridley driving around in my Mustang.*

I wandered to the upstairs section of the video store and pretended to browse the titles.

What the fuck am I going to do? I can't go back to the apartment. I don't even have the money to catch the bus back to Montrose. Where am I going to go?

I sat down in the middle of the aisle, pulled my knees up to my chest, and wept.

I heard the sound of footsteps coming up the stairs. It was the girl from behind the counter. She looked at me with pity, walked over, and sat down next to me. "What's your name?" she asked.

My heart reached out toward her. She couldn't have been older than 16, but she had so much motherly compassion. "I'm De'Vannon," I replied, wiping tears and snot from my face.

"Where do you live, De'Vannon?"

As soon as the tears had stopped, they started again. For the first time in my life I couldn't give an answer to this question. *Holy shit. Am I homeless?* I couldn't help but face my new reality. I didn't have the strength to respond with the only truthful answer which was "nowhere", so I buried my face in my knees again and sobbed.

I could taste the tears on my lips, and they were bitter. I hated the situation I was in and I blamed myself for it. Eventually I got tired and stopped crying. When I calmed down, the girl said, "You gonna have to learn to survive."

I looked up at her. The intensity in her eyes matched the tone of her voice.

"The streets won't be nice to you. They gonna take try to take everything from you. You have to learn to pay the price to survive. Everything gonna cost you something."

"I don't have any money," I interjected.

"What do you have?" the girl asked.

I had some crack. I presented it. Without saying another word, she plucked a rock from my bag and stood up. I got the sense I was supposed to follow her. We walked downstairs. Another girl had taken over the shift at the counter, and she pretended not to notice as we walked behind her to a door I hadn't noticed earlier.

The passage was short, dark, and narrow, but when it opened up, I quickly understood what the girl had been trying to tell me upstairs.

We were in a theater, and standing in the aisles were trains of men waiting to fuck one woman who sat up on the stage. The seats were littered with naked men giving and receiving blow jobs, and the back of the room was lined with plywood stalls, from which I could hear muffled moans and screams.

"If you wanna make money, you have to use your body," the girl said, and she motioned for me to follow her out of the theater and into a different room. She continued to talk, but I tuned her out. *This cannot be happening,* I thought to myself. *Surely, I have some dignity left! I'm not going to sell my body for a living! If I don't find a way out of this mess I've made, I will sooner die than sell myself to survive.*

"We give you one night to think about it," the girl said, and then she left me in the room.

I put my phone on the charger then pulled out my pipe and smoked the rest of the crack I had left. *This is not happening,* I told myself as I lay down on the hard linoleum floor and fell asleep.

* * *

The buzzing of my phone woke me up. It was Casey calling.

"Where the fuck are you?"

"Why?" I asked, groggily.

"The lawyer I was telling you about is ready to meet you. Now where the fuck are you?"

I didn't want to tell Casey the truth, so I tried to remember what else was on the block by the video store.

"Burger King," I lied.

"Okay, I'm on my way," he said, and then hung up.

The girl working out front said nothing as I left, and as I heard the door swing shut behind me, I prayed to never step foot in a place like that again.

I was waiting outside the Burger King when Casey arrived. He took one look at me and said, "You look like shit." I looked down at my shirt and noticed that I had bloodstains on my torso from my attempts to inject myself the day before. "You can't meet my lawyer looking like that."

He drove us to a Walmart, handed me $50 cash, and sent me in to buy more presentable clothes.

I found an extra small shirt that I liked and picked out the smallest pair of jeans I could find, which was a size twenty-six. The shirt fit me like a poncho, and Casey made an effort to keep his tense lips shut as I walked out looking just as much the fool as I did when I entered. *At least these clothes are clean.*

The narcotics lawyer's name was Miller, and I heard him before I saw him. Loud groans echoed from Casey's living room as we entered through the back door to his kitchen.

"Miller!" Casey shouted.

"Almost done!" came a hoarse cry from around the corner. Another moan eclipsed Miller's reply.

"Fuck!"

There was a minute of silence as Casey and I waited in his kitchen. When Miller finally rounded the corner, I saw a tired young man with dark bags under his brown eyes. "That's one hot ass fucking gimp boy you got there!"

Casey shrugged as he poured Miller a glass of water.

When we were all settled at the kitchen island, Miller explained what I was being charged with: a bag of 0.3 grams of cocaine, a bag of 0.3 grams of methamphetamine, 35 Adderall pills (which Miller said was a schedule-two drug), 12.1 grams of Lyrica, and eight meth pipes with residue.

"What the fuck?" I exclaimed. "The only shit in my place was the Adderall, and that wasn't even mine! And I cleaned those fucking pipes right before the raid!"

Miller took a patient sip from his water. I couldn't tell if he was bored, tired, or just a walking dead man. The bags under his eyes held his face in a perpetual zombified state of *Dude, I'm just doing my fucking job*. "There's not much we can do about the Adderall if Ridley was working with the cops and planted it. The good news is they can't get you for dealing with that shit. The other shit, though, that'll be tougher to prove. They'll probably throw in a lot so even if the jury agrees some of it is not legit, they'll still think at least one of the drugs was probably yours. But if you ask me, I don't see this going to a jury. I'm not saying you'll get off scot-free, but if you stay out of trouble, I think we can strike a favorable deal with the prosecution. Just stay low and don't do anything stupid. You'll be fine."

I looked at Casey and shied away from his scowl. *Lay low, stupid*, I could practically hear him say in his posh diction.

After the meeting, Miller left to attend another appointment (which I guess meant he had another boy-toy to fuck). As soon as the door closed behind Miller I turned on Casey. "Fuck you. I'm going with my own lawyer." "*But. 'I'm going to need some more money first.*

* * *

"I got two fresh sheets of ice," Scarlet said. "How much you got?"

The walk to Scarlet's place had taken me all night, and the sun was just peaking above the horizon when I had knocked on her door. I'd been wandering the streets of Houston for a few days hopping from one trap house to the next. I needed a favor, and Scarlet cooked the best T in town.

"I have nothing," I said, embarrassed. I hated being broke. It made me feel powerless.

"Damn, son! It's not like you to pack lighter than your own bodyweight! Well shit, I'll see what I can get you. It's not like me to front, but I happen to know you got a handsome clientele list."

I walked inside and waited in the kitchen while she went to her lab and emerged with a bag of clear crystals.

"Now here," she said, handing me the bag of crystals. It was over an ounce. I could easily sell it for a few thousand dollars. "Get the fuck out and go sell this shit. I expect six hundred dollars back from you in a couple days tops. Now I gotta go feed my baby. Fuck, he's fatter than you already."

I wanted to smoke some of the meth immediately, but I got out of Scarlet's way. I would need to be able to pay her back if I was going to have any hope of getting more from her. I knew she wouldn't front me twice.

The walk to Nora's mansion took all day. I snuck into a gas station bathroom to get high about halfway there. The sun was low in the sky when I arrived at Nora's door.

"Token!" she exclaimed, overjoyed to see me. She gave me a big hug, squeezing me so tight that her triple-Z boobs nearly suffocated me. She laughed. "Come in! Tell me, what's been going on?"

I thought about telling Nora about the drug raid, but then I worried she might kick me out if she knew the cops had an eye on me, so I said, "Well, my car got stolen." That was true, and it could help explain why I'd been absent.

"Oh my God! What the fuck?"

"And I know the fucker who did it, too. He probably skipped town already."

"Have you thought about hiring Cole to get him?"

I thought of the tattooed hitman. *"I'll kill anyone for a thousand bucks,"* he'd said, *"no questions asked."*

Ridley definitely had done something to fucking deserve it. That fucking snitch! I had been contemplating revenge against him, and Cole had definitely been on my mind. But what was left of my Christian values prevented me from taking the steps necessary to take the life of my archnemesis. "As much as I would like to off Ridley, I don't want blood on my hands! I just want my damn car back!"

Nora waved like it was nothing. "Suit yourself. If someone stole my shit, I'd have Cole stuff their dick down their face. Anyways, I'm sure you'll pick yourself up again. Whatchu got today?"

I pulled the bag of crystals out of my backpack and spread them out on the counter.

"Your glass is always the best, Token." Nora pulled out a handful of $100 bills and gave me all but one. The last one she rolled up and then snorted one of the crystals after crushing it with her Black Amex card. High class.

I was sad to hand over so much Tina, but I needed the money. *A few flips like this and I can put myself back on top again. No problem.* Nora told me about the latest parties she'd attended while I charged my phone.

It was midnight when I left her house. Walking through her neighborhood, with mansions lining both sides of the street, I felt lonely and out of place.

Who am I kidding? I'll never pick myself back up from this.

* * *

I lost track of days and nights as I wandered around Houston. Every so often I would find a private spot to smoke some dope, but other than that I just walked.

I could feel the smog begin to layer itself on my skin, and eventually I was revolted by my own odor. *I smell like walking death.*

There was no sleep and food was hard to come by. All I wanted was to kill time in peace, as high as I could possibly be, and beg my disease to take me sooner rather than later. Either that, or I needed a miracle.

Eventually my body demanded sleep. I revolted at the thought of it, but I could no longer keep my head up straight. I hardly had the strength to stand. *Maybe there's a dope house I can crash at.* I leaned against the nearest wall and looked up. It was the middle of the day and the June sun was blinding. When I figured out where I was, I picked the direction for the nearest trap I could think of and started walking.

"Token?" Mac opened the door to his drug den. "Holy shit! What the fuck is going on, man?"

He hesitantly pulled his hand up to his mouth, trying to be casual, but he was clearly horrified by my smell. He blocked the doorway.

"Can I crash for a bit?" I asked.

Mac looked at me, contemplating my request. "Go straight to the fucking shower, okay?"

I wanted to collapse on his couch the moment I stepped in, but I did as

I was told and headed for the bathroom. The other tweakers pinched their noses as I passed, occupied by the gay porn on the television.

One of them tried to resume a conversation that was happening before I entered. "So, yeah, Thiago got arrested, man. Can you believe that?"

The shower was miserable. I hated the weight of the water falling on my head. But I couldn't deny I was relieved to sense the odor wash away and down the drain. When I got out, I swapped my dirty clothes out for a new pair in my backpack, but realized I was out of underwear. *Mac won't mind if one pair goes missing, right?... No! Don't become a dope fiend. Don't steal shit!... What am I supposed to do, put on that rank underwear I just took off?*

I crept across the hall to Mac's room and nudged the door open. When I was sure it was empty, I slipped inside.

My heart sank. Dirty clothes littered the bedroom floor. And my underwear collection garnished the display. *This motherfucker!*

I stuffed as many pairs of my stolen underwear into my backpack as I could fit, and then put on four more. Then I marched back out of the room, across the hall, through the living room, and out the door.

"Yo, Token! I thought you were gonna hang!" Mac called.

I didn't answer. I kept walking. And walking. And walking.

Did one of them say Thiago got arrested? Shit! But wait, I know where he parks his car. Maybe I can sleep in it tonight.

I found the block Thiago's car was parked on and wandered around the neighborhood until the sun was down. My body struggled for sleep, but I kept it up and moving until I was confident I could sneak into the car without being seen.

Thankfully, I didn't have to break into his car since it was already unlocked. I slept in his backseat for the next two days.

Once I woke up I couldn't keep still. The sun was almost gone so I felt it was safe to emerge from Thiago's car and see where I would end up next. Even though I hardly ate or drank anything, I eventually did need to shit every so often. I tried to hold it in until I could crash at someone's house, but this time it was an emergency. I thought of going into a nearby store to use their bathroom, but then I thought about the looks I would get. *They might even tell me to leave.* I was tired of the humiliation. I was tired of being rejected. So, I found a tree in a nearby park, dropped my pants, and dropped a fresh river of shit at the base of the trunk. I wiped my ass with some leaves, and then covered the shit with some more leaves. Then I kept walking.

* * *

It was good to see Thiago after he got out of jail, but he wouldn't let me stay at his place when he went out for work. Thankfully, he did allow me to shower at his place before my court date. My phone charged in his living room while the warm water dissolved weeks of summertime dust and smog from my greasy skin. When I was finally done in the shower, I texted Halle to let her know where I was.

Halle stood tall, confident, and pissed. She wore a tight black dress, pitch black shades, and trademark six-inch stilettos. Her black Mercedes-Benz cowered behind her. I tried to keep my head up as I approached her, but she sucked her teeth and I cracked.

"I know! I'm sorry, okay? But what the fuck was I supposed to do about a fucking raid at my apartment, even if I did stay low?"

"Do you have the money?" she asked bluntly.

I handed Halle an envelope with $2,500 in cash. It was almost everything I'd earned since leaving Scarlet's, who I had not paid back yet. Halle snatched the envelope and peaked inside, her eyes brightening at the sight of the money.

"Okay," she said, opening the door to her car and sliding in. "Let's fuck some shit up."

* * *

"Hi, Mother."

"*Hey, sweetie. How are you?*" My mother's voice sounded calm on the other end of the line, but I could sense some tension.

"I'm okay." I kept my voice down, conscious of the people walking outside the court's chambers.

"*You don't sound okay. What's the matter?*"

"Um," I took a deep breath. Part of me wanted to return home to Baton Rouge, but a more stubborn part of me wasn't done with Houston. Plus, Halle warned me the best deal she could probably get me would be strict probation. I wouldn't be allowed to leave Houston for some time. "No, nothing's the matter, Mother. I'm just tired."

"Is work getting to you? You're still working, right?"

I fell silent. I didn't expect my Mother to ask so bluntly whether I was working or not. I hadn't clocked into work in over six months.

"Honey, I know you haven't found the right job since leaving the military, but you gotta stick with it. You'll get something eventually."

I gulped. "Yes, Mother. I know."

We were quiet for some time.

"What's going on, De'Vannon? This doesn't sound like you."

"I'm just tired!" I snapped back in a panic. She was asking way too many questions. Was she onto me? *Why did I even bother calling?*

"Okay, well get some rest then," my Mother said, signaling the end of our talk.

"Yes, ma'am," I said, and hung up.

I needed to get high. *How the fuck am I gonna get high if I can't pay Scarlet back?*

* * *

Astram's bathroom smelled of moss and sea salt, and his cum had notes of lime and almond. He sighed as I finished sucking off his soft, delicious dick. Then he passed me a teener of crystal, pulled up his baggy cargo pants, and walked back to the living room of his trap house.

"Okay, what does everybody want?" Astram asked. Several heads in the dope shack perked up. We all eyed the baggy cargo pants hanging onto his skinny ass.

"Yo, I'll take some Skittles!" someone chimed in.

"Reese's!"

"Lots of Reese's!"

"Yo, I'll take a burger!"

"Fuck you! Where the fuck is he gonna swipe a burger from?"

"M&M's and a Sprite!"

"Sprite for me too!" I yelled from the bathroom.

When we'd given our orders, a skinny Astram walked out. One hour later he returned much fatter.

* * *

"De'Vannon! Where are you?"

"Oh, I'm just out walking. Why? What's up?"

"Your dad and I are at your apartment, and there's a lady here saying you don't live here anymore? Did you move?"

"You're here in Houston?"

"Yes! Where are you? I want to see you!"

I felt my stomach tie up into a knot. "Um. What hotel are you staying at? Do you want to meet–"

"De'Vannon, where are you living?"

I couldn't avoid the truth any longer. I couldn't think of any lie I could get away with. There was only one answer to my Mother's question. Tears formed in my eyes as I formed the words on my lips, "Nowhere."

The silent response was torture. I started to weep.

"Where are you right now? We'll come and pick you up."

* * *

My parents' white pickup gunned around the corner and came to a screeching stop in front of me. I was seated at a bus stop and didn't have time to stand before my Mother jumped out of the truck and pulled me into a tight embrace. It was a short hug, probably because I hadn't showered in a week. She hurried me into the truck and we drove to the Marriott Hotel on Westheimer.

My parents rushed me through the lobby to the elevator.

In the room, my Mother said, "Leave your clothes in the bathroom when you're done. You just wear a bathrobe until then, okay?"

I nodded without saying anything. I was ashamed. I felt guilty cleaning myself up in a bathroom my parents had spent their money on because of me. But it was a relief to get off the streets.

When I saw myself in the mirror, I was surprised at how skinny I'd become. My cheeks were chiseled down to the bone, and my flesh was gaunt. I could count my ribs, and even wrap my arms around my torso in a self-hug and lock my fingers behind my back. *Damn! Look at that skinny ass!* I thought. *Sexy!* My fingernails and toenails looked like they belonged on a crow. I couldn't remember the last time I had clipped them or even brushed my teeth.

I considered smoking a little meth in the bathroom, but remembered I'd have to cover the smoke detectors first, and I didn't want to look suspicious. *I could just run steaming hot water and then smoke... but how am I gonna face my parents high on meth?*

The urge to tweak pulled on my conscience. My skin itched and begged for a hit as I forced myself to shower, put on the bathrobe, and exit the bathroom.

"Are you working?"

"No."

"Are you on drugs?"

"Um, No." I said looking at the floor.

My dad shook his head while my Mother pulled out a piece of paper with scribbles on it. Sitting on the bed across from my parents, I listened as my Mother began recounting the research she'd done while I was in the shower. "Your cousin Harriet works at the Veteran's Affairs here in Houston. She said they have a food kitchen. You're clearly not eating anything, so go there for meals. And the VA also has a program to help you find a job." My dad shook his head again. "First thing tomorrow we're taking you there, you hear?"

I pursed my lips. *This is going to make it really fucking hard to get high.*

"You have to do this for me, okay?" my Mother said, trying to keep her voice calm. I could hear a slight quiver, though, as if at any moment she might burst into tears. "Your dad and I can stay for about a week, and we can help you get a hotel room some nights after that, but you need to pick yourself back up."

I nodded. This was no multiple-choice test. There was only one right answer. "Yes, Mother."

"Good. Now let me see the size of your clothes, and your dad will go buy you some new ones for tomorrow. I'm not letting you out of my sight until you're at the VA office, okay?"

"Mother, just because I don't have a place to stay doesn't mean I have nothing to do."

"I'm not negotiating with you! Do you understand? You are staying with me until I know you can stand on your own!"

I sat in silent tension as my Mother examined the clothes I'd left on the bathroom floor. My skin burned. I needed meth.

* * *

I walked into the Houston VA Regional office and hospital at 10am and stood uncomfortably in line. It took so much effort to avoid scratching my arms. My neck prickled, and I worried that at any moment I might break out sweating. I ground my teeth in agitation as I waited in line.

When I got to the front, the old man behind the counter looked at me and grinned. He had a bushy white mustache and was sporting a black cowboy hat. Suddenly, he pointed his stubby finger at my face and exclaimed, "Yeah! Afghanistan! Right?"

I gulped and gave a slight grin, neither confirming nor denying his assumption. I had never served in Afghanistan. *Damn, do I really look like I've just come back from a fucking war?*

"How can I help you?" the man asked.

I was about to explain that I needed work, but something within me revolted. *I don't want to work. I want to get fucking high!*

"I need help getting off drugs," I said. I wanted to believe it, but I knew I was just leading the guy on. He sympathized and gave me some paperwork to fill out. I sat down against the far wall to complete the paperwork, but then I got to the line asking for my address. *Can I just leave that blank? Fuck it, why don't I leave the whole thing blank! I'm only here because my Mother is making me.*

"De'Vannon?"

I looked up. It was my cousin, Harriet. She sat down next to me and handed me a different form. *"Compensated Work Therapy,"* it said.

"Fill this out," she said. "Your Mother told me about your situation, so don't worry about your address. I'll handle that. Also, we don't advertise this too much, but if you need housing vouchers, the VA can give you a monthly stipend for rent. They're available if you ask for them. And if you need money, you can apply for a pension, too. There's lots of help for you here. In the meantime, finish this form and I'll get you signed up to work. Then you'll just have to pass a drug test."

Harriet stood to leave, but then she paused. "De'Vannon, I'm sorry to see you like this, but I'm here to help. Let me know if you need anything." And she was gone.

I felt sick. Harriet was sweet, and I didn't want to let her down, but there was no way in hell I could pass a drug test.

My parents left Houston after one week, but not before buying me a hotel room close to the VA hospital. They paid up front for a month. They wanted me close to the VA in case I needed emergency medical attention and so I could get to work without a car if I got a job there. They hoped I would work with my cousin and begin to improve. What they didn't understand was that I had lost the will to live and wasn't seeking to improve at all.

* * *

"I'm sorry, it's a busy day, hun, and we can't spare you a meal." The VA kitchen had been a reliable place to grab a meal before, but for some reason the lady at the front was stopping me today.

"What do you mean?" I asked. "I'm here, I'm homeless, why can't I get something to eat?"

The lady raised her eyebrows at me. "You don't *look* homeless."

I was stunned. "You mean to say I have to *look* homeless to get a meal? Nevermind that I *am* homeless, I have to *look* homeless, too?"

"I'm sorry, hun. We just don't have much food to spare, today. You look alright. We can't feed you."

I watched as all the other homeless veterans ate their first servings and then went back for seconds. I was beyond furious but mostly I was hurt. Typical VA bullshit.

I walked away starving. *Fuck this. If I look good enough to be turned away at the VA kitchen, then I must look good enough to go to a fucking bar. FUCK! I miss dancing!*

* * *

The music from Fancy's pulsed into the parking lot. I could feel it vibrate welcomingly through every skinny bone in my body. I wanted to dance so bad. I wanted to remember the feeling of walking into the scene and hearing the DJ play my favorite song. I wanted to have fun again.

The meth was no longer satisfying. Every day was a hunt for a kind of satisfaction that was always just out of reach. The joy of the high only ever seemed to exist in retrospect. I looked forward to the process of getting high, but the high itself never seemed to be high enough. It always fell just short.

I needed to remember my old love.

I needed to dance.

I walked up to the door where the bouncer I'd bought so many drinks for in the past checked IDs. I skipped the line and walked right up to him. "Hey Diego! I'm back!"

"Who the fuck are you?" he said.

"Come on, Diego. It's Token! Don't tell me you've forgotten me."

Diego gave me a puzzled look. "Nah, man. I don't know you."

I exhaled exasperatedly. "Fine. Well, maybe Grayson will remember me. Can you let me in?"

"Leave Grayson out of this," Diego said, suddenly aggressive. "Now go find trouble somewhere else."

"Trouble?" I said, trying to sound as offended as possible. *He's got to be playing with me. There's no way he's not letting me in.* "Diego, I just want to dance."

"Well, you can fuck off and leave us all alone, okay?"

"But–"

"I'm serious, bro! Fuck off!"

"Diego, stop fucking with me. It's Token, remember?" I stepped toward the rope that separated me from the music but Diego muscled up in front of me.

"Are we gonna have a problem?" he said, glaring down at me.

"Are you seriously not gonna let me in?" I challenged him.

Diego spoke into a walkie-talkie, "Backup to the front."

"Aw, fuck! Come on, Diego! What's the deal?"

"The deal is if you don't fuck off in the next minute, then the police will get involved."

"Why don't you just check with Grayson? I know Grayson!"

"I don't know how you know Grayson, but I'm sure you're no good for him."

I felt tears well up underneath my eyes. I had to get inside, one way or another. If Grayson could vouch for me, maybe I had a shot.

I lunged for the door.

Diego caught me. It was like running into an iron wall. He shoved me down on the concrete. A siren sounded and tires screeched as a cop car pulled up behind me.

"No!" I screamed and tried to run for the door one more time. Diego blocked me again, and soon two more pairs of arms latched onto mine and dragged me from the premises. Everyone standing in line to get into the club had looks of shock and disgust plastered across their faces.

In the parking lot, away from the line, the cops warned me to walk away. I could see my dream of dancing the night away was just that: a dream. Everything I wanted was just a few feet away. I walked off and wandered the streets aimlessly for another ten days. When I finally stopped to rest, in an alley behind a Chinese restaurant, my sleep was empty and dreamless.

* * *

"Mother, stop sending me favors."

"Baby, what are you talking about?"

"It's not helping, okay? Stop wasting your money on me."

"Honey, if I know for one night that you're safe in a hotel room and not on the street, then it's not a waste of money for me!"

"It's not fixing anything!" my temper erupted. "Just stop! Either I'm gonna fucking die out here, or some miracle has to happen, but this is not fixing anything, so please just stop!"

After I hung up with my Mother I looked nervously at my phone as I waited for the bus to take me to Montrose. I'd tried to ask Scarlet to front me some more T, but she wouldn't answer my calls. Now my skin burned for the relief of a high that was seemingly unattainable. I ground my teeth as I stared at the menu bar. It only had five percent battery left.

I had no money to take the bus, but I figured most times no one checks the bus passengers for tickets. The odds were in my favor.

A black sedan with tinted windows pulled up right in front of me and the passenger side window slid down. A man wearing dark shades looked at me from the shadow of the driver's seat. "Need a job, son?"

"What kind of job?" I asked, hesitantly.

"I stole a check. If you cash it for me, I'll split the money with you."

I thought about the offer. *Shit, I ain't got nothing else to do, and I'm flat out of money.* "Sure," I said. "Why not."

As we drove, I shuffled my feet next to a black backpack.

"Oh, sorry about that," the man said. "Here," he pulled into a parking lot, "just throw that out. I've no more use for that." Without giving his instructions a second thought, I opened the door and tossed the backpack out. Then we continued to drive.

In the parking lot of a Bank of America the man handed me a check, and a pen to endorse the back. It had the names of a couple in the top left corner with an address located in Corpus Christi. The check was worth $10,000. I shrugged. *Sucks for them.*

"Oh, and feel free to leave your bag here. No need to give security a reason for alarm. Just make sure you have your identification on you."

With my passport in my pocket, I walked into the bank and right up to the teller. I handed the lady the check and explained I wanted to cash it.

"Do you have a form of identification?" she asked.

I handed her my passport. She looked at it, and then looked at the back of the check for a long time.

A fat security guard approached from down the hall. *Oh, fuck!*

I turned to run. I weighed a pound and could easily outrun the guard.

"Wait! Stop!" he yelled.

The desperation in his voice awoke something within me. *Do I really want this? They have my passport! If I run, I will always be running.*

I stopped running. The guard detained me.

While waiting for the police to show up, I pulled out my phone to call the man who had set the whole thing up. I thought if I could prove I wasn't the mastermind behind this sham I would be shown mercy and not be taken to jail. And he still had my backpack in his car! But my phone was dead. I was shit out of luck.

CHAPTER 19: STUNT QUEENS

Normally I would have liked the fact that there was no sunlight in jail. But without dope, the vampire in me faded and the agony of my humanity set in.

Just a couple days, I told myself. *Then Casey, or Scarlet, or Thiago, or Halle, or fucking somebody will bail me out.*

Everything was indoors. The primary purpose of Harris County Jail is for it to be a "temporary" holding facility while cases are processed. At least this is what I was told when I asked why we were never allowed to go outside. *Prison* is where convicted criminals get the added perk of sunlight. In County, though, there was no way to conceive of the passage of time.

Just a couple days… but how long is a fucking day in here?

I kept my back turned on the shared bathroom which was exposed and open for all to see. Four toilets sat side by side. There was one shower and one sink. There were no doors and no partitions of any sort except for a waist level brick wall which spanned the length of the four toilets. For what good it did the wall may as well have not even been there. There was no privacy in the tank, but I held onto whatever dignity I had left. My bowels cramped, begging for relief. *Just a couple days. There will be another bond, a miracle, or something. Then I can shower. Then I can shit. But not here. Not fucking here.*

My face itched. The stubble was no longer stubble, and the oily residue building up at the roots of my beard burned. I tried not to agitate it. I sat still, staring at the concrete floors; the concrete walls; the concrete ceiling. The tank was stuffed with at least thirty bunk beds and damn near sixty inmates. Only a few inches of mattress separated me from the wire frame of my bottom bunk. I thought about tucking the thin sheets neatly in place, just like my days in BMT, but I never did. No one ever made their bed.

"Hey Crunch Bar! How you doin'?" one man flirted. The glass door of our tank was soundproof, but with a little wave he succeeded in getting the attention of a man in the tank across from ours who was lifting weights using bags filled with what I presumed was water.

Our tank was the "gay" tank, and the other tank was the "straight" tank, but that didn't stop the weightlifting man from smirking and playing along.

"Ooo! I think Crunch Bar likes me!"

"Tell Lilo to shut the fuck up!" another man shouted from the back of our tank.

"Who was that? Red?" the man named Lilo asked, still in a flirtatious tone. "How you doin' Red?"

"Fuck you!"

"Oh, I wish you would fuck me, baby. You cute piece of ass. Mmm-mmm! When I leave, I might get another DUI just so I can come back and see you, honey!"

Red screamed and kicked his bed. I could see Crunch Bar laughing in the tank across from us. Lilo shook his ass as he walked away from the glass and back to his bunk. His wristband said "Daniel McCarthy," but no one went by the names on their wristbands.

* * *

"It's so fucking cold!"

"It's always fucking cold!"

"Shut the fuck up!"

The tank was freezing at night, but I was sweating a river. I wanted meth... no. I *needed* meth. And though everyone complained about the cold, it was my shakes that drew the most attention.

The next morning, they gave me the nickname "Paris," after Paris Hilton. It was a sacred title for the wildest drug user in the tank. I also learned that "Lilo" was short for Lindsay Lohan, and that Daniel got that nickname for keeping pace with Ms. Lohan herself and her trips to jail. When it came to DUI's, Daniel had nine.

* * *

My stomach screamed at me. *Eat the fucking food!* I stared at the food on my tray that had been delivered to the tank. Everyone else around me ate greedily. I could hear them slurp the soup and smack their lips as if they were all crowded around me. Food was a rare commodity here, and if I didn't eat my food soon, someone would come asking for it. I hadn't yet discovered what would happen if I refused to give it away.

But my spoon stayed frozen in my hand. I still hadn't taken a shit yet, and I knew that the second this food entered my system I would need the relief. *I should just give in. No one's coming for me. No point in starving, especially if there's no dope.*

Reluctantly, I dipped my spoon into the bowl, fished out a carrot slice with some broth, and raised it to my mouth. It was bland, and in desperate need of salt, but it was warm enough. I consumed the rest of it quickly.

Then I ran to the toilet. I had finally caved in. To my surprise no one stared at me as I sat there which was a huge relief.

* * *

"What are you in for?" Topper asked me.

"Forgery of a financial instrument," I said.

"No fucking shit! Me too! What's your story?"

I told Topper about the man who picked me up in a dark car and told me to cash a stolen check. When I shared about the backpack that had been in the front seat with me before I tossed it out of the car, Topper exclaimed, "Yo! That was my fucking backpack! Holy shit!"

"What! No way!"

"Well, shit happens! Next week we'll probably meet the guy who tossed your shit outta the car. Anyways, most of the other guys are convinced you're a dealer of some shit."

My ears perked up. "Why? What do they wanna buy?"

"I don't know. Everyone here's into something different. Hell, I've talked to some guys who are schooling me on how to actually forge some fucking financial instruments!"

I nodded along. "Hey, is there any way I could get a Sprite in here?" I wasn't sure how long I'd been off meth, but I still craved the sugary carbonation.

"You could probably order something like that if you've got money on your books," Topper answered. "But you gotta have people on the outside funding you. Then you can order all the honeybuns and pickles and shit. Hell, if you wanna pay a little extra, some of these guys can take honeybuns and make a fucking cake outta them."

This shit I gotta see.

* * *

My Mother started putting the maximum $150 per week on my books, and I ordered my honeybuns and pickles and shit.

"Hey Hollywood! I hear you can make a cake out of honeybuns."

Hollywood gave me a wry smile. "Which honeybuns, Paris? The ones in that bag there, or the ones you got hiding in the back of your orange jumpsuit?"

"In the bag," I said as nonchalantly as I could. My stomach twisted in a knot at the thought of sex, though. *Don't they know I have HIV?*

Hollywood smirked. "Alright, I can make you a sweet thang, but it's gonna cost you all those pickles I see in that bag."

What the fuck kinda steep pricing is this? I tried to keep a straight face as I passed the honeybuns and pickles to him. "Show me what you can do."

* * *

SNAP!

I flinched as a big fist swung by my head and snapped its fingers damn-near inside my ear.

A big ass queen named Juicy got in my face. "Fuck you!" A spritz of spittle misted my face. Juicy opened up his arms wide, begging me to stand up and confront him. He must have weighed over 300 pounds, and I knew from when I was processed that I barely weighed 130.

I wiped the spittle from my face.

"What's the matter, bitch?" Juicy clapped his hands right in front of my face, causing me to flinch again. "Fucking come at me!"

Don't throw the first blow, the voice inside my head said. *Don't give this bitch what he wants.*

Juicy was about to talk more shit when from across the room I heard someone pipe up, "Ayyyy! Turn that shit up!"

There was a TV mounted on the wall, and someone reached up to turn up the volume. The "Bootylicious" music video by Destiny's Child was playing.

"HEEEEY!"

Suddenly the whole tank was a party, and every ass in sight was twerking. I took the opportunity and evaded Juicy, joining in the fun. I hadn't danced in so long.

"Turn that fucking shit down!" Juicy yelled from across the tank. We all ignored him.

"Bite me, Crunch Bar! Come bite this ass!" I could see Lilo up against the glass door with two other guys twerking their asses in the direction of Crunch Bar and the other guys in the "straight" tank.

"You like this shit, Crunch Bar?" Lilo hollered.

Crunch Bar was smirking, but he crossed his arms and yelled something.

"How about now?" Lilo's ass was twerking like a machine. Crunch Bar mouthed something I'm sure would've amounted to a catcall as he applauded and laughed.

* * *

Hollywood presented me with a cake. I had to do a double-take to make sure what I was seeing was real. *How the fuck did he do that?*

Thick, glazed icing coated the entire surface area of this seven layer cake, and when I cut into it I couldn't tell the difference between one honeybun and the next. *He must have smushed them all together or something!* However Hollywood transformed my honeybuns into a cake, I stopped caring as soon as I took a bite. The sugar-sweet doughy texture of the honeybuns was still there, but it was now a cake!

"How is this fucking for real? This is fucking art!"

Hollywood gave me a sly grin. "You ain't seen nothin' yet, Paris." He held out his hand. In it was a ring made out of tightly woven plastic that looked like it could slip right onto my finger. I picked it up and was immediately stunned by the ring's intricacy and structural integrity.

"Is this from one of the plastic trash bags?"

Hollywood nodded. "You can have the ring in exchange for one of those boxes of chocolate chip cookies I see you got by your bunk. Or a bag of chips."

I gladly traded the cookies.

Junk food was currency in jail, and it turned out I was the only one getting the maximum amount of money placed on my books each week.

* * *

I woke up to the sound of crunching by my ear. My eyes fluttered awake, and then–

SNAP!

I immediately knew it was Juicy snapping his fingers by my ear, but that didn't stop me from jumping awake, startled.

Juicy was down at my eye-level, and his eyes shone with an evil glee. Cookie crumbs spilled carelessly from his mouth as he ground my snacks to dust between his teeth. He was smiling. He wanted me to see that he was enjoying stealing my food.

Don't react. Don't react. Don't react.

"Whatcha gonna doaboudit?" Juicy asked through a muffled mouthful of cookies.

Don't say a word.

I kept quiet, staring Juicy down. I watched as Juicy finished my box of cookies, and then stood up and walked back to his bunk. I felt my blood burn within me. I had more cookies, but I hated him. *Why the fuck has he got it out for me?*

* * *

We all watched as the tank door opened at the sound of the buzzer and a new guy entered.

Well, I thought he was new.

He walked right over to a vacant bunk, set his shit down, pulled out his toothbrush, and then went to brush his teeth as if he had done this a thousand times before.

"Hey Lilo," he said as he passed Lilo's bunk.

"Hey Courtney," Lilo replied.

I turned to Topper. "Courtney?"

"Courtney Love," he said.

"Aaaah."

* * *

"Well, if you ask my brother, he'll only say he likes ecstasy. But if you put cocaine in front of him, he won't say no to that either."

I wrote down the info about Elo's brother as fast as I could: *Elo's bro - X, but also coke.*

"Now most of the boys he hangs out with like speed, but my bro says they're particular about who they buy from."

"I'm sure I can sway them," I said. "Trust me, my shit's the best."

"I believe it, man. Pinkeye was telling me he knows some homies who bought from you. Sounds like you're legit, man."

Topper peaked over the top bunk. "So, hey, Paris, what else do you sell?"

"You name it, I got it," I said.

"Okay, dope. Cuz I'm gonna have a mad craving for some weed when I get outta this shithole, and I suppose I'll be getting out around the same time as you given our shared circumstances."

"Yes! Let's hang out, get high, and go find that motherfucker who played us!" I wrote down on my legal pad: *Topper - weed.*

My list of new clients was growing. I had made some great connections. Jail was like a convention of criminals! Business was going to be good when I got out. I had filled almost three pages of names, contact info, and drugs of choice by the time Courtney came over to me and leaned next to my bunk. "Yo, did you roll with Casey?"

I looked up at Courtney suspiciously. "You know Casey?"

"I know *of* Casey. I heard he was sporting a flashy Black, gay dealer around. I also heard he got shot in the face last week."

I felt the blood drain from my face. *Casey got shot? He's the most cautious dealer in the game! How the fuck did that happen?* I tried to stay calm, but Courtney could see that I was shaken.

"Don't worry, honey, he's fine. Just cut his cheek up real bad. Left a nasty scar the way I hear it. But he a'ight. Shit, he got himself a new truck all bulletproofed and everything. Hell, he's even hired a team of bodyguards to protect him whenever he leaves his house! Shit, he'll be fine. Just thought you would wanna know."

I nodded and looked back at my list of orders. *If people can get to Casey, what's to stop them from getting to me?*

* * *

"Yo, do you know how to pass a kite?" Topper asked me.

"No. What?"

"A kite. You know, just a folded-up note. If you wanna communicate with the boys in the other blocks, you gotta know how to pass a kite."

"Why would I want to communicate with guys in the other blocks?" I asked.

"Why the hell should I care?" Topper retorted. "Maybe you just wanna know their dick size. It don't matter. But you should know how to pass a kite."

"I'm not interested."

"The fuck you mean you're not interested?"

"I'm just not."

Topper was silent for a moment, and then let up. "Shit, a'ight then. Suit yourself."

I was relieved when he let the topic go. I didn't want to learn how the whole system worked. I knew there was a criminal underworld of its own within the confines of this jail, but I didn't want anything to do with it. I wanted to get out, and then stay out. *This cannot become my normal. No matter how long I'm here, I can't let myself think this is fucking normal!*

* * *

"Hubert, you got a hearing in an hour," the guard said through the intercom. "Make sure your ass is ready."

I showered and got myself cleaned up, and when the time came, I let the guard put the handcuffs back on me. He then led me away from the tank. We walked down a confusing series of corridors. The walls became narrower, but I could sense the air lighten the farther away from the tanks we walked. I had hoped there would be some windows letting daylight in as I was in desperation for even a glance at a ray of light. I couldn't remember the last time I had seen the sky, the sun, the moon or even felt the wind on my skin. No windows ever appeared.

Suddenly I was in a courtroom. The air was so fresh and breathable, but my stomach was in my throat in apprehension. Normal civilians lined the benches behind two tables where attorneys were seated. To my relief, Halle was one of them, and I settled down a bit as I was escorted over beside her.

The hearing was brief, but those few minutes standing by Halle's side gave me reassurance that I could get through this. I tried not to look across the aisle at the prosecutors' table. The lead prosecutor was a short woman with skin that was practically gray, long black hair, deep cut wrinkles, and a horribly bent and crooked nose. She looked like the Wicked Witch of the West. When she gave me a sharp glance, I flinched and looked back at the table in front of me. *Maybe she is the Wicked Witch of the West. But does that make Halle the Good Witch? ... Nah. Halle's the motherfucking house that's gonna crush this bitch!*

* * *

"Stay outta trouble in there and I think I can get you probation," Halle told me after my court session had ended. I nodded as the guard tore me from Halle's side and led me back to the stuffy corridors. It was a longer walk back to the tank than I remembered, and I was light headed by the time I returned. Afterward, I lay on my mattress lost in thought.

Stay outta trouble. I can do that. Whatever it takes to get outta here.
SNAP!

Juicy's fingers rang even louder than they had in previous instances in my ear, and I clapped my hand to the side of my head.

"Fuck off, Juicy!"

"Make me!"

SNAP! SNAP! SNAP! SNAP! SNAP!

"Bitch!" he yelled, opening up his arms again, inviting confrontation. I didn't move. I just scowled at him. "Yeah," he said, "that's all you'll ever be. A prissy fucking little bitch. *With AIDS!*"

I couldn't help but wince at his last remark. I clenched my teeth, forcing myself to remain silent. That was the last time I ever shouted back at Juicy.

* * *

Of the items we were allowed to order in jail, lotion was one of them, and I was fascinated by the selections available. It was while I was browsing the different aromas and ingredients in one of these options that I came across one word: methylparaben.

Methylparaben? METH-ylparaben? METH!?

I ordered the lotion on the spot.

* * *

Hollywood showed us how to tear the fabric of our bed sheets and fold them to make sexy outfits. The Destiny's Child dance parties were quite regular, and we were ready to put on a performance for the boys in the tank across from us.

I loved being dressed up in something other than orange.

When Destiny's Child finally came on the television, we all started singing the lyrics to "Say My Name."

"Come on, Crunch Bar! Say my fucking name!" Lilo shouted.

"You tell him, girl!" we yelled, backing him up. Then we all laughed and went along with our rendition of the song. Crunch Bar and some of the guys in the straight tank whistled, even though we couldn't hear them. At the end, we all bowed, and they gave us a standing ovation.

Suddenly, Lilo ripped off his white, folded, makeshift miniskirt and thrust his dick in the direction of the straight boys.

I could see them all mouth, *"Oh, shit!"* and they shielded their eyes as they retreated back into their tank. Most of the guys around me laughed, but I couldn't believe what I had just witnessed.

I can't let myself think this is fucking normal!

* * *

"Alright, McCharthy, today's your day," came the guard's voice through the intercom. "Let's go."

Time seemed to stand still as every head pointed in the direction of Lilo. I could see him gulp, but at the same time smile. "Cool. Good luck, y'all. Peace!"

Lilo jumped up and sprinted for the door.

Simultaneously, dozens of the other guys jumped down from their bunks and swarmed Lilo's bunk where his leftover snacks remained. I watched in stunned silence as this wake of orange vultures grappled for bags of chips and cookies. Juicy hauled several guys aside as he muscled himself to the center of the pack and collected two arms full of snacks for himself. By the time the snacks had all been collected and the crowd of guys returned to their bunks, Lilo was gone.

* * *

"Yo, Topper, you okay?" asked Hollywood.

Topper was leaning over a toilet, clutching his head. Suddenly, he puked.

"I don't feel too fucking good," he murmured, letting spit drool into the murky water in the toilet bowl.

"Ah, shit." Hollywood jumped up, ran to the door, and pounded on it. "Guard!"

Moments later a guard stood outside our tank. He looked inside curiously, but didn't make any motion for the lock. "What's the problem?" he asked gruffly through the intercom.

"Topper's mad fucking sick," Hollywood explained. "He just puked his guts out in the toilet. I think he needs to see a doctor.

The guard craned his neck to see Topper clutching his head over the bowl of the toilet. "Nah, he'll be alright," the guard said.

"Yo, he's *not* alright!" Hollywood snapped back. "He needs a doctor, man! What's the problem with that?"

The guard shrugged passively. "Not my problem," he said, and walked away before Hollywood could say another word.

"Motherfucker," Hollywood muttered under his breath, but loud enough for me to hear.

When the guard was out of sight, Hollywood walked back to where Topper sat on the concrete floor. Spit hung on his lip, and his face was notably paler.

"Yo, Topper," Hollywood said, crouching down near Topper's eye-level, "need us to pull a stunt?"

"Fuck, man," Topper groaned. "Whatever it takes."

"You got it. Lie down, close your eyes and I'll count to three."

Topper eased himself back onto the floor as gently as he could, but his movements were rough. Hollywood cushioned his head with his hand before it hit the floor.

I turned to Courtney. "What's happening?" I whispered.

"Girl, we bout to pull a stunt!" Courtney said in a hushed tone. "You'll see."

Hollywood raised a fist in the air, and then pumped it. *One-two-three.*

"AAAAH!"

"HEEEEY!"

"GUAAAARD!"

"HEEEELP!"

Everyone started screaming and making a commotion. A bunch of guys ran over to the door and pounded the fuck out of it. "GUAAAARD! GUAAAAARD! GUAAAAAAAARD!'"

Four guards came running over.

"He fucking passed out, man!" Hollywood screamed. "He needs a fucking doctor!!!"

"Oh my God I hope he doesn't die! Oh Lawd Jesus!!!" Courtney screeched.

The guards ordered us to bring Topper to the door. They retrieved a stretcher and came back with an extra guard. Topper was loaded onto the stretcher and carried away.

"Fucking homophobes," Hollywood muttered when they were out of sight.

* * *

My lotion arrived.

"Whatchu got there, Paris?"

"I got lotion that I think has meth in it."

"What the fuck? For real?"

"Yeah! Meth-yl-par-a-ben," I said, slowly reading the name of the ingredient on the back of the bottle.

"Ha!" Courtney laughed. "Girl, You really think that'll get you high?"

"Well, I'm gonna lather this shit all over me and find out!"

"Alright, *Auntie Lotionelle*. You do that."

I did exactly that. I stripped myself of the orange jumpsuit and slathered the lotion all over my body. And then I waited.

And waited.

"How you feeling, Auntie," Courtney asked.

"Fucking wet," I said, disappointedly. Everyone laughed. "And sticky too," I added, which got me a little more laughter.

"Hey, don't worry about it, Lotionelle. Maybe you can slip through the crack in the door now and make a run for it!"

"Ha-ha," I said sarcastically. I put my orange jumpsuit back on.

Fuck! I really thought that would work! Well, at least this lotion smells nice.

I ordered another bottle of that lotion, determined to make the next one last a bit longer.

* * *

"Hubert," the guard said, "let's go. I'm taking you to the I.D. Clinic."

"Ooo," I said, getting up and going to the door. "Am I getting my picture taken?"

The guard rolled his eyes. When I turned around so he could handcuff me, I could see Juicy shaking his head. *Did I miss something?*

The guard led me through another maze of corridors and eventually into a brightly lit room with tile floors instead of concrete. Then a man in a white robe emerged from a back door. He wore square glasses and had neatly gelled brown hair, and he carried himself confidently. As he approached me, he smiled and held out his hand.

"Hi, De'Vannon, I'm Dr. Raymond. Welcome."

I shook the doctor's hand, but looked around puzzled. *This is a medical place? What does I.D. stand for?* Dr. Raymond continued with his introduction.

"You look good, De'Vannon! Just by looking at you I can tell you've put on more tone since you first got processed back in September. I'm hoping our talk today can help accelerate your already improving health. How does that sound?"

"That sounds fabulous," I replied, "but I'm a bit confused. What does the I.D. stand for? I thought I was getting my picture taken."

Dr. Raymond laughed. "I'm sorry about the confusion. We try to be gentle with the terminology, but I can see where you might have been misled. In all honesty, the I.D. stands for 'Infectious Diseases.'"

I nodded. *I'm here because they want to do something about my HIV. They might actually try to help me! Dammit, I don't need their help!*

"De'Vannon, it's no secret that you have HIV, and it's also no secret that you haven't been taking any medication for it. Now look, your reasons for that up to this point are your own and I respect that. Under the care of the County, though, we can't just let your health deteriorate. De'Vannon, it would be irresponsible of me to not try to help your medical situation. And I *want* to help, but I also *want* to make sure the medication I prescribe is something you're comfortable taking. I want to work with you. Are you willing to work with me on this?"

I watched Dr. Raymond talk, and looked for any sign of ingenuity, any hint of deception. I saw none. *Dammit, if he wasn't so fucking nice to me, I'd get up and walk right out of here! I don't want anyone to fix my problem! ... But I have no reason to say no to his help. He really wants to help, and it would be rude of me to refuse his offer.*

I nodded in response to the doctor's question.

"Good. That's good," he said. "Now tell me, what is your current understanding of HIV?"

I gave a wry chuckle. "The way I see it is that it's a fucking death sentence."

"Mmm. You're not alone in seeing it that way. What makes you think it's a death sentence?"

"Everyone I've ever known to have had HIV has died," I said. "And not from old age. From AIDS."

"No one can be forced to take the medication. And the medication certainly won't solve all of your problems. People may still judge you for having HIV, and your feelings about the disease are your own, but what I know to be true is that with consistent ingestion of the medication, the HIV can be practically nonexistent in your body. It won't go away completely, but this medication can reduce the prevalence of the virus to a count so low that it may as well not even be in you at all. You can have, for all intents and purposes, a normal life, whatever normal means to you. You may even be able to have sex again without the fear of transmitting the virus. That is, assuming you find a partner who's comfortable with it."

"I can have sex again and not have to worry?"

"Yes," Dr. Raymond insisted. "If you take the medication."

"How long will I have to take it for?"

"I'm sorry to say, the rest of your life."

"And what if it doesn't work?"

"Well, considering you had no plan to do anything about the virus before today, I would say you have nothing to lose by at least trying."

The way Dr. Raymond explained it made sense and I couldn't argue with his logic. *I might as well try it and see what happens. Maybe it won't work and I'll die anyway. Or maybe it will, in which case I'll have a lot of shit to sort out... but I'll only worry about all that if these meds actually do work.*

* * *

I don't know how many days, weeks, or months passed, but one day the guard brought me back to court. Halle was there.

"What's up, motherfucker?" Halle said with a smirk. "Are you ready to leave?"

My mouth crept into a smile. "What did you do?" I asked.

"I'm *about* to get you probation, stupid." And that's exactly what she did. By the end of the court hearing, I had been awarded probation. I would soon be released.

I couldn't stop smiling as I spoke to Halle before going back to the tank. "Halle?" I asked.

"If you thank me, I'm gonna cut you with my stilettos."

I grinned. "How long was I in jail for? It felt like two whole fucking years."

"I bet it did," she said. "Tomorrow's Thanksgiving. You were in the tank for two months."

I gaped. "Fuck!" I couldn't believe it. It was like time had slowed down in jail. My beard was thick and lengthy, and I felt that if I went another day without meth or dick that my skin would peel itself off and go find my vices without me.

Halle put a firm hand on my shoulder. "This is a big win," she said, looking me in the eye. "Don't fuck this up."

I nodded, not because I understood, but because I knew if I didn't then Halle would move her hand to my beard and force my head to nod.

"Alright, baby," Halle said, "I'll see you down the road. Your parents will pick you up when you get out on tomorrow."

Dammit. The last people I wanted to see were my parents. My jaw hurt from grinding my teeth for two months of craving meth, and no amount of methylparaben lotion was going to calm me down. I wanted more than anything to go straight to a dope house.

True to Halle's word, when I was released the next day, my parents were waiting right out front of the jail with the truck pulled up and waiting for me. I was leaving with my parents whether I wanted to or not.

CHAPTER 20: NOT AGAIN

My eyes hurt from the sunlight. I hadn't been outside or seen real sunlight for two months, and the brightness hurt worse after jail than when I was high on meth. It only made my craving burn hotter.

"Hey, can you drop me off here?" I asked my parents.

"No," came my dad's gruff reply. "We're going home and not coming back until your hearing to get your probation transferred to Baton Rouge."

Home? He means Baton Rouge! I panicked. I had only just gotten out of jail, and I wasn't ready to leave Houston yet. *If I leave Houston now, then I'm a failure! I can't give up yet! I can still make this work!*

"Excuse me!" I said, immediately raising my voice. "I just got my freedom back! You cannot make me go or stay any place I do not want to!"

"You're not free!" my dad yelled back. "You're on probation! There's a fucking difference!"

"If you drive me all the way back to Baton Rouge, I'll just skip back here on the next bus. You might as well save me the bus ticket."

My dad was about to say something, but Mother spoke first. "Pull over. We can't make him do anything he doesn't want to."

My dad was silent for a minute as we drove, but at the next stop light he put the truck in park.

"We will get a room at the Extended Stay America Hotel in Greenway Plaza," my Mother said. I knew what she meant. She and dad would be staying until I was either back in jail or done with my next hearing.

I didn't acknowledge my Mother, but jumped out of the truck as quickly as I could. *Ok, where am I. And where is the nearest trap? I'm over-fucking-due for a hit.*

* * *

"What are you thankful for this Thanksgiving?"

"Fuck you! Pass me the damn pipe."

I had ended up in a dope haven in South Houston, and I was thankful to be high again. I didn't care for all the banter, though.

Suddenly the front door burst open. "Yo! There's a block party down the street with a shit-ton of bikes just lying around on the lawn unchained!"

All the tweakers in the house got up and bolted out the door. Seconds later I was alone in the house. It was just me and the pipe.

Fucking dope fiends, going out to steal shit, I thought as I rummaged through someone else's backpack for their stash of meth. I found it and swiped a crystal. Then proceeded to crush the crystal with a knife from the kitchen. I organized the dust into a neat line. *Oh, how I missed this shit.* I snorted the meth and eased back on the couch.

When the other tweakers returned and crowded the room with a shit-ton of bikes, no one paid me any mind, even though the evidence of my dope hit was still in plain sight on the table. And for a few minutes, the tension in my jaw lessened, and I relaxed.

* * *

"Most people don't do well on probation. In fact, most people don't make it a year. But that doesn't mean all people don't make it. Mr. Hubert, I want to give you the best possible odds at success, even if the odds aren't very good. I'm transferring your probation from Houston to Baton Rouge because you clearly have a better support system there with your family and your church. You will be required to perform regular check-ins at the probation office in Baton Rouge. Best of luck to you."

The probation officer dismissed me and I left with a subdued smile on my face.

I gave Halle a big hug. To my delight, she hugged me back. Then she said, "Ok, you ain't outta this shit yet. Next time I hear from you I want it to be because some bitch is suing you for half your well-earned money. I love kicking a greedy bitch's ass in court. Either that or because you just wanna get drinks. No more of this drug money bullshit, you hear?"

I nodded, not because I wanted to, but because I knew Halle would karate chop my nut sack in half if I gave any hint of disagreement.

Three hours later I had walked from the Probation & Transfer Office to a drug shack in Montrose. And the meth was flowing.

* * *

"Yo, Token, can you help me distract a store clerk so I can swipe a carton of cigs?"

"Nope!" I said.

"Okay, well Dooby found this car key on the ground near a parking lot. We're gonna go out later and try to find the car and take it to a chop shop. Wanna join us then?"

"Hell, no!"

"What the fuck, man? Why not?"

I don't wanna be a thieving ass dope fiend, motherfucker! I thought.

"I don't wanna do that shit! Leave me alone!"

The tweaker did leave me alone. He found some dumbass to help him and Dooby out, and the three skipped out. They didn't come back.

* * *

My Mother bought me a new pair of orange Chuck Taylors. Someone else bought Suggs a new car.

I knew there was no way Suggs had bought his own car because his trap was still as grungy as it ever was, and I knew he'd sooner spend a car's worth of money on dope before dropping it on a brand new ride. Also, the shiny black sedan had a bright red ribbon crowning its roof. It was fucking weird. I wondered if Suggs had become an informant, but I went inside his house anyway. I'd walked miles to his place from my parents' hotel room, and I was thirsting for ice.

The walking was getting easier, and that wasn't just due to my new kicks. The HIV medication I'd been prescribed in jail was working. *I'm not dying anymore...*

Fuck! I'm not dying anymore, and I haven't paid taxes or bills or shit in a year! How the fuck am I going to rebound from that?

I tried not to think about the problems that came with no longer dying. I was now less than five feet from my next high.

"Token! Welcome back, yo!" Suggs was already preparing a syringe to shoot up with. There was another tweaker I didn't recognize cleaning a pipe. I was about to sit down across from this dude and join the fun when Suggs grabbed my shoulder. "Listen, yo, I got some people swinging by in a little bit. We should totally hang out after, but if you wouldn't mind checking in next door for a bit while I take care of those friends. I promise you my neighbor's got what you need next door."

I looked at Suggs confused. "I've got what I *need* right here."

"I know, Token. I know. But just for a bit, okay?"

"No," I objected. "They're not here yet. I can leave when they show up."

"I gotta insist, man. Trust me, the dude next door will take care of you. And after those other friends leave, I got you, too."

Suggs was unrelenting. *What the fuck is going on?* The dope was within arm's reach. *Grab and run?* I thought. *No, I'm not here to make enemies. Damn! I'll just do what he says, and when I'm back, I'm getting even more fucked up!*

Suggs pointed me to the neighbor who would apparently have dope for me, and I walked over. As I did, a truck turned onto the street and parked next to Suggs's new bow-tied vehicle. It had tinted windows and the type of doors where the front doors have to open first before the back doors can be opened. Two guys I didn't recognize got out of the front doors and entered Suggs's home. I almost thought they were undercover cops but I wasn't sure. Something didn't feel right but I pushed my better senses aside in order to feed my craving.

I knocked on the door of Suggs's neighbor. A short dude with a deep five-o-clock shadow opened the door and the smell of strong coffee hit me in the face. He squinted up at me as if staring into the sun, even though it was the middle of a cloudy night.

"What do you want?" he grouched.

"Suggs said I could come over here for–"

"Ah, fuck," the guy grumbled. "Alright, come on in." I entered. Candles cast a dim light over the otherwise pitch-black space. If they had a scent, it was masked by the coffee. "Just sit your ass down over there," the guy said, pointing to a wall where I could make out the shape of a cushioned bench. "I'll get you a Sprite. That's what you boys like, right?"

I nodded, unsure of what to make of this man's sour hospitality. "Do you have anything to chase it down with?" I asked as friendly as possible when the man brought my glass of Sprite.

"This is what I got, kid," the man said, raising and dropping his arms. He seemed almost disappointed to be unable to give me what I wanted, even though his voice suggested he hated the very essence of my existence in his home.

"Suggs said you–"

"Suggs said what? That you could come over here? Yes. That I got dope for you? No. Now please, don't ask me any more questions."

Wait, so Suggs lied about this guy having dope for me? What the fuck is actually going on?

I sat awkwardly on the neighbor's bench and drank my Sprite. *This would be so much better with meth.* I loved the way the sugary carbonation interacted with the tingling of my meth high. I longed for the itching in my skin to turn to the tingling, sensual fuzziness of a high. I wanted the substance that would suddenly make everything fuckable. I wanted the rush of blood and the electricity in my limbs. *If it turns out I'm not dying anytime soon, I'm gonna need a hell of a lot more meth.*

Inside my head I begged Suggs's strange friends to leave, trying to will them to get out of his house and fucking go.

I wasn't even done with my Sprite when I heard a vehicle door open and close. I walked over to a window and watched as the truck pulled out of Suggs's driveway and drove quietly away. Without saying goodbye, I left the neighbor's house and hurried back to Suggs's place.

To my surprise, the meth was just as I had left it, and so was the tweaker I didn't recognize still cleaning his pipe. It was as if the two other people had never even shown up.

I forced all the questions I had out of my mind, and made a b-line for the ice.

"Easy, Token," Suggs said as I fumbled with the syringe and rubber tourniquet. "Yo, lemme help you out. I don't want you fucking up a vein all over my table."

I let Suggs prepare the syringe while I wrapped the tourniquet around my bicep. I watched him obsessively, jealous that I wasn't getting to do my own process, but eager to feel the high. Suggs dissolved a large blue crystal in a little bit of water. I watched the rock dissolve and the blue color swirl around in the fluid. For a second, I thought it flashed an aquamarine color. Suggs filled the syringe halfway then inserted the needle into a bulging vein in my left arm. As he drew the stopper back I saw a little of my blood enter the syringe and mix with the meth mixture. My heart raced in anticipation as Suggs pushed the stopper toward me, sending liquid ecstasy coursing through my body.

I orgasmed, feeling my own cum wet my pants. I tried to stand up to get to the couch, but my legs flopped and told my brain to fuck off. So, it did.

I laid on the floor in a sexual daze and watched as the heavens of a water-stained ceiling indoctrinated me into their euphoric cosmos.

* * *

People were laughing. I couldn't tell which people, but the Batman level hearing of my crystal high told me people were laughing… at me.

"Look how fucked up he is."

"Dude, he fucking jizzed himself."

"Holy shit, he's a fucking goner."

"Yo, don't take a picture. What the fuck?"

"I wanna show this fool to Danny."

"Just call Danny and tell him to come over! And call Lenox, too!"

I tried to roll my body in the direction of the hushed, giggling voices. My vision swirled and I couldn't feel my body move. "Uhm–" I murmured unwillingly. "Uhla– Ah–"

Suddenly there was a whole chorus of laughter all around me.

How many fucking people are here? I tried to orient myself and my head spun. I shut my eyes. The laughter continued. *I'm gonna have to wait this shit out.*

* * *

It took me hours to finally sober up and get my shit together. All my clothes were strewn around me. I pulled them back on.

"Yo, how are you feeling, Token? All better now?" It was Suggs.

"Yeah, I'm cool," I assured him.

"Cool, bro," he said. "Yeah, and I know you're good for this shit, too. Thanks for coming around." *Am I good for this shit? It's not like I have any money to pay him back.*

I knew I had overstayed my welcome, but I didn't want to leave. *Where else am I going to go? The dope is here. People are here. Why should I leave?*

Tap. Tap. Tap-tap. Tap. Tap.

The sound had come from a window behind me. Suddenly people started to leave.

Was that some kind of code knock? I got up to leave as well.

"Token, you don't have to leave, man!" Suggs called from across the room. He was opening a backdoor, and the two guys Suggs had kicked me out for before were now entering the room.

"No, I'm gonna go," I responded, beginning to move toward the front door.

"Yo, Token, what's the rush, man? Listen, if you gotta go, these two guys will give you a ride."

I looked hesitantly at the trio across the room from me. Everyone else had left. It was just me and them. "Where?" I asked.

Suggs shrugged. "They'll drop you off on a bus stop, man."

I thought about the truck I had seen these guys drive up in earlier. *If I'm in the back, I'll be trapped until they let me out. IF they let me out. Did Suggs really mean DEAD on a bus stop?*

I grabbed the front door handle and burst out into the night. I realized I had left my backpack behind and in it were my meds and my clientele list. *FUCK!* I heard the rumble of shoes chase after me, but I didn't look back. I made it from Sugg's house in the Astrodome Area to a park far down the road and sprinted across a field, overlooked by The Museum of Fine Arts.

Halfway across, I looked over my shoulder. There was only darkness behind me. If there was anyone chasing me I couldn't have heard them over the noise of my own panicked breath. At the far end of the lawn, I jumped the fence and continued to run.

I ran through block after block of residential neighborhoods crying for my Mother like I was a baby again. Every time a car turned onto the same street as me, I didn't wait to see if it was the truck before hiding behind a tree or sprinting around the nearest corner to try and shake it. For all I cared, any and every car was after me.

Finally, I found a trail that could take me most of the remaining distance to the hotel my Mother would still be staying at. And I ran as fast as I could. When I finally emerged within a few blocks of the hotel in Greenway Plaza, I kept myself hidden in back alleyways. I scouted the block of the hotel for any sign of the truck. I didn't see it.

Covered in sweat, I entered the hotel and made my way toward the elevator praying no one would stop me. No one did. One minute later I was knocking on the door of my Mother's hotel room.

I had no idea how late (or early) it was. The door opened.

My Mother looked at me through a veil of distress, and slowly her eyes widened. She grabbed my arm, pulled me inside, and slammed the door.

"Why do you have to keep doing this, De'Vannon! A Mother can only take so much!"-

"Where's dad?" I asked.

"He went back to Baton Rouge," came the curt reply. "But he'll be back tomorrow morning." Suddenly, her hand gripped my arm again and she shoved me into the bathroom. She didn't say another word as she closed the door.

I stood in silence for a moment before leaning down to take off my shoes. I had ran so far and so fast that my orange Chuck Taylors were no longer orange, but coated in a grimy layer of black tar and dirt. And the laces were shredded to the point that the shoes could no longer be tied.

As I washed the dirt and sweat from my body, I wondered about my Mother. I had never put her in a position to shed tears for me before. But on the other side of the door, hidden by the sound of the shower, I wondered if she was crying now.

After I showered, I fell into a deep sleep laying next to my Mother as she held my hand, gazing down upon me with an unconditional love that only a Mother could give.

* * *

"We're going home," my Mother said the next morning. She began packing her suitcase while I stared at her in dumbfounded silence. I had no intention of leaving Houston. After a minute she gave me a sharp look. "Now I'm not asking you, De'Vannon. You're coming back home with me."

"No," I said. It was all I could think to say, but I said it as forcefully as I could.

"De'Vannon," my Mother retorted on the verge of yelling. "I'm not asking."

"I'm not going," I said, matching the resoluteness in her voice. "This is my city, and you can't force me to leave."

My Mother huffed. I knew she was trying to find the right words to convince me, but I also knew those words didn't exist. "De'Va–"

"I refuse," I said. The air of finality filled the room, and my Mother closed her eyes, knowing she had lost. Then she finished packing her bag in silence.

As she stood to leave the hotel room, she grabbed my hand and slapped a piece of paper into it. "I'm going back home. And when you're ready, I hope you come home, too."

The paper in my hand was a one-way Greyhound bus ticket to Baton Rouge. I gave my Mother a weak smile and nodded to reassure her that I understood, and then watched as she dragged her suitcase out the door to head to the lobby to check out.

Now what? I thought to myself. I had no intention of using the ticket. *Now I need to score some more dope.* And so, I started walking. *Something will come along. Maybe Scarlet will loan me some dope to do business with.*

Five hours later I found out that Scarlet would have none of that *loan shark bullshit*. "Get your lazy ass some money, and then you can buy whatever you want from me! But don't you ever come to me for charity again!" She had slammed the door in my face a bit harsher than I thought was necessary.

And so, I walked. And walked. And walked.
Something will work out. Something has to work out. I can't leave Houston a failure.

* * *

I hadn't taken any HIV medication in over two weeks, but I couldn't afford to think about that. I needed Crimson's help, but if he wanted to have sex again then I was in a tough situation. I tried not to think about the possibilities. *I just need his help. That's all.*

To my delight, he answered the buzzer on the first ring.

"Token? Is that you?"

"Yes, doll," I said flirtatiously. "Now let me in." He did.

Crimson gave me a quick hug when I entered, but I could feel him recoil slightly as he pulled away. I knew I smelled bad, but I was hoping he'd look past that.

"How are you?" I asked. "How's the repair shop?"

"It's good," Crimson said, nodding nervously. He was being short with me, I realized. "Yeah, it's good. What can I do for you?"

I hated the way he asked me that. *He already assumes I'm here to get something from him. I mean, I am here to get something from him, but still! Why does he have to assume the worst from me?*

I hung my head. "Look, Crimson. I'm trying to get back on my feet." I held out my hands as if to say *look at me*. "And as much as I hate to have to ask for your help, I'm here to ask for your help."

Crimson nodded a little more intently now. My honesty was having a positive impact. "That's good, man," he said. "I want you to get back on your feet, too." I smiled hopefully. "I'm not going to give you any money, though." My smile vanished. "Look, man, I know what it's like to hustle. And I know that money isn't everything. You need tools and resources. So if you have a plan, tell me what you need *other than money*."

I opened my mouth, but realized I didn't have an answer. I had no plan. All I wanted was money and dope. So, I closed my mouth.

I could see Crimson's shoulders deflate in disappointment, as if he could see right through my poorly woven facade.

"Do you have a laptop?" Crimson asked suddenly.

"No," I said. All I had was a cell phone.

"How about I buy you a laptop. That's probably the best tool you can have."

I smiled. "Thank you, Crimson. I'll need something to carry it in as well, though." A laptop wasn't what I wanted, but it assured me that I still had Crimson's friendship and support. And that was worth something.

* * *

I didn't like the added weight of my new laptop on my shoulders, but I did love my new backpack. Walking became more burdensome. All the weight I'd gained in jail dropped off of me as if it had never been there. The "homeless shuffle" of constant coming and going came back like muscle memory. It seemed like I was always walking.

"Hey, Mr. Brown!" I waved to a fellow homeless veteran I had talked to a couple times before.

"Hey there, Token!" he waved back, but he didn't stop walking.

"Where are you off to, Mr. Brown?"

"I'm going to a mental hospital, Token. Every so often I go in and tell them I'm suicidal. They'll keep me there for at least the next three nights because of a coroner's requirement or some shit. That's a few nights I don't have to worry about where I'm gonna sleep and eat. I'll still see you around, though!"

My mouth hung agape. *What a way to rig the system!* I continued on my way, wondering if I would ever do what Mr. Brown was doing. *Could be helpful in a pinch, perhaps.*

I continued on my way. And then I stopped again.

"Ahhh!!!"

My right foot cramped and curled up inside my shoe.

Gritting my teeth, I focused on my foot. I forced the muscles to untangle themselves. I willed my foot to uncurl and bear the little weight my body had left. After several minutes, my toes were straight again. I pushed my weight down on my foot as if to seal it in place.

And then I continued to walk. *I can't keep going like this.* I fingered the Greyhound Bus ticket in my pocket. *I can't keep going like this.*

* * *

I managed to get my hands on some T and saved a small piece for the bus ride. I fidgeted most of the way, itching to just pull out my pipe and smoke it in front of everyone, but I resisted the urge. I tried to ignore the odd looks I got for grinding my teeth so loudly.

I tried to sleep but couldn't. The daylight was blinding. I just stared at my feet and waited.

Then at one of our stops I heard a male voice say, "Tickets?"

I looked up. Two cops had got on the bus and were checking tickets. *Shit, my ticket is in my backpack with my pipe and dope!* I was about to try to quickly pull my ticket out, but the cops were moving too fast. Everyone else had their tickets out and ready to show. I leaned away from my bag. *Better if I get kicked off for not having a ticket than having them see what's in my backpack.*

My knees shook nervously as the cops made their way through the bus. Then they saw me and stopped checking IDs. I looked pleadingly at them, praying with my eyes that they would go easy.

The cop closest to me looked at me like he knew I was guilty but couldn't prove it. He then took a deep breath and sighed, as if to say *I don't want any trouble either, man. I just want to do my job and go home.* The cop turned around and patted his partner on the shoulder, signaling it was time to go. The cops got off the bus, and I was on my way home again.

I was thankful.

*   *   *

It was odd being back in the hood in Baton Rouge. Nothing had changed. The only thing that was different was the fact that I was in possession of a sliver of dope, but I didn't know anyone I could party with.

No matter how hard I searched on Craigslist or any other dating app, no one in Baton Rouge seemed to be into ice. Crack was the drug of choice in the hood.

There was a VA outpatient clinic in Baton Rouge that I visited at my Mother's request. It was a short line to get to the woman at the window where I explained, "I need a medical checkup."

While I waited in the lobby, I listened in on a conversation between two other veterans.

"Frankie said the first thing he did when he got back from Afghanistan was cash in on his pension."

"For real? What did he do with all that money?"

"Good ol' Frankie went and bought himself a new car!"

A lightbulb flipped on inside my head. *I still have a pension from working at CenterPoint Energy that I had completely forgotten about. I bet I can cash that in, too!*

"De'Vannon Hubert!" a nurse called.

I got my physical and bloodwork done. I weighed 135 pounds. "When was the last time you took your HIV medication?" the doctor asked me.

"Uh, I honestly don't know," I said.

"And what about medication for Hep B?"

I smiled sheepishly, indicating the answer would be the same.

"Ok, I'm going to order you a new antiviral prescription. I need you to pick it up and start taking it *immediately*. Ok?"

I did as I was told.

* * *

The results of my blood work indicated that my T-cell count was around 500, which the call from the doctor indicated put me at high risk of full-blown AIDS.

"*A healthy T-cell count is around 1,000*," the doctor said on the phone. "*Are you taking your new medication?*"

"Yes, I am," I answered truthfully.

"*Good. You should start regaining weight soon. If you don't, give me a call, okay? I insist.*"

I agreed to the doctor's request, even though I knew my weight was not going to increase anytime soon.

It had been surprisingly easy to get my pension money from CenterPoint, and I wanted to re-up on as much dope as possible. Tina was nowhere to be seen in the hood, and with a fresh $10,000 I could start a whole new operation in Baton Rouge!

I couldn't wait to visit Casey and make the biggest dope purchase of my life!

* * *

I found a black fanny pack lying around my parents' house and swiped it before heading for the bus to go to Houston. It felt funny around my waist, but I liked the look of it. Casey wasn't so impressed.

"What the fuck is that?" he said the moment he laid eyes upon me in his kitchen doorway.

"It's a fanny pack," I said gleefully.

"Shit, Token, just when I think you've managed to lay low, you pull shit like this!"

I shrugged. "You know me!"

Casey cracked a smile, and for the first time in our relationship he laughed. "Welcome back," he said, motioning for me to come inside.

"It's good to be back," I said, entering.

The scar under Casey's jaw where he'd been shot was hardly noticeable. If I hadn't known to look for it, I wouldn't have known he'd ever been hit. I was about to ask Casey about the incident when I heard a groan come from his living room. I gave Casey an inquisitive look. *What is the deal with him and Lorenzo?*

Casey gestured to the living room with an open palm, inviting me to examine. I did.

Hogtied, gagged, and naked in the middle of the floor was Lorenzo. He moaned again.

"You better not cum on my carpet!" Casey yelled from the kitchen.

I guess everyone's got their thing, I figured.

"Now, what can I do for you, Token? Need work?"

I pulled out a thick stack of bills and handed it to Casey. Casey counted out the $2,500 and raised his eyebrows.

"That was the max I could withdraw from the ATM," I said. He gave me a wide grin and bagged me a quarter pound of blue dope shards.

I extracted one crystal from the bag and put the rest in my fanny pack. Casey retrieved his pipe for me to use, and I got right to smoking.

"Hey, have you heard from Miles?" I asked.

"Miles? Who the fuck is Miles?"

"You know, the tweaker who first introduced you to me. Seems as if he's fallen off the grid."

"Oh, that Miles. Huh. No, I haven't seen him."

Casey seemed puzzled, but he didn't press the issue. And just like that,

I was on my way out his door to start a new operation in Baton Rouge.

* * *

The high kicked in before the bus arrived. *Fuck! I won't be able to do this bus ride without fucking the seat in front of me!*

I needed someone to screw. *But who?* I thought of Blaze. We'd had sex only once before and his place wasn't too far. Just a quick cab ride over to the Galleria Area. And besides, I was back on antiviral medication thanks to the VA. It was time to have some fun.

I wasn't sure if Blaze was going to answer the door. But after several seconds, the door opened and Blaze was standing in front of me. "Token?" he asked, unsure of what he was seeing.

"You guessed it!"

"Holy shit. Okay, yeah, come in."

"What's going on?" he asked.

"I'll tell you what's going on," I said, pulling out my quarter pound of meth from my fanny pack.

Blaze's eyes widened. He stuttered at a loss for words.

"Honey," I teased, "don't tell me you don't party anymore. You can't hide behind these blackout curtains and tell me you're not down for a good time."

Blaze nodded eagerly. "Fuck it, man. Let's roll."

Blaze got a syringe and a tourniquet. I happily joined in the process. I loved the process almost more than I loved the high. I was going to offer to shoot Blaze up first, but before I could speak, he had wrapped the tourniquet around my arm. I didn't protest. "Make sure you fill that whole syringe with crystals," I demanded. Blaze obeyed.

He slid the needle into my vein. The warmth flooded my entire body, and he barely got the needle out before I shivered and ejaculated. The room spun. *Blaze is gonna have to shoot himself up.*

Moments later, Blaze grabbed me by the belt of my fanny pack and threw me on the couch. He mounted me and began unbuttoning my jeans. The air was as cool as an ocean breeze on my ass cheeks, and his dick was as warm and smooth as honey whiskey. There was no foreplay. He pounded my ass and I moaned with pleasure. My body shook and pulsated, and I felt another orgasm coming.

I felt warmth spread in between my ass cheeks as jizz filled my asshole and overflowed. I came at the same time, screaming with delight. And then Blaze collapsed on top of me, crushing me under the comfort of his sweaty body. We laid there breathing heavily and enjoying the high. *I just want my whole life to feel like this,* I thought as the darkness of the room bloomed, invisible fireworks erupting in the void.

I was about to ask if I could stay the night when Blaze said, "Listen, I need to go run a quick errand. Would you mind waiting outside until I come back?"

"Ugh, do I have to?" I wined into the couch cushion.

"Unfortunately, I must insist," Blaze said. He got up and the cool air quickly filled in the absence of his body. Shocked into motion, I put my clothes on and collected my dope. It still felt like a quarter pound.

Blaze locked the door as we stepped outside. "I'll be right back."

"Can't I come with you?" I asked.

"No need," Blaze said. "Just wait right here." He turned and left, leaving me standing awkwardly on his front doorstep.

"You can't trust him," a voice in my head whispered. *"He's going to get a friend to rob you! What tweaker wouldn't fucking rob a dealer with a quarter pound of meth!"*

The voice in my head was right. There was no way Blaze was just running an errand. My heart started hammering inside my chest. *"Do you want to be a standing target or a moving target? Move!!!"*

I kicked my feet into motion and ran. The wind felt weird, as if it were scratching my face. I didn't know where to run, so I aimed for the nearest alleyway.

In the shadows, the sounds of the Galleria echoed and ricocheted and morphed into the pitter-patter of footsteps creeping up behind me. But every time I turned around, only darkness was behind me. *"You can't hide from the shadows in the shadows, De'Vannon!"*

I bolted out of the alleyway and into the heart of the Galleria Area. Faces blurred past me, until one finally hit me. "Sorry!" I screamed.

The man growled. "Watch it!" And then his face morphed and twisted and sickened. Suddenly, it was no longer a man's face growling at me, but a brown and black bloodshot demon's face.

"Ah!!!" I screamed and ran as fast as I could. Cars honked and swerved as I sprinted across all eight lanes of Westheimer Road.

Finally, the hotel my Mother had stayed in when she first came to my rescue was in sight. I bolted into the lobby and ran to the check-in counter, my fanny pack flapping away in front of me.

The woman behind the counter jumped when I collided with it. I immediately started listing off my demands. "I need the first room available. Preferably with a queen bed. No full or twin-size bullshit, please. And if the minibar is stocked, that would be great, but really, I just need a room! What's the first one you have available? I really need to get up there, now!"

The woman typed away at her computer frantically trying to keep up with my demands. "Okay, slow down, baby," she said in a motherly voice, "I wanna help you, but please slow down."

I stopped talking, but proceeded to jump in place, tapping frantically on the counter.

"I'm gonna need a card to put on file, dear."

I pulled my wallet out and slapped my card down in front of her. She swiped it and handed it back. An agonizing minute later, she handed me a hotel room key card with a number scrawled on the envelope.

"Thank you!" I yelled as I took the card and ran for the elevator. But when the elevator didn't open right away, I turned for the stairs and ran up the stairs.

"Keep moving. Keep moving. Keep moving."

The voice in my head was incessant. Even after I got in my room and collapsed on the bed, the voice continued to preach on, *"Keep moving. Keep moving. They know you're here. Keep moving!"*

The voice was right. The voice had to be right. The woman at the desk probably switched a silent alarm or something. It was only a matter of time before cops raided the room and arrested me.

I jumped up from the bed and ran out again, down the stairs, and back across the lobby into the street. Outside, a line of cabs waited. I jumped in the first available one and shouted to the driver, "Take me to a different hotel!"

"Buckle your seatbelt first, buddy," the driver retorted.

"Fuck you!" I jumped out of that cab and got into the next one. "Take me to a different hotel!"

The engine ignited and the driver drove off. Five minutes later I was at a neighboring hotel. I ran across the lobby, slammed into the check-in counter, and began rattling off my same list of demands.

"Whoa, whoa, whoa! What's going on?" the lady behind the counter cut me off.

"I need a room! The first one you have available! Now!"

"That's right," said the voice in my head. *"Keep running. Don't stop until you're clear of all the cops."*

"Hey, buddy, what's going on?" A big security guard had walked up behind me.

"I just want a room!" I screamed.

"I hear you, man. Look, this probably isn't the place for you, but if there's somewhere else you can go I'd be happy to take you."

The security guard sounded genuine. Either way, he wasn't going to let me get a room. I took him up on his offer.

The guard led me around the counter to a back office, which led to another door, which opened up outside to a small lot with a line of golf carts. At the end of the line was an SUV, which the guard invited me to get into. He started driving toward Westheimer. "Alright, where are we going, buddy?"

"Montrose," I said.

"You got it." When we got to Westheimer, the guard turned in the direction of Montrose.

Within thirty seconds of us turning onto Westheimer, a Houston Police Department patrol car pulled up alongside us.

The side window of the patrol car rolled down, and a police officer leaned out like he was about to say something, but then the security guard driving me raised a hand and waved the police officer away. The cop didn't say a word. Instead he leaned back in his car, rolled up his window and drove away.

I fidgeted nervously in the SUV. "So, what's your story, man?" the security guard asked.

I proceeded to tell him about growing up in Baton Rouge, going to the Air Force and living in Arizona, working as a kickass recruiter in Southern California, and then making my way to Houston where I served at Lakewood Church before getting kicked out and hitting a downward spiral. The security guard was silent throughout my whole recollection. When I got to the present moment, we were in Montrose. I thanked the security guard for the ride and got out of the SUV. And then it was back to wandering.

The voice in my head returned. *"What are you doing, fool? You think that patrol car just left you alone? They're tracking you! Probably by phone!"*

I panicked again. I pulled out my phone and powered it off. Then I ran for Thiago's place.

When I knocked frantically on his door, he was home. "Thiago!" I exclaimed, and gave him a big hug. "Oh, thank God you're here!"

"Sure, man," Thiago said hesitantly. I could feel him stiffen the longer I embraced him, so I let go. "What's going on?" he asked.

I closed his door and deadbolted it. Then I ran to his window and peeled back the blackout curtain.

"Yo, Token? What's going on?"

The courtyard below Thiago's window was flooded with men in plain clothes, but they all seemed to be looking about scratching their heads. *"Undercover cops. They know you're here."*

"Um," I started, wondering how to explain my situation to Thiago. "I think the cops are after me," I said plainly.

"You *think* the cops are after you?"

"I mean, it's hard to say," I stammered. "Like, I think all the guys in the courtyard below are undercover, but they're in civilian clothes so I don't know."

"Right," Thiago said. He sounded unconvinced.

Thiago joined me by the window and looked down. I pulled out my phone. I held down the power button on my cell phone. I felt it jolt with a little vibration as it sprang to life. Moments later, all the men in the courtyard sprang to life.

"He's here!" one of them yelled. Then they all ran for the entrance to the building.

From where Thiago and I were standing we could hear footsteps begin to echo from the hallway. I looked at Thiago as I panicked.

"Hide in the bathroom," he whispered to me. "I'll deal with these guys."

I ran to the bathroom, yanked the battery out of my cell phone, crouched in the tub, and tried to be as quiet as humanly possible.

There was a pounding on the door. Then some muttering voices that I couldn't make out. The muttering went back and forth for some time, but I never heard Thiago open the door. Eventually, everything was quiet.

The bathroom door opened. "You're all good, man," Thiago said, still whispering.

I shook my head. I didn't want to leave the tub. I was tired of the cat and mouse chase. If I was safe, I wanted to just stay put. And if I wasn't safe, I didn't want to risk falling into a trap. "I just want to stay here, man," I said to Thiago.

Thiago shrugged. "Suit yourself, bro. But listen, I've gotta go to work at eight in the morning, and you can't stay here while I'm gone."

I looked pleadingly at Thiago, begging him to change his mind.

"No, no exceptions. If I'm gone, no one stays here. This isn't a fucking trap house."

"Fine," I said begrudgingly.

Thiago left the bathroom, leaving me huddled in the tub, cradling my fanny pack.

"You're running out of options" said the voice in my head. *"What are you gonna do?"*

"Shush," I muttered. "Fuck off, I don't want to worry about that right now."

I sat in the tub and waited for Thiago to kick me out. Slowly my high faded.

* * *

At 8am when Thiago kicked me out, I panicked and sprinted to the nearest coffee shop where I sat fidgeting with my cell phone. *What should I do? I can't just get on a bus, they'll be looking for me. And I can't power on my phone or they'll locate me in an instant.*

I was out of options. If I was going to get caught, it had to be without the drugs. But it would be better to not get caught at all. *Is there a way I can dump the drugs and evade arrest?*

Yes, there was a way.

One last dash.

I stood up and wailed, "Oh my God! I'm having, like, chest convulsions!

I need you to call an ambulance! I'm gonna die!"

A worker ran to my aid. "Oh my gosh! Are you okay?"

"No!" I screamed. "I need you to call an ambulance, now!!!"

She pulled out her own cell phone and dialed 911. When the operator confirmed that an ambulance was on its way I asked the worker, "Do you have a bathroom? I need to use your bathroom." She showed me to their bathroom and punched in the code on the keypad to unlock the door for me.

"Holler if you need anything," she insisted. "I'll be right here."

I locked the door, opened my fanny pack, and threw my bag of drugs into the toilet. *What am I doing? ... I'm flushing $2,500 worth of ice down the drain is what I'm doing.*

I hit the handle on the toilet. A burst of water erupted into the bowl as the contents were flushed down the pipes and away forever. Then I exited the bathroom.

I breathed heavily, acting as if my lungs were in agony. Finally, the red and white lights of an ambulance arrived. Paramedics rushed into the coffee shop with a stretcher and laid me out on it. They rolled me out of the coffee shop and into the back of the ambulance. As I passed the driver's seat, I heard walkie-talkie chatter, *"Copy, subject is in the ambulance. Units are in route."*

Fuck! Was that the police?

"Do you have an insurance card and a form of identification?" one of the paramedics asked.

Careful to maintain the illusion I was in pain, I pulled out my wallet and gave the woman my VA card.

"De'Vannon, did you use the bathroom in that coffee shop?"

Why does she want to know that? Could they really predict that I'd flush my dope down the drain? Do they have some way of retrieving it from the plumbing to use as evidence?

"No," I said flatly.

On cue, I heard the siren of a police car accompanied by the sound of tires screeching to a halt. The car pulled up right behind the ambulance. From the back of the ambulance, I could see two officers look at me and speak into their radios. They wanted me badly, but they remained in their patrol car. For the moment, I was out of their reach.

"Mr. Hubert" said one of the medics, "there's nothing wrong with you. You can go."

"I want to go to the VA hospital," I insisted.

"Mr. Hubert, we've checked all your vitals. There's nothing–"

"No, I want to go to the VA!"

As long as I'm under the care of medics, I think I'm okay. I don't think the police can take me from an ambulance. That theory seemed to be holding up… until I was put in handcuffs.

No, this can't be the end. I can't go back to jail! I'll never get probation again!

I was placed in the back of a patrol car. "I'm telling you I need to go to the VA! Take me to the VA!"

The car started moving. *Where are they taking me?*

I panicked. I needed a way to get out of the vehicle. *Maybe if I fuck up their cruiser, they'll let me outta here.*

I tried to shit myself. I squeezed my abdomen and twisted my torso. I succeeded in farting.

"Ah, what the fuck? Did you just take a fucking shit back there? Oh hell no!"

I farted again. I felt the car immediately accelerate. The next time it stopped was at the VA Emergency Room. *They didn't take me to jail after all!*

In the VA ER, the cops finally uncuffed me. The waiting room was packed with people in civilian clothes, and they all cast frequent glances in my direction. There didn't seem to be anything wrong with them; no reason for them to be in an emergency room at all.

I sat in the waiting area but couldn't keep still. Nurses took my vitals and did bloodwork twice. I waited to see what would happen. At least, I tried to wait, but my skin began to itch again.

Why did I throw away my dope?

I wanted a Sprite. I saw a vending machine in the hallway and stood up to walk over to it. Almost immediately, a lady stood up and followed me. She acted as if she was waiting behind me for the vending machine while I stared at the bottles in front of me, but I knew she was really watching me.

I've gotta get out of here.

I made my way toward the doors.

"Code green! Code green!" someone shouted over the intercom. I turned to look, and six VA security guards were running in my direction. I sighed. I didn't want to run. I walked back to the ER waiting area and sat back down.

Almost a full hour went by before the nurses took me to a room and took even more vitals. "Have you taken any drugs?" one of the nurses asked.

Why is she asking that? Is she trying to get a confession that I broke probation?
"No," I said.

"Nothing in the past seventy-two hours?" the nurse asked again.

"No," I insisted. "I haven't done anything."

The nurse huffed and left the room. I thought I heard chatter in the hallway. *Are they talking to the police? Are the cops here? Are they going to arrest me and take me in anyway?*

Am I completely surrounded? Is there no way out of this?

I got up to leave again. I made it to the lobby without anyone yelling "code green," but then I heard someone say, "Paging Doctor Strange." I b-lined it for the door. Suddenly, everybody in civilian clothes in the lobby stood up and crowded in front of the exit, blocking my escape.

The nurse came running into the lobby behind me. "De'Vannon?" she said, hesitantly. "Look, all these people are here for you, okay? Now come back to the room."

I felt defeated. There was nothing I could do other than do what I was told. I was powerless, and I hated it.

I followed the nurse back to the hospital room and sat down. She prepared a dixie cup with a concoction of pills and had me take them all. And then everything went black.

* * *

I woke up to the feeling of something scraping against the bottom of my foot.

"You gave him too much," a voice said.

"Hmm?" I stirred.

"Oh, good!" the doctor said. "You've given us quite the scare, Mr. Hubert. You've been out cold for three days. Ready to go home?"

Home. The word echoed in my head. *Yes, home.*

I asked to use the telephone and called my Mother.

"De'Vannon? Where are you, boy?"

"Oh, I'm in the Houston VA hospital. In the psych ward."

I heard my Mother sigh. Then the speaker on her end of the line got muffled. I thought I heard my dad's voice. When my Mother got back on the phone she said, *"Okay, you take the next Greyhound Bus back, right away."*

I explained the plan to the hospital staff, and they gave me papers to sign myself out. When I looked at the date on the papers, I realized it was my 30th birthday. *Fuck me. This was not at all how I had imagined my 30th birthday would be.*

I felt like I had reached a new low as I made my way to the bus station to head home to my Mother.

EPILOGUE: BITTERSWEET

(2013-2022)

2013 – LOUISIANA

I was down in New Orleans, high and sketched out once again and on the run from someone, but I wasn't sure who. But in case it was the cops I checked into a civilian mental hospital and told them that I was suicidal. This guaranteed me at least three days to hopefully get the heat off me and protect me from incarceration. Baton Rouge is only about an hour away from New Orleans, but I didn't have a car and I had no way to get home.

On the third day when I was due to be discharged, I asked to be released into the custody of the VA. The VA psychiatrist agreed on the condition that I go directly into rehab. I gave my consent to her request, and she prepared my transfer.

The psychiatrist sent me to the VA hospital in Shreveport which is in the northwest part of Louisiana, and over 300 miles and at least 5 hours away from New Orleans. She said this was the best choice since it was far away from everyone I knew which meant I could focus on rehabilitating without getting distracted, or getting into any more trouble. An Acadian Ambulance drove me all the way to Shreveport from the mental hospital in New Orleans, and I spent the next two weeks in a psych ward where

I wasn't allowed to go outside. I was hardly allowed to leave the floor I was assigned to. All the furniture was bolted to the ground, and in the rooms adjacent to mine were guys talking to themselves, taking shits on the floor, and constantly getting thrown into isolation. I made macaroni art and leather coin purses while I watched the world outside my window move on without me. I hated every minute of it. All I could think about was getting high the moment I got out.

After I was released from the psych ward I went to live in a half-way house in Shreveport for 45 days. During this time, I attended a substance abuse program at the VA and got exposed to Alcoholics Anonymous for the first time. It sucked that there was no from of treatment available specific to my addiction and I never quite felt like I fit in or belonged in the rooms of AA. With this reservation in my mind, I was never completely open to healing and rehabilitation and so I rebelled.

After rehab ended, I scored a hit of dope and took the bus back to Baton Rouge. My parents were ready to bet on me again and they bought me a used Ford Focus as a gesture of good will. That was a happy surprise for me. The first thing I did was visit Evangelist Nelson.

* * *

As I stood in the open doorway of Evangelist Nelson's home, she gave me a long, hard look. "Lord have mercy, child. You ought to be hospitalized! There isn't a shred of meat on you, nor a glimmer of life in you."

I was crestfallen.

Evangelist Nelson saw my face sadden. "Come in and sit down, child." Once we were at the kitchen table, she started up again. "Look, De'Vannon. God's still putting breath in your lungs for a reason. You have to find out what that reason is. But before that, you have to be willing to *live*. Are you willing to live?"

"Yes," I said, taken aback. "I am." I meant it. Since getting out of jail and realizing that the HIV medication could work, I wanted to make my life work, too. But as I looked back at Evangelist Nelson who was still pressing the same question on me with her gaze, I began to discern the nuance in my answer.

"I don't want to die," I said. *I'm not actually sure if that means I want to live.*

"De'Vannon, if you want to live, then you have to fight for life. You have to fight for *your* life. And if you don't fight for your life and God still puts life in you, then I'm gonna be fighting for you every night in my prayers. Child, your heavenly Father is going to war for your soul. But there's a war of both good and evil that's raging inside of you that ultimately only you can fight. And you can win, but first you have to be willing to fight."

I hung my head. *Since when did life get to be so intense?*

"And child, look at me," Evangelist Nelson said. I obeyed, lifting my gaze to meet hers. "You're not alone. You never have been. You know I'll always be in your corner."

"I know you've always got my back. I was so lonely out there in Houston. I walked the streets by myself for months, but it felt like years. People avoided me because I smelled like a grave. And when I needed help, the only people who showed up for me were my parents, my attorney, a tweaker named Thiago, and my gay drug dealer."

"Your drug dealer isn't gay," Evangelist Nelson said almost immediately.

"What?" *How could Casey not be gay?* "But he has a boyfriend." I didn't know if I could call Lorenzo gagged and bound by Casey's side a "boyfriend," but I didn't know what else to call him.

"Have you ever seen him do anything with this *boyfriend*?" Evangelist Nelson asked.

I thought about all the times I had been around Casey and Lorenzo. I had never actually *seen* Casey do anything sexual with Lorenzo.

"This drug dealer of yours has a wife and an entirely separate life," Evangelist Nelson said. "This boyfriend is a disguise. If anything, he only likes seeing gay men get humiliated. He's a very dangerous man, De'Vannon. If you ever happen to see him again, walk away."

I was silent for a long time as I played back every memory I had of Casey. *Has he been pretending this whole time?* It didn't matter. If Evangelist Nelson said he was dangerous and that I should never see him again, I was never going to see him again.

Evangelist Nelson waited patiently as I pondered. I could sense her warm spirit reaching out to me. In her silence was an offer for help, relief, and solace that I didn't know I needed. We continued in the silence and I felt the stillness begin to heal me.

Then I wept.

"Alright," Evangelist Nelson soothed. "I've got you, son. I've got you. It's going to be alright."

I wept for a good long time. Evangelist Nelson didn't speak until I had calmed down.

"You are stronger than you know, De'Vannon. But you're also more injured than you realize. You still have wounds from Nico that haven't fully healed." She paused and collected her thoughts, remembering the man who had haunted me during my teenage years. "He was so angry... *Oh, he was so very angry*. Did you know he had AIDS?"

I shook my head. "I was told he had cancer."

"Nico willingly stopped taking his HIV medication to increase his viral load, and he was having sex with all kinds of people trying to infect them. He was trying to infect you too. And he knew that without the medication he was going to die."

I couldn't believe what I was hearing, but it all made sense.

"Your soul has deep scars," Evangelist Nelson said, gently. "Your scars need tending to. Healing is hard work, child. Do you understand what I'm saying?"

I didn't know what to say. I didn't know how to heal, and I didn't know how I was ever going to rebuild my life.

"What else is troubling you, De'Vannon?"

An angry tension gripped my throat and I let my thoughts run wild: *I want revenge against all the fuckers in Houston who fucked me over and took everything from me!!! Fuck that damned informant!!! Fuck them all!!! Maybe I can go back there, find them and...*

"De'Vannon," Evangelist Nelson said with a new intensity in her voice, "whatever you're thinking of doing, it isn't going to help you. Whoever hurt you back in Houston, you need to let them go."

Suddenly I was in tears again. I was thankful that Evangelist Nelson understood me, and the fact that she did made me feel seen and loved.

"Okay," I said through my tears. "I'll try."

Evangelist Nelson took my hand. "Look, I'm not saying the road ahead of you is easy, but please believe me when I say, child, prayer changes things."

* * *

It was really hard to pass a drug test, but I finally succeeded and enrolled in the VA's Compensated Work Therapy program. I had three felonies, so I couldn't find work anywhere, but through CWT I found tax free minimum wage work as a janitor at the VA Outpatient Clinic in Baton Rouge.

When my first direct deposit for $250 arrived in my bank account I fell down on my knees and cried. It was the first time since I had left CenterPoint Energy that I'd earned legitimate money. Suddenly the prospect of having a future begin to drift into focus.

I got pissed off one day and walked off the janitor job. I had been there for over a year and a half, but it was time to move the fuck on. There was only two of us janitors for the whole building and the other guy was a full-time employee. He vexed me and made my life at work a living hell. He would do things like take a shit, intentionally make the toilet overflow, and then leave work for the rest of the day. Since I would be the only janitor left I had to literally clean his shit up. Some of the other full-time employees were abusive as well, and no matter how much I protested I was never heard. Whenever there is a dispute, veterans in the CWT program are never believed over a full-time VA employee, even if the VA employee is in the wrong.

* * *

Trying to rebuild my life, after having lost everything, is the hardest thing I have ever had to do. On minimum wage I was going nowhere fast. I needed more work. I tried another job where I helped build and refurbish furniture.

The team I was assigned to would go to offices and put cubicles together. We would also take in scratched up tables and chairs, and make them look brand new. It paid better than my janitor job had and I liked working with my hands, but I couldn't stand my boss.

This time my boss was a mean, domineering woman who could not be satisfied. There was never any sense of gratitude for the hard work me and my team were doing. I hated how thankless the work was, and after a couple months I quit.

* * *

I didn't know where to find meth in Baton Rouge, but I would make frequent trips down to New Orleans attempting to get engaged in the night life there. I made connections with a couple meth dealers, but eventually shit got really sketchy and my trips became less frequent. I had a genuine will to live, and New Orleans was becoming as unsafe for me as Houston.

Slowly, meth became more of a peripheral indulgence in my life. Crack on the other hand was in full swing. In the hood, crack is everywhere. I could spin in a circle blindfolded and point to any random house and the odds were good that I could find crack there.

Ever obsessed with the process of ingesting drugs, I found out how to shoot up crack on Google. But I actually felt like I was making an improvement. Compared to meth, crack wasn't nearly as hard on my body. In a way, crack was my gateway drug to sobriety.

* * *

The relationship between my dad and I worsened. I hated having to move back in with my parents at the age of 30, and we both hated living with each other. No amount of improvement in my situation was good enough for him. He verbally berated me. I was desperate to leave, but I couldn't afford to live on my own.

One day while I was picking up my prescriptions at the VA, I started talking to a veteran about a program through the VA where we could get help with housing. *This was the same program my cousin Harriet at the VA in Houston was telling me about!*

"Wait, where do I find more info?" I asked him.

"You don't," he said. "They don't advertise this shit. And it ain't gonna be easy to get. You have to really push hard for it. I'm still pressing the issue myself."

The next day I made my way to the VA and told the lady at the front desk, "If I have to keep living with my dad, I am going to kill him! I can't do this shit anymore! Is there anything you can do to help?"

Startled, the lady dug in her desk for a pamphlet and handed it to me. It had information about housing assistance programs on a city-to-city basis.

I found out that in Baton Rouge I could be given $600 in housing support each month. *Plus, a utility allowance!* I applied for the program.

Since I was already enrolled in mental health at the VA, they assigned me a case manager and a social worker to evaluate my circumstances. They wanted to know where I was living, who I was living with, and how many "instances of homelessness" I had experienced between couch surfing my way through various trap houses. I checked all the boxes and they were able to obtain vouchers from the regional Housing Authority for me. They also got me connected with the State so I could start receiving Food Stamps.

My Mother and I spent the next month researching Baton Rouge's apartments and made sure I got one that was perfect for me. We found a place about two miles from my parents' house. My parents furnished the apartment for me and did everything they could to help me succeed.

When I moved out of my parents' house I only had one suitcase to pack. But it was a miracle. I had my own place again!!!

* * *

I did a web search for "food delivery," interviewed at the first place I saw listed, and got hired immediately.

I hustled in my little Ford Focus my parents had got for me trying to make the hours work to my advantage. It was a grind. The company I worked for took a large cut of the payments, and after paying for gas I wasn't earning a lot. And people don't tend to tip delivery drivers well at all. Still, it was a net gain of something, so I kept at it. I knew the odds of me finding work anywhere else were slim to none due to my felonies.

One afternoon I pulled into a restaurant's parking lot to pick up a food order. As I got out of my car, a man who looked like he was just out for a jog walked up to me. There was what seemed to be electricity in his eyes. I immediately felt strange in his presence.

"Have any money?" he asked. "I need some money to buy gas for my car."

I only had 36 cents in my pocket, which felt like having nothing at all, so I responded: "No."

"Not even change?" the man pressed, as if he already knew I had change in my pocket.

"I'm sorry," I said, and turned to lock my car door. *What am I doing?* I wondered. *It's only 36 cents. It's like having nothing at all anyway.*

I changed my mind and turned to go give the man the coins in my pocket... but he was nowhere to be seen. There was a black truck parked near me, and I went to check the other side of it, but the man was gone. There were no other cars in the parking lot. In the split second it had taken me to change my mind, the man had had vanished.

Did I just meet an Angel?

In that moment I felt more comforted and watched over than I had in years. It was God's way of personally reminding me that I was in fact *not* alone.

That night I dreamed for the first time since being kicked out of Lakewood Church. I started dreaming a lot about everything that had happened to me in Houston. I would wake up in my bed sideways and in a total panic. Evangelist Nelson said I was reliving everything I had suffered in Houston. I felt like all the negativity from the bad experiences that I had suffered through had been locked inside of me, but it was now coming back out. It was like going through everything all over again.

* * *

I finally committed to an idea I had when I was living in Montrose building up my underwear collection. *Why don't I sell underwear?* The answer had always been *because I don't need the money, and I'd much rather wear the underwear.* Well, now I *needed* the money. I got on my laptop and began my research.

Finding a wholesale underwear supplier was an ordeal, but the people I eventually found are who I still source from to this very day. I ordered a bunch of merchandise and set up storage in my apartment. *Okay, now I have to sell all this shit... and not wear the product.*

There were two flea markets I visited that were willing to bring me on. One was in Baton Rouge and was run by a friendly group of people who loved the idea of an underwear shop, but they didn't have sufficient air conditioning in their building. The other flea market was a bit of a drive over to Denham Springs, but they had air conditioning. And since Southern Louisiana summers can melt the black off of asphalt, this girl *had* to have her AC!

I went with my parents to Walmart and bought "Mickey Mouse Yellow" paint. We spent the next two days painting the inside walls of the booth, and when we were done it looked fabulous. I chose yellow because that is the color of attraction, spiritually speaking. My parents also helped me buy stickers, plastic bags, cleaning supplies, and hangers to display the underwear on. We also bought PVC pipe to build a dressing room. I was ready.

The rent was $250 per month, and I moved my store in. I named it DownUnder Apparel. To my delight, the ladies who ran the other booths loved me and my store and were quick to welcome me into their community. It helped that I had a large poster in the back of my booth depicting one of my model friends posing in nothing but underwear and holding a soccer ball. My booth was polarizing, but popular with the ladies running the other booths, and that mattered the most.

I wanted to sell kinkier shit, but the flea market had rules: no jockstraps and no thongs. I sold swimwear, briefs, boxer briefs, but nothing too revealing. The women tried to encourage me to sell that stuff anyways.

"You can just hide the kinky shit behind the counter or something!" they would say to me.

I loved their support and their ideas, but my response was always the same. "I don't want to get kicked out!" This was probably my only shot to make this business work, and I could not afford to fuck it up. Thankfully, the ladies were understanding. My first sale was to one of them buying something for her lesbian daughter, which warmed my heart.

For the sake of variety, I did reach out to other wholesale vendors to buy stuff like tank-tops, bowties, socks, gloves, etc.

The flea market was open every day and had tons of traffic, but because of my other job I would only go to my store on the weekends. The ladies watched over my booth during the other days of the week, and if they were able, they would facilitate transactions and hold the money for me until Friday. I became a part of the flea market family, and from the get-go business was good.

I only made about $250 in profit for the first several months, but I was never in the red.

There was one other male vendor at the flea market and he had the *hots* for me. It also turned out he was a meth dealer. I told him I wasn't buying, but because he wanted to stick his dick in me, he gifted me with a *shit ton* of meth. He wasn't my type, but I wasn't saying no to free meth, so I took the gift and managed to stave off his sexual advances. This was a setback because I had managed to maintain my sobriety for several months until this happened.

My sleep worsened, and the drive down to the flea market on the weekends became more unbearable. Furthermore, I was beginning to feel less safe in the evenings when I packed up and closed for the night. I was seeing some sketchy-ass dude poking his head around corners and glancing in my direction.

Then one day a man in a big white cowboy hat came up to me and asked, "Hey, are you the *underwear dealer* we've been hearing about?"

I didn't know who he meant by "we," but it was clear to me that the people in Denham Springs were talking about the gay Black guy selling underwear at the flea market. I got a feeling that I shouldn't be sticking around much longer.

I made one last trip to the flea market to pack up my booth and leave. Then I never went back.

* * *

I had a friend who recommended I try using WordPress to build a website for DownUnder. She helped me lay the foundation, and suddenly I was selling underwear on the internet.

I learned that I could have my wholesale supplier dropship orders directly to my customers so merchandise didn't have to go through me, which helped ease my expenses dramatically.

I started blogging about underwear, and I tried all kinds of different advertising. The strategy that worked best, though, was time. Sales didn't come in as quickly as I wanted them to so I had to learn to be patient.

About a year later I was invited to a party and I met someone who felt like he could improve my business. He looked at my website and suggested we build a whole new version of it on Shopify. Apparently, Shopify was created for ecommerce shops and DownUnder could go a lot further on that platform as opposed to WordPress. He only charged me the bare minimum it would cost to do the work, and over the course of a week he made it look like a fully professional website, SEO optimized and everything. Sales only continued to go up from that point on.

* * *

After I got burnt out on delivering food I found work waiting tables at Another Broken Egg. I happened to have a friend who worked there and she helped me get hired.

Working as a waiter was a relief from the craziness of food delivery. I didn't have to work late because Another Broken Egg was a breakfast establishment, and I ended up working less hours for the same amount of money. It also helped that I didn't have to pay for gas every day.

Being a waiter also helped me learn how to deal with society again. Large groups of people would come in expecting to be seated immediately. It was common for arguments to break out when people with reservations were seated before them. Mediating these fights helped me learn that most points of conflict in life are of very low consequence. At first, I was extremely uncomfortable around unhappy customers, but I learned that nothing bad ever came of their displeasure. No one was going to hire a hitman to come and kill me because I couldn't accommodate their ridiculous expectations.

* * *

It came into my mind to revisit my dream of being a massage therapist. I had never gone back to my massage school in Houston after receiving my HIV diagnosis. I had felt far too filthy to touch people on most days and that was not a suitable mindset to have when I was trying to be a massage therapist.

I looked up massage programs in Baton Rouge, found one that had night classes, and signed up. My tuition was still 100 percent covered by the G.I. Bill, and I wanted to retake the full year-long program because I figured I would be rusty on everything I had learned before. I was one of twelve students in the class, and I hated most of the others. They complained about having to learn all the anatomy of the human body, and one guy wouldn't let any of the other males practice on him. I tried to ignore their negative attitudes and just kept my head down and focused on my own learning.

Only six of the original twelve students in my massage course finished it with me. A massage clinic tried to recruit us, and while a couple people took the offer, some of us had bigger plans for our careers. I had no intention of working *for* someone, especially when it came to something I loved as much as being a massage therapist.

I graduated from massage therapy school in 2018 and enough time had finally passed since my felonies for me to be eligible to be licensed for massage in the state of Louisiana. Even though enough time had passed since my felonies, I still had to appear before the Louisiana Board of Massage Therapy to explain my past. I felt like it was an unnecessary step, but they said they wanted to be "thorough." Thankfully I was cleared. This allowed me to open my own private massage therapy practice and quit waiting tables. I went all-fucking-out!

My plan was to offer more than everyone else and charge less than everyone else. I ordered a custom table, over 60 essential oils, hot stones, Himalayan salt stones, and the best of everything I could get my hands on. Energetically speaking, my massage room was perfectly balanced.

I was at a wine party one night and I shared with some friends about my plan for my massage therapy practice. One of my friends asked, "So what's going to be the name of your practice?"

I paused. I hadn't actually given it a permanent name yet. But then one friend had an epiphany: "You know, since you have a mole in the middle of your forehead, a perfect third eye, I think it might be nice to name it something related to vision." The idea was well received, and that night I began looking up different ways to describe the third eye in different languages.

The moment I saw the word for "vision" in Swahili, I knew that had to be the one. *Maono*. I loved that it started with an "M" as did "Massage." It was perfect. *Maono Massage & Wellness* was born! The same friend who designed my website for DownUnder set up another website for Maono. I had custom scrubs made, as well as custom polo shirts, a shit-ton of business cards... anything I could get the name of my practice printed on, I did.

I spoiled my clients and made it hard for them not to want to keep coming back to see me. I set flat rates for my sessions and I never upcharged for any services. Whatever a paying customer wanted in the time allotted to them, I provided. I only scheduled four people per day so I could take my time with each client and make sure they never felt rushed. When they came in, I immediately donned them with a neck warmer and then poured them a drink (wine or champagne). Word of mouth spread quickly.

Within a couple months I was making a profit! *Business was good!*

A few months after I opened my practice, I was browsing through some boxes of books at my parents' place that were left over from when my grandmother died, and I found an old book called "Hands-on Healing: Massage Remedies for Hundreds of Health Problems." My grandmother had never mentioned massage therapy to me, but I discovered that she was fascinated with alternative healing as well. I felt like Jesus was doing a work to make sure that passion stayed alive in my family.

One day a friend invited me out to a bar at 7pm, but I had a massage scheduled at that time. When I explained my scheduling conflict my friend said, "Chyle, you don't need to stay open late like that anymore!"

His words shocked me, but before I pushed back, I considered what he was trying to tell me. I did some quick mental math and realized, *He's right!* I was finally at a place where I did not have to take clients late and sacrifice my social life. After hearing his advice and realizing I had paid my dues, I adjusted my availability for future appointments.

* * *

I continued to attend Pentecostal services at Evangelist Nelson's church, but the whole experience was tarnished by my having flashbacks of Lakewood. I didn't feel accepted. I wouldn't have attended church at all if it wasn't for Evangelist Nelson being there. After a while I started to experiment and seek out spiritual community elsewhere.

Evangelist Nelson made sure I was seeing her for monthly counseling sessions, but I still wasn't fully committed to her church. I knew the people at her church didn't like the LGBTQIA+ community either. Evangelist Nelson seemed to be the only soul that was different.

She was so far and beyond the theology of any denomination when it came to her Godly obedience to love other people. The only reason she didn't fuss about the rules with the male leaders was because she didn't want to cause division. Thankfully she still made time to minister to me personally.

It wasn't until I visited a Buddhist temple out of curiosity that I began to understand what it looked like to have respect for people of different faiths and lifestyles. I wasn't trying to convert, and the people there weren't trying to convert me. In fact, we had really interesting discussions about what we believed and got to know each other really well. The temple was immaculate and the grounds around it looked like paradise. I also couldn't help but notice that they never asked for money (and they seemed to have plenty of it).

I did further research about other religions online as my desire to expand my perspective intensified. I knew I wasn't going to get an objective education in a church building, so I explored and continued to visit other places on my own.

One night when I was leaving a Buddhist temple, I got a call from Evangelist Nelson. *"What's going on, De'Vannon? Where are you right now?"*

"I'm actually leaving a Buddhist temple," I explained.

"Oh, well I guess that's why the Spirit told me to call you. Ok, read the 23rd Psalm."

Evangelist Nelson hung up. I appreciated that about her. She didn't criticize me for going to another place of worship or even tell me not to go. I don't really know why she told me to read that Psalm, but when I did, I felt reenergized and better aligned. *I know Buddha is not the God that I serve. I know I will only ever worship Jesus. But where? It's so hard to find Christians who are accepting of openly gay people like me, not to mention recovering drug addicts with a criminal record.*

*   *   *

Evangelist Nelson faded quickly in her last month. She was 80 years old, and she knew before anyone else that her time had come. She told us several times throughout that final month, but most of us were in denial.

"Oh, no, Evangelist, this'll pass. Whatever this is, it'll go and you'll recover. Don't worry" people would say.

What we didn't realize, though, was that Evangelist Nelson wasn't worried. She was fearless and ready to go be with the Lord. It was the rest of us who were worried. We couldn't imagine going on without our powerful spiritual leader.

One of Evangelist Nelson's final prophecies that she shared with us was that *we wouldn't recognize this world in three years.* Three years later was the outbreak of the coronavirus pandemic. When I think of this prophecy, I am reminded of a vision my grandmother told me about when I was younger: she saw the sun as though it were a huge, flaming ball of fire taking up a large part of the sky. The vision shook my grandmother so much that her knees buckled and her legs gave out. She fell down against the side of her vehicle and immediately called Evangelist Nelson. Evangelist Nelson said it was a Doomsday sign.

Speaking personally, I was in complete denial that my Evangelist could ever die. She always had so much life in her, and I couldn't imagine a world without her healing presence in it. But her heart and lungs weakened and sure enough she ended up in the hospital.

I visited Evangelist Nelson as frequently as I could. So did much of her family and other people from within the community. One night, after everyone had left, I decided to stick around in her hospital room. For some reason I couldn't bring myself to leave her side. Her husband was sleeping soundly on the couch. She and I talked like the days when I was her altar boy in her office before a church service. The three of us being there together reminded me of old times when it would be just us sitting up in the pulpit at church on so many Sundays.

"De'Vannon, call my daughter in Texas, will you? I want to talk to her."

I grabbed her cell phone and dialed her daughter's number, and then a few other numbers of people she wanted to talk to. After she had called all the people she wanted to, her breathing quickly worsened.

"De'Vannon, I have to go to the bathroom," she said. This meant I had to find a nurse to assist her since she couldn't get up on her own. I retrieved a nurse and waited outside the room. I waited but the nurse didn't come out.

Standing outside the door I could hear my Evangelist ask for help breathing and then she let out a loud howl that echoed down into the furthest reaches of my soul. Then all I heard was silence. The nurse walked out of the room and went back to the nurse's station.

I rushed into the room and found Evangelist Nelson's eyes closed. She looked like she was sleeping. But she wasn't breathing. And the heart rate monitor showed that her heart was slowing down, the gaps between the beats increasing. I panicked.

I ran to the nurse's station. "She's dying!" I yelled. "Do something!"

"We have orders not to resuscitate," the nurse said calmly.

"So you're just going to let her die?"

The nurse gave me a weak smile.

I ran back to the hospital room. The heart rate monitor beeped slower, and slower. Eventually the beeps just stopped. I couldn't believe this was happening.

I called my Mother. "Evangelist Nelson has died! I'm at the hospital. Please come!"

I didn't cry as I stood over Evangelist Nelson's lifeless body. As her friends and family arrived I simply told them what happened and left it at that. I felt devoid of all emotion.

"De'Vannon!"

It was my Mother. I turned and ran into her arms. The moment we embraced, the dam in my heart broke and I began to sob bitterly. I could hardly stand, but my Mother held me up.

I had lost one of the most loving people in my life and the wounds were catastrophic, but the longer my Mother held me the more I was assured that I would heal; I would recover. I would not let the work Evangelist Nelson had done in my life be in vain.

I cried for what I'd lost, but I saw someone die with grace and peace, and that changed my perspective about life and death. Her funeral had the church packed full of people who were just as surprised as me that someone who had lived so powerfully in the Spirit had died. But Evangelist Nelson said she had completed her work and that she was glad to finally be with Jesus. She got her wings like she wanted, and I know one day I'll be joining her.

After Evangelist Nelson died, I tried to continue going to the Pentecostal church where she'd ministered, but it never felt quite right for me to be there without her. Looking up at her empty chair on the pulpit caused me grief that I couldn't handle. I felt like a lost and wandering soul because my leader to whom I was fiercely bonded was gone, and nobody could replace her. I parted ways with the Pentecostals and never looked back.

* * *

Around the time the coronavirus pandemic hit I ended up joining a Crystal Meth Anonymous group and got myself a sponsor. Zoom meetings made it possible for me to find support groups literally all over the world. I was thankful to find a meeting in San Francisco with a group of people I felt like I could relate with better than the people in Baton Rouge. After reaching my peak in CMA, I started studying Rational Recovery and other alternatives to the Anonymous movement which I felt were more in line with my way of thinking. The desire to let drugs go was only part of the battle. Out there in those streets is a strong sense of community and for a time that community had accepted me whereas the church had not. There came a point where I wasn't even enjoying the high anymore, but I found I was still seeking community in old places that were not congruent my new lifestyle. It was hard to say goodbye to the people, places, and things that once made me feel loved and accepted, but I had to.

* * *

During the pandemic I also attended the Hypnostist Motivation Institute online and became a Certified Hypnot. My original intent was to couple hypnosis with massage therapy, but the pandemic crushed that dream.

Due to COVID-19, I made the decision to close down my massage therapy practice. I felt like the pandemic was the sort of thing we had talked about in our Ethics class while I was still in training for my massage license. The government said it was safe to do massages, but my heart told me otherwise.

I'm now trying to make the best of DownUnder Apparel in the online retail space. I started a podcast (Sex, Drugs & Jesus) and wrote this book. I'd love to be able to say that I've finally arrived, but the truth is that I am in a constant state of evolution, and I have so much more to learn.

* * *

Whether my story feels like a mirror image of your life or just some crazy fucked up nightmare, I hope my final words resonant with you on some level:

Even when you feel abandoned and all by yourself, *you are not alone*. God is with you. He's fighting for you, and he wants to fight with you. He always has, and always will. There is literally nothing that can separate you from his love.

My goal in writing this memoir was to be painfully transparent, with the aim of inspiring more open-mindedness and empathy with regard to people going through, or who have gone through, similar struggles. I also hold the hope of helping others avoid the troubles I have been through or at the very least to know that *you are not alone* if you are going through similar struggles as you read this.

I would like to encourage everyone to pay close attention to their spiritual health. It is very easy for us to become casual in the way we approach spiritual matters, or to not deal with such matters at all, but our spirits and souls are a significant part of our being. If we fail to feed them in some way, then we will fall out of balance. If this happens, then we can never truly be whole. I know not everyone is going to follow Christ like I do, but everyone should decide on some type of spiritual path, no matter what it is.

Have you been hurt by the church? Do you know someone who has been treated poorly by the church? I know this can be incredibly discouraging, but please consider a spiritual path again. Attending church is not necessary for a healthy spiritual life, though they can provide community for those who benefit from such company. There is nothing more meaningful or important to your spiritual walk than your alone time with whoever you choose to believe in. Churches are a mere accessory to your spiritual journey which you can choose to use, or not.

To my 2SLGBTQIA+ FAMILY, I beg you to stop attending churches that do not affirm our lifestyle. It is one of the most abusive things you can do to yourself. Such places do not deserve you. They do not deserve your gifts. They damn well do not deserve your financial resources. The Gay Dollar is strong, and it should not be found in such places. Further, a church that thinks our lifestyle is a sin but "no different than any other sin," is included in this abusive category. There is nothing wrong with you at all. Periodt!!! There are several affirming denominations out there to select from, and — even if you live in a town without options — with a good internet connection you can attend these denominations' services online.

Thank you so much for reading my story. I appreciate it immensely. Feel free to reach out to me and just remember that everything is going to be alright!

The following story is a snapshot from my early teen years in which I went through a very traumatic experience involving some very dark spiritual elements. Had I not lived through this myself I might find such a story hard to believe.

Witchcraft is real.

WISDOM & WITCHERY

(1997)

I was excited to be Evangelist Nelson's first ever altar boy. It was my chance to be *special*.

But when I showed up to church to prepare for service, I noticed a new man sitting at the piano. And the choir director was nowhere to be seen. The new man started to sing and play a worship song, and I wondered if he might be the new choir director.

Since my seat was in the pulpit, I was right next to the piano, but I faced away from it. I tried to steal looks at this new mystery man, but I had to sit with my back to him.

He wore studded earrings and wireframe glasses. He had flawless caramel skin and a jawline that looked like a lethal weapon. His muscles pressed up against the sleeves of his shirt as his hands danced across the keys on the piano. Then he started to sing. The microphone wasn't turned on yet, but his voice was booming wonderfully. I was enchanted. *Who is this man?*

After the opening song, Evangelist Nelson stood up and gestured to the man at the piano. "Good morning everyone, this is Brother Nicolai, our new choir director!"

Nicolai stood and waved. A warm aroma of bergamot and lavender caressed my nostrils. I started to sweat beneath my altar boy uniform. My attraction to this man was instant and torturous.

After church, I hurried to wrap up my altar boy duties and rush out to the dining hall where Nicolai was surrounded by congregants.

"I'm De'Vannon." My voice cracked. I held out my hand. When Nicolai shook it, his middle finger tickled my palm. My stomach turned upside down as a shiver went up my spine.

"It's a pleasure to worship with you, De'Vannon," he smiled. "I'm Nico. Do you go by Dee?"

He let go of my hand. I felt goosebumps stand up on my arm. *No one ever calls me Dee.* "Yes, sir," I lied. Then Nico turned to greet another family, as he *winked* at me! I was dizzy.

* * *

Our church went on a trip to Orlando, Florida, just as a hurricane was predicted to hit. During the ride I kept wondering whether our bus was going to turn back, but we went further into the thick of the storm. When we arrived the palm trees were nearly horizontal from the hurricane force winds blowing through the city. I was relieved when we finally made it to the hotel. The wind howled all through the night.

By morning, the rain had calmed enough for us to go to Disney World.

Before we entered the park, we had to wait in line for thirty minutes. By the time we were through, I needed to use the bathroom, but that had a line, too. I barely made it.

Then I waited in line for another forty-five minutes to ride Space Mountain. But when I was finally buckled in and ready to go, the wind and rain picked up again and they shut down the ride. I was furious.

I met up with my brother, and while we waited in line for food Nico caught up with us. After lunch, Nico and I went to try our luck at Space Mountain, but it was still closed.

"Hey, man, nice jacket," Nico complimented me.

"Thanks," I responded. I was wearing a windbreaker since the weather was kinda cool in the aftermath of the hurricane.

"Hey, can I check it out?" Nico asked.

"Sure," I said, flattered that he wanted to see my jacket. "No problem."

"Thanks, brother," he slipped it on. "I appreciate you."

After a few minutes, Nico walked off and I couldn't find him for the rest of the trip.

Weeks later, back in Baton Rouge, I was falling asleep on the top bunk when the smell of Nico's cologne wafted over me. I dreamt vividly of him that night, and when I woke his scent was still in the air. It hung on me even after a shower. No one else seemed to notice it, though.

* * *

Mother and dad hosted a housewarming party. I saw a lot of people from church, but there were also some faces I didn't recognize. And then there was Nico, his trademark cologne lingering in the wake of his booming voice. He was wearing a tight, black, button-down with small white birds spotted all over it, and white shorts that stopped at least three inches above his knees. A golden necklace hung just beneath the top of his shirt's neckline, beautifully framing his dark chest hair. I found myself following him at a distance.

I was mesmerized by his presence. He commanded his space with an enviable comfort. I wanted to be with him the way I was with Dillon, but every time I caught his eye, he looked away. I chased.

He evaded. To the bathroom. He was clever.

I wandered over to the platters my Mother had set out on the dining room table. There were more cheeses than I could name, crackers with green seasoning on them, and crackers with raisins baked into them. There was also traditional Southern bar-b-que and jambalaya, which I immediately loaded onto a plate. I wasn't sure which of the unfamiliar cheeses I wanted to try first, though. I decided I was going to try all of them, so I reached for the slices nearest to me. As soon as my fingers touched a soft, white slice, I heard a soft voice in my ear.

"Good choice," Nico muttered. "You wouldn't want the Gruyére making your breath all nutty. Unless nutty is your preferred palate." Nico's breath was minty, and the bergamot of his cologne was overpowering.

As I turned around, his eyes hooked me in a hypnotic stare. They were black and shone like obsidian in the dim light of the dining room.

"Fresh air?" he invited, before brushing past me toward the front door. I left my loaded plate on the table and followed him, dumb with desire, and numb with lust.

The cool of the night washed over me like a dive into a pond underneath the stars. Crickets making love drowned out the commotion of adults making friendly indoors. I followed the essence of Nico around the corner to the side of my new house and into a narrow walkway. He stood patiently in the shadows between two windows. The perfect blind spot.

I felt my heart lurch toward him with a tug, and my feet followed.

"Do you still have my jacket?" I asked. And he answered with a kiss.

* * *

I couldn't get my mind off of Nico. I couldn't forget the minty taste of his soft lips and the tingling sensation it left behind. And I could never escape the scent of his cologne.

Every night after sundown he would call my house and I would drag the phone down the hallway from the kitchen to my bedroom.

"What are you doing *right now*?" Nico asked one night. I could sense the seductive pressure in his voice, and I teased for more of it.

"I'm in my room," I said, "stretched out on my bed."

Nico ran his tongue across his teeth, and the sound reminded me of our kiss. I wanted to taste that tongue again, and for a second, I thought I could.

Suddenly, Mother was at my door. "De'Vannon, dinner's on the table. Make sure you get some."

"Okay," I said.

"Who are you talking to every night in there?" she asked.

"Nico," I said. "We're just discussing church business."

"Okay. Well, make sure you get some food." And then she left.

"Liar," Nico chuckled.

"I just became a manager for my high school's wrestling team," I told him.

"Oh?" Nico sounded disinterested.

"Hey, this is a big deal!" I said. "I think I'll enjoy this better than being a wrestler and I won't have to worry about winning matches all the time."

"I want to see you again," Nico said.

"I want to see you too," I whispered.

I dreamt of Nico that night. We were making out on the walkway beside my house. The next night I dreamt we were making out in my room.

Every evening was the same, I spent hours talking to Nico instead of doing my homework. Then I dreamt about him all night. Sometimes my dreams were pleasant and sometimes they were nightmares, but they always had Nico in them.

* * *

"So, if you see a man at a café and you want to find out if he's gay, what might you do or say?"

Nico had spent the past week lecturing me on the secrets of gay culture. He was teaching me what to do and say in different situations to communicate with other people who might be gay. I hadn't paid close enough attention.

"I don't know, tell me," I said, trying to sound cute on the phone.

Nico sighed. After a minute he asked, "Are you looking forward to the church's summer trip to Mexico?"

I perked up. "What? I didn't know our church was going to Mexico."

"Oh, shoot. Maybe no one's supposed to know, yet. But yes, we're going to have a retreat in Laredo this summer. We'll be at a nice hotel with a swimming pool and everything."

I marveled at the thought. I had never been out of the country before.

"Want to room together?" Nico asked.

I did not hesitate. "Yes!"

* * *

The bus ride from Baton Rouge to Laredo, Texas was nine hours, not including breaks for gas and food. About a dozen families from the church were packed onto this bus. Some of them started complaining only a few hours in, but I didn't mind the long ride. I was sharing a seat with Nico.

I rested my head on his pecs, and he draped his arm around my shoulder. The smell of his cologne was as real as it had ever been, and I was comfortable. By the time we were halfway to Laredo, I was asleep in Nico's arms. If the other adults noticed what was going on they didn't say anything about it.

The hotel in Laredo was on the border of Mexico. Room keys were handed out and we were sent to bed. I was rooming with Nico and two other boys.

I wondered if Nico and I were going to share beds, but it turned out Nico had brought a sleeping bag to sleep on the floor. All night long I peeked over at Nico. I wanted to sneak over and kiss him, but he was asleep. I stirred restlessly, the long nap on the bus ride taking its toll. I silently begged Nico to wake up, but he didn't. Eventually, I gave up, and shut my eyes.

The sun shone through the blinds bright and early the next morning. When I checked the clock on the stand between the beds, it said 6:00am. I groaned. I couldn't have gotten more than a few hours of sleep.

At breakfast I felt nervous. I could barely eat anything. On the far wall a TV showed the news. The word "PapaNazis" was in big, bold print on the station's news banner. "I just can't believe Princess Diana is truly dead," someone behind me muttered. She sounded on the verge of tears. I wanted to turn around and ask what happened, but I couldn't turn away from Nico.

Nico sat across from me and smeared cream cheese from a packet onto the face of his raisin bagel. I gulped. The bagel looked good, but all I could smell was his cologne. I couldn't eat if I tried. He looked up at me, then at my full plate.

He winked.

I felt my stomach lurch. His scent filled my nostrils again, and I was hungry only for him, but something didn't feel right.

"Are you wearing your cologne?" I asked in a hushed voice.

Nico shrugged. "I haven't showered yet."

I couldn't help it. I was salivating, and my arms were getting tense in my lap. I tried to eat a bite of my bagel, but it felt dry and bland in my mouth. Nothing else could satisfy me. I needed to *have* Nico.

A little girl from our church ran up to our table and asked excitedly, "Are you guys going to the pool? We're gonna have a big water gun fight! Come on!" Without waiting for a response, she ran off.

Slowly, other people from the church finished their meals and left for the pool.

"Are you going to the pool?" Nico asked.

I hesitated, trying to guess how he wanted me to answer. "I need to put on my swim trunks first."

He nodded. "Me too."

When we got back to the room, Nico said he was taking a shower and he glided past me into the bathroom. He didn't close the door.

I stood frozen between the bathroom door and the exit. I wanted to join Nico in the shower, but I was suddenly terrified. My heart pulled toward Nico, but my feet wouldn't move. My head was spinning between lust and logic.

I needed fresh air. I left the room and headed for the elevator. My stomach tightened into a knot, squeezing me from the inside the whole ride down. The elevator doors opened and I saw our whole church group engaged in a wild water gun war. It was chaos and laughter, and it was practically raining with the amount of water that was being thrown around. I didn't join in. I walked to a vacant bench and sat, contemplating.

Essence of Nico filled my nostrils, and my heart pulled up from within my chest. Then, suddenly, I felt ready. I b-lined it for the elevator and jabbed the up arrow with full conviction that I was about to have the best experience of my life. And nothing was going to get in my way.

The elevator doors opened and Evangelist Nelson stepped out in a yellow sundress. She grabbed my elbow with a talon-like grip and pulled me away from the elevator. I had no choice but to follow. My heart screamed as the elevator doors closed without me inside, but I didn't make a sound. Instead, my head grew dizzy and numb.

Evangelist Nelson sat me down on a bench by the pool. "You're staying down here, you hear?"

I nodded, and she let go of my arm. The scent of Nico's cologne still lingered in my nostrils, but it no longer smelled good. It smelled damp and moldy, like bergamot and lavender that had been wasted in a trashcan for too long.

I shook my head, and laid down on the bench, ignoring the occasional burst of water that rained down on me. This wasn't how the trip was supposed to go.

I was afraid to go back up to the room. I imagined Nico still soaking in the shower, waiting for me to come up.

When evening came, Nico came down to the pool area, grabbed me by my arm, and pulled me off to the side. Nico glared at me. His eyes were deep and dark, almost like a shadow. He began to breathe heavily.

"Why?" It wasn't so much a question but rather a growl, from a lion to a cub. "Why didn't you come back up earlier?"

I said nothing. I didn't want to share about Evangelist Nelson because I didn't want to believe she knew about us.

Nico had madness and rage in his eyes. "We're done!" he said.

I was shocked. I was prepared for him to be mad at me, but his words stung in ways I had never been hurt before. I was beyond terrified.

I ran back up to the room and hid under the covers. The image of Nico's dark eyes haunted me.

It was as though Nico's true nature had finally been revealed, and I had seen him for the angry monster he truly was. And yet, the smell of his cologne still persisted to fill my head.

* * *

"God does not condone homosexuality," Pastor Nelson, Evangelist Nelson's husband, said sternly to the packed congregation. I tried to tune out the preacher's words, but I couldn't shake the ripple of nods around me as pious adults up and down the aisles silently agreed with him. It had been a week since the trip to Laredo and I felt like the pastor was talking directly to me. I was furious, but I didn't hate him.

It was Nico I hated.

I glared at Nico where he sat proudly on the front row of the church. The edge of his lips curled into a fake smile as he nodded along with Pastor Nelson's fiery words. Even worse than Nico, though, was the woman. The sight of her made my blood boil. Her hair was tied back in a neat ponytail, and she held her arm around Nico's waist in an excessive show of affection.

She's faking it, I thought to myself. *There's no way Nico could have been hiding his fiancé from me this whole time.* But there she was, the woman who'd moved from California to be with Nico. I wanted to puke, and the lingering scent of Nico's cologne didn't help.

The next day after school I met Evangelist Nelson at her house. I'd been assigned special counseling sessions after the Laredo incident, but I was embarrassed to talk about what had happened.

"What did I do wrong?" I asked. Tears were welling in my eyes.

"Nothing, my sweet child," Evangelist Nelson looked at me with compassion.

"De'Vannon, *he wronged you.*" She spoke sternly. "The truth is, child, your soul has been tampered with in ways it was never meant to be. Nico has been burning candles and practicing witchcraft on you, soliciting the help of demons to try and possess your soul because he wants to have you all to himself. His actions have caused your soul to be ripped and torn." I shook my head. *Witchcraft?* It sounded not only inconceivable but also unfair that one human could wield such power over another. But then I thought about the scent of his cologne that followed me everywhere, and his haunting presence in my dreams and it all made sense. Evangelist Nelson continued. "What he's done to you is wrong. It was wrong of him to make you feel jealous. And I'm so sorry he did that to you. But now it's up to you to let go of your anger toward him. If you remain angry you are only hurting yourself. I will work to break this spell from off you, but some things take time. I need you to be patient."

* * *

My dreams about Nico turned into pure hell. I felt like I could not escape him no matter where I went. I dreamt of him every night and his scent followed me every day. Then one Sunday morning as I sat at the kitchen table and stared at a sheet of math problems through weary eyes. *Nico,* the thought entered my head, but his scent did not follow this time.

Suddenly, it was gone.

It was like an invisible weight had been lifted off my shoulders. I stood up from the kitchen table. *I'm free,* I realized. Relief washed over me. It had been six months since Nico turned on me: six months of nightly nightmares and daily despair, as Nico's scent haunted me everywhere I went. But now my head finally felt clear. I bolted from the kitchen and out the front door to go for a walk along our driveway where my grandmother was already strolling along.

Winter never smelled so good. My nose stung from the cold wind, and I delighted in the novelty of the sensation. The scent of bergamot and lavender was gone. I started to skip down the driveway. *I am free!!!*

Nico never haunted my dreams again.

The next time my family drove to church, Nico looked awful. He was pale and emaciated. His skin was covered in sores and boils. His lips were purple, and he could barely stand without his fiancé's help… and a cane.

"What's wrong with him?" I whispered to my Mother.

"I heard he has cancer," she replied.

Two weeks later, our church held a memorial service for Nico. He was 24 years old when he died.

ABOUT THE AUTHOR

De'Vannon Hubert is a native of Baton Rouge, Louisiana, but his favorite city is Los Angeles, California. He is a graduate of Baton Rouge Magnet High School and an honorably discharged veteran of the United States Air Force. Aside from this, De'Vannon is a graduate of both Embry-Riddle Aeronautical University and the Hypnosis Motivation Institute. He also graduated from the Medical Training College of Baton Rouge and is a Licensed Massage Therapist. He is the host of the Sex, Drugs & Jesus podcast and is the owner of DownUnder Apparel. He also enjoys spending time with his two Maine Coon Mix cats, the amazing Mr. Felix D' Kat & the lovely Ms. Felicity Cleopatra.

SEX, DRUGS & JESUS PODCAST
www.SexDrugsAndJesus.com

RETAIL STORE
www.DownUnderApparel.com

EMAIL
DeVannon@SexDrugsAndJesus.com

Made in the USA
Monee, IL
08 June 2022

a65cf872-51fa-4075-b196-f7158f45653bR02